HARRY FOWLER

University of Pittsburgh

CURIOSITY AND EXPLORATORY BEHAVIOR

The Macmillan Company, New York
Collier-Macmillan Limited, London

FIRST PRINTING

Library of Congress catalog card number: 65–14071

THE MACMILLAN COMPANY, NEW YORK
COLLIER–MACMILLAN CANADA, LTD., TORONTO, ONTARIO

Printed in the United States of America

DESIGN: STANLEY S. DRATE

Foreword

"The Critical Issues in Psychology Series," paperback source books for the undergraduate in psychology, are designed to provide authoritative and provocative reviews of selected topics germane to a spectrum of courses. Each volume offers an original inquiry into major facets of the point at issue and a set of illuminating reports carefully chosen to represent salient positions of historical or current significance. This combination will afford instructor and student opportunity to read stimulating, even challenging, argument with primary sources in hand.

Interest in the topic of this volume, *Curiosity and Exploratory Behavior*, is only a recent development in psychology. Experimental psychologists, long concerned with motivational processes induced by deprivation of biological needs, have been slow to investigate these commonplace behaviors. Once such investigations were initiated, however, they proliferated rapidly, and today this topic is afforded the attention so long denied it.

Harry Fowler is Associate Professor of psychology at the University of Pittsburgh, and has taught there since receiving his Ph.D. in experimental psychology from Yale. He is the author of a number of experimental and theoretical reports on the problem of curiosity and exploratory behavior, having been for the past several years in the forefront of this new field of experimentation. His active interest in and investigation of the learning, motivational, and perceptual processes relevant to this kind of behavior make him well suited to evaluate the complexities inherent in the subject.

MELVIN H. MARX, *General Editor*

Preface

JAMES B. CONANT ONCE REFERRED TO THE DEVELOPMENTS within the areas of the physical sciences as "an interweaving of fruitful concepts." This felicitous phrase now seems quite fitting for a behavioral science like psychology, for within its brief history, psychology has been characterized by continuous interchanges of concepts, concepts prompting varied researches that, in turn, have generated additional problems and new conceptualizations. The central purpose of this book is to illuminate this characteristic development of psychology, relatively free of the actual complexities of research and methodological minutiae. Specifically, its goal is to describe the role of certain of psychology's more "fruitful" concepts, and through selective reference to the content area of curiosity and exploration, illustrate the manner in which these concepts have exerted a guiding influence on the development of this science.

I have tried to satisfy this purpose through an explanatory interpretation, bridged to articles selected to represent the significant empirical and theoretical developments within the scope of exploratory behavior. The essay itself is divided into four chapters covering fairly distinct segments of the problem in rough historical progression. Because this book is intended primarily to supplement texts for undergraduate courses in experimental psychology, motivation, and learning (or their theoretical counterparts), an attempt has been made to keep the level of exposition relatively simple, particularly at the beginning of the discussion, where focus is on the nature and function of theory and the multiude of conceptual developments preliminary to the intensification of research on curiosity and exploration in the early 1950's. Comparable simplification has been attempted with the variety of concepts introduced, such as information-theoretic ones, and the incentive-motivational construct, together with its underlying anticipatory-response mechanism. Hopefully I have not distorted their meaning or their intent. In this context, it seems appropriate to note that the application of the incentive-motivational construct to exploratory phenomena (Chapter III) represents its formal introduction to the area; similarly, much of my personal research reported in relation to this concept, and its inclusion in a broader drive-incentive formulation, is here published for the first time.

My indebtedness in writing and editing this volume is to many individuals whose thoughts and comments have shaped my own. I am especially grateful to Austin Jones for detailed and constructive criticisms of the entire manuscript. My thanks are also due Janet Tyler, Barbara Harris and Sandra Senior for painstaking clerical assistance. Most of all, for patience and understanding during this preoccupation, I thank my wife Dolores.

Grateful acknowledgement is also made to the following individuals and organizations for their kind permission to reproduce the articles selected for reading: G. W. Barnes, A. Baron, D. E. Berlyne, R. A. Butler, J. F. Dashiell, W. N. Dember, W. Dennis, D. G. Forgays, M. Glanzer, H. F. Harlow, D. O. Hebb, C. Leuba, H. Levin, N. E. Miller, A. K. Myers, and P. G. Zimbardo; the American Psychological Association, Southern Universities Press, and the Williams and Wilkins Company, Inc. Finally, I should like to acknowledge that the previously unpublished research reported herein was supported in part by a grant (MH 04549, currently, HD 00910) from the National Institutes of Health, United States Public Health Service.

HARRY FOWLER

Contents

PART ONE

Inquiry and Argument

CHAPTER I

The Problem and Its History

WITH THE ADVENT OF PSYCHOLOGY AND THE TWENTIETH
century, a diversified group of behaviors was brought under intensive experimental analysis, but for a good many years, those activities
that came under the labels of curiosity and exploration received
little consideration. In fact, prior to 1950, systematic investigations of
these behaviors were unavailable, and the few, isolated bits of
research that had appeared on the subject served only to reflect
its perfunctory treatment. This early indifference toward curiosity
and exploration was due primarily to the psychologist's concern
with the biological significance of behavioral events; under the
prevailing Darwinian influence, behaviors such as food and water
seeking required urgent study because of their crucial function in
providing for the organism's well-being and, hence, its survival.
In this regard, curiosity and exploratory behaviors seemed of little
consequence.

Once the phenomenon of exploration began to receive serious attention in the early 1950's, the impetus for its continued analysis
was of sufficient intensity to promote a wealth of findings within the
short span of the subsequent decade. Two factors were of promi-
nence in fostering this recent concern with exploration. First, many
investigators came to recognize that a good portion of the organism's
behavior, especially man's, was characterized not so much by those
activities that served to maintain its biological well-being, but rather
by those pronounced and prominent tendencies that it had to

explore, to investigate, or, in general, to seek out new forms of stimulation. In this respect, then, investigations of curiosity and exploratory behaviors were just as important as the intensive study that had earlier been given to the "more basic" activities of seeking food and water or escaping from pain.

A second, if not related, factor that prompted research in the area of exploration was the concern expressed by other investigators that any general theory of behavior that neglected curiosity and exploration would be seriously deficient. Indeed, with preliminary analysis of these behaviors in the early fifties, serious doubt was cast upon the adequacy of the concepts and principles that formed the bulwark of contemporary theory. And, as investigation proceeded, the findings uncovered were of sufficient consequence to call for both the modification of existing theory and the development of new conceptualizations. These developments have currently led the behavioral investigator to a threshold of new problems and still additional challenges; but, with all of this, there has occurred a further and progressively more rapid development of his science.

The purpose of this essay is to present and critically discuss the developments that have marked research in the area of curiosity and exploration; and, in so doing, to describe the nature of these behaviors. To comprehend and appreciate the significance of these developments, it is necessary that they be viewed within the framework of the total problem to which behavior theory is directed. Thus, in this chapter, attention will initially be drawn to the nature of this problem, and then, briefly, to the ways in which it has been approached within the relatively short span of psychology's existence.

THE PROBLEM OF BEHAVIOR VARIABILITY

Broadly viewed, the problem facing the psychologist interested in curiosity and exploratory behaviors is the same as that confronting the psychologist interested in food and water-seeking activities or for that matter any class of behaviors. In essence, this problem is one of understanding and explaining *behavior variability*. In coping with this problem, the psychologist is confronted with the task of specifying those relationships that may exist between the behavior being observed and the relevant conditions and factors, environmental or biological, that affect the behavior. In and of itself, specification of these relationships (or empirical laws as they are also called) requires answers to questions of the following sort: What are the conditions and factors that produce the behavior—that is, what factors make the organism act? Aside from the initiation of activity, what conditions underlie the different levels of performance or the different strengths of response that are observed for different animals or for the same animal at different points in time? And still further, what factors relate to the animal's engaging with a particular degree of vigor in one type of activity rather than some other?

These questions have often been used to describe the problem area of *motivation*. In the present context, the term *behavior variability* is employed rather than *motivation* because the area for the latter is by no means clearly delineated. Questions similar to the above also confront the psychologist interested in the process of learning; indeed, the task of distinguishing the learning process from that of performance or motivation seems to be an ever-present one. It is similarly noteworthy that the above questions have often been posed in the form "Why?" rather than "What are the conditions and factors?" This is somewhat unfortunate because, strictly speaking, the scientist is not interested in the reasons for a particular event, behavioral or otherwise, but rather the *mechanics* underlying the event. This issue may be posed in its broadest framework by noting that the scientist is not concerned with why the universe, including its behavioral component, is as it is; instead, his concern is with the orderliness and "workings" of the universe or various aspects of it.

The fact that the behavioral scientist is interested in the "mechanics" of behavior should imply that his task is not complete once the conditions and factors relating to a particular behavior have been discovered and isolated; or, for that matter, how or in what ways these conditions affect the behavior. Specification of these determining conditions and the relationships existing between them and the behavior under study can only provide a collection of unrelated empirical laws. Thus, were the task for the behavioral scientist complete at this point, the empirical laws on food-seeking activities would be unrelated to those on curiosity and exploratory behaviors, or those on fear and pain-terminating activities, or those on any other behavioral category designated. Moreover, the facts ascribed to a particular behavior, such as food seeking, would be related only insofar as they came under this behavioral heading, and this, in itself, can be an arbitrary matter. For these reasons, the behavioral scientist must attempt some sort of integration or *systematic interpretation*, both within and across "behavioral categories," of the empirical laws that have been ascertained.

The Use of Conceptual Schemes

To effect a systematic interpretation of behavior, the psychologist must specify and describe those processes that underlie behavioral variability in all of its aspects, from the initiation, maintenance, and termination of one behavior to the selection of another. Unfortunately, the processes underlying behavioral variability are not *directly* observable, even at a physiological level of inquiry. Reference can be made to these processes in terms of physiological events, but this does not solve the problem of specifying them or their functions, because their presence has already been alluded to and inferred from the behavioral events observed. Moreover, if an attempt were made to describe these processes solely in terms of physiological events, it would still be incumbent upon the investigator, in this case the physiologist or physiological psychologist, to specify and describe those processes that underlie the events that he observes, and so on in an infinite regress through each of the "more basic" levels of scientific inquiry. For this reason, the behavioral scientist or any other must resort, at his own level of discourse and inquiry, to *conceptualizations* of the processes presumed to determine the events he observes.

From his own observations, then, and also those reported by other behavioral scientists, the psychologist attempts to infer those concepts or conceptual processes that may be useful in integrating the facts of his science. As a scientific investigator, however, his methodological approach requires that the phenomena with which he deals be publicly rather than privately observable, and therefore communicable to and assessable by other investigators. For this reason, he must make certain that the concepts he employs are adequately defined in terms of observable events—that is, specified and described in terms of particular conditions or sets of conditions and the effects that these conditions have on behavior. Thus, in current psychological theorizing, a motivational concept or process, such as hunger, is typically defined in terms of the amount or length of food deprivation that has been imposed upon an animal; in addition, its motivating or "energizing" function is given expression in terms of the variations in behavior that the defining condition of food deprivation may produce as, for example, in the rate of bar pressing for food, speed of running, strength of pull, amount eaten, and so forth.

The interpretive or integrative utility of this motivational concept is not realized, however, with the specification of a single defining relationship such as that noted with the condition of food deprivation. To serve in an integrative capacity, the concept must "tie in" or bring together a number of empirical relationships. Thus, the concept is also defined, as in current theorizing, in terms of a host of other conditions or variables, such as extremes of temperature, amount or length of water deprivation, intensity of electric shock, loudness of sound, and so on, and correspondingly, its "energizing" function is expressed in terms of the effects that these variables have on behavior. In this fashion, different sets of empirical laws relating to a number of conditions and variations in behavior are unified under a common conceptual scheme, and a systematic interpretation of behavior is effected.

Specific Requirements for a Concept

The extent to which a concept or conceptual scheme may serve in an integrative capactiy will certainly be an important consideration in determining its usefulness. Nevertheless, there are two additional considerations that relate to the adequacy of the concept itself. The first of these considerations is whether the concept is *meaningful*—that is, whether the properties or functions ascribed to the concept are adequately reflected in the behavioral events that are produced by the conditions that define the concept. By ascribing an "energizing" or "activating" function to a motivational concept and defining it in terms of amount or length of food deprivation, for example, we must be able to demonstrate that when this motivational process is made operative, by depriving the animal of food, the level of performance or the strength of the particular behavior performed by the animal is, in fact, elevated or increased—for example, frequency of bar pressing for food is heightened, speeds of running are faster, amounts eaten are greater, and so on. In addition, it will be necessary to show that the strengths of these behaviors are greater with longer periods of food deprivation because, according to our definition, the animal's motivation has been increased. These demonstrations, which provide the concept with an "operational" definition, will also be required with the other conditions—water deprivation, electric shock, and so on—used to define the concept, especially if it is to serve in an integrative capacity.

The second consideration regarding the adequacy or worth of a concept is whether it is *fruitful*—that is, whether on the basis of the concept and the propositions specifying its functions and defining conditions, we can predict new events and thereby generate additional research. Although these predictions are typically derived on the basis of a theoretical system comprised of a number of concepts and propositions describing their functions, in the context of the motivational concept referred to and the conditions that have been specified as defining this concept, we may infer that any condition of deprivation or intense stimulation may motivate the organism— that is to say, energize its responses. And on the basis of this proposition, we may hypothesize that the strength of the animal's responses will be greater when, for example, conditions of oxygen deprivation or intense light are imposed upon it. More directly, perhaps, we might predict that by subjecting the animal to combinations of the conditions defining the motivational process—both food deprivation and loud noise, for example—their energizing effects will summate, causing the strength of the animal's responses to be greater than when either of these conditions is operative alone. The utility of these predictions and those derived from other concepts, or concepts in combination, rests with the fact that the findings of the research that these predictions may generate, should serve, if in agreement, to promote the generality of the conceptual scheme or theory employed, and, if in opposition, to spur us on to appropriate modifications of the theory or to new and hopefully better conceptualizations of behavior variability.

The quest for concepts that are sufficiently meaningful and fruitful to enable an integration of the facts of one's science remains as the unending task to which the investigator must put himself, for herein lies understanding in a scientific sense. With the concentrated research efforts that took place within the context of curiosity and exploration in the early 1950's, this same task prevailed; findings were uncovered that were embarassing to contemporary theory and, therefore, required understanding in their own right. Although quite significant in itself, the task of developing adequate conceptualizations for these "deviant" behaviors of curiosity and exploration represented only a portion of the total problem of understanding and explaining behavior variability in general. As such, the import of the developments that marked research in the area of exploration can only be viewed within the framework of this total problem and its relatively brief history.

EARLY CONCEPTUALIZATIONS

From antiquity until not more than a century ago, the problem of behavior variability was treated quite differently for man and lower-order creatures. Man was viewed as a rational being whose behavior involved reflection and judgement; the acts of animals, on the other hand, were cast as being blind, mechanical in nature, and without such reason or reflection. With this man–brute dichotomy of behavior, it was averred that a rational *soul* governed Man's acts, whereas only natural or divinely implanted *instincts* directed the behavior of other creatures. This conceptualization, which seems to have originated with Stoic philosophers of the first century A.D. (see Wiln, 1925), was rather flattering to man, because it placed him in a community shared only by other rational beings, namely his gods. Moreover, with the propagation of a similar doctrine by Christian theologians, man was afforded the unique position of being able to differentiate "good" from "evil," to act accordingly, and thereby to earn his own salvation. Unfortunately, with both of these philosophies, sacred and secular, the premises concerning the behavioral differences between man and the lower-order animals were without empirical foundation; they had not been inferred from objective evidence or observation, but merely dictated by the assumption of these philosophies that animals lacked a rational soul (see Beach, 1955).

With the appearance of *Origin of Species* in 1859, the man–brute dichotomy began to lose credence; Darwin's espousal of a biological continuity between these species suggested a similar continuity in their behavior, a notion that was made explicit by him in his later writings (Darwin, 1872). Proponents of evolutionary theory were then led to accept (rather uncritically) the proposition that all behavior was governed either by instincts or by a rational soul. Hence, they sought to demonstrate both that animals could reason and humans had instincts. Apparently, this influence prevailed on some of the early psychologists of the time, for in his monumental text *The Principles of Psychology*, James (1890) averred that man had more instincts than other animals, so many, in fact, that they tended to obscure one another. In the course of this intellectual ferment, the instinct concept gradually came to replace the animistic notion of a soul.

The Instinct Concept

The writings of McDougall (for example, 1912, 1923) provided the instinct concept with a formal introduction to psychological thinking. For McDougall, instincts were innate predisposers of purposive behavior—that is, native propensities that initiated man's behavior and directed him to particular ends or goals. Accordingly, instincts were given the specific function of predisposing the individual (a) to perceive and attend to particular stimuli or stimulus objects, (b) to become emotionally aroused in their presence, and (c) to make specific acts directed toward these objects. Because these instinctive acts were capable of being elicited by ideas or thoughts of the objects, in addition to the objects themselves, and also capable of being compounded, integrated, and even modified by learning (a notion that received earlier expression by James, 1890), McDougall felt that he could account for the varieties and complexities of human behavior on the basis of a dozen or so instincts. Thus, the instinct concept was to serve in both a descriptive and an explanatory capacity, designating certain if not all of the components of the behavior observed as being innate or unlearned and also accounting for the behavior's occurrence.

Under the prevailing Darwinian influence, McDougall's instinct doctrine gained considerable popularity, because it served to bridge the gap between animal and human behavior. Nevertheless, the success of the instinct doctrine was short-lived, for soon psychologists and sociologists alike began to question the concept's adequacy. The sociologist Bernard (1924), for example, argued that proponents of the doctrine could not agree on the number or kinds of instincts that were to be designated in accounting for all of human behavior. Indeed, even McDougall had to increase the number from time to time. Moreover, some of the instinctive acts, such as parental love and self-assertion, for which specific instincts had been posited, actually varied from culture to culture, suggesting that the responses involved in these acts were influenced by the specific conditions of these cultures and, thus, were the products of learning rather than any native or innate propensity.

Arguments regarding the learned aspects of various behavior patterns that had been labeled as instinctive were also posed by psychologists like Dunlap (1919), Kuo (1928), and Watson (1925). More important, however, these critics asserted that the instinct concept did not explain behavior but merely provided a redundant description of it. To say, as McDougall had, that exploration was due to a *curiosity instinct* or that seeking food was due to a *food-seeking instinct* was without meaning, for when one asked how we know that there are these instincts, the answer could only be that the animal explores and seeks food. Thus, the presence of an instinct was inferred from and at the same time used to explain the behavior observed. With its circular definition, the instinct concept could hardly serve as a scientific explanation of behavior. As a result, investigators soon turned their attention to an analysis of the environmental conditions and biological processes that presumably affected the so-called instinctive acts, and out of these endeavors, a new conceptualization was formed.

The Drive Concept

The development of the new concept of *drive* was actually coincidental with that of instinct. As early as 1918, while McDougall was propounding his instinct doctrine, Woodworth used the term *drive* to designate an *energy dimension* of behavior. And while battle cries over the instinct notion were being sounded in the twenties, other psychologists, notably Moss (1924), Richter (1922, 1927), Carr (1925), and Dashiell (1928), were advancing the basic thesis that behavior was dependent upon the animal's drive state.

For both Moss (1924) and Richter (1922, 1927), drives were internal, biological disturbances that drove or forced the animal into activities that restored the natural balance or equilibrium of its internal state, a condition to which Cannon (1932) subsequently gave the label *homeostasis*. Thus when an organism was lacking of food, for example, the resulting internal disturbances aroused or stimulated the animal into "random," restless activity that persisted until food was obtained and the drive sufficiently reduced. When this imbalance recurred, the process was repeated; with time and similar experiences, however, the random activity was gradually excluded, because those movements or responses leading to food became more strongly associated with the stimulation (for example, the stomach contractions) characteristic of the imbalance brought about by the lack of food. Thus with this drive conceptualization of behavior, a basis was laid both for the initiation or arousal of general activity and the subsequent selection of specific behaviors that restored the natural balance of the animal's internal state.

A similar thesis was expounded by Carr (1925), who posited hunger, thirst, sex, pain, and extremes of temperature as some of the fundamental or primary motives that dominated the organism's behavior. These motives, or drives as they were also called, were characterized by relatively intense, persistent stimuli that affected the organism until it responded in such a way that its "organic needs" for food, water, and so on, were satisfied. Hence, motives or drives served, through the responses that they directed, to sustain the biological well-being of the organism and, in the case of the sex motive, the species itself. Because Carr (1925) felt that the individual animal would not be motionless in the absence of these drives, he gave particular emphasis to their *directive* function, in contrast to Moss (1924) and Richter (1922, 1927), who stressed their *energizing* or *activating* property. Carr's view was also expounded by Dashiell (1928), who argued that spontaneous activity could occur simply as a result of the metabolic functioning of the organism. Nevertheless, Dashiell (1928) ascribed both energizing and directive functions to the primary drives, because, along with their characteristic stimulation, they served both to get man into action and to influence the course of his behavior.

The varied and complex actions of both men and animals seemed not to be explained, however, simply on the basis of the energizing and directive services provided by the primary drives, especially because much of their activity, a good case of which was exploration, apparently occurred in the absence of these drives. For this reason, Dashiell (1928) suggested, as Tolman (1925b) had earlier, that the drive conceptualization could be extended to include *secondary* or *learned drives.* Through the action of stimulus substitution (classical conditioning), those neutral stimuli in the animal's environment that were consistently associated with a primary drive state could come to elicit, independently, the energizing and directive forces that typically resulted from conditions of deprivation and intense external stimulation. As early workers in the field of curiosity and exploratory behavior, both Dashiell [1] [1] and Nissen (1930) felt that the drive state and the restless, seeking activity of a food-deprived animal, for example, became conditioned to those novel or unfamiliar stimuli with which the animal was consistently brought into contact. Consequently, these novel stimuli served in and of themselves to arouse "a new type of drive behavior."

CONTEMPORARY THEORY

In contrast to the instinct notion, the drive concept proved to be a hardy one. Throughout the thirties, forties, and fifties, reference to the concept was encountered more and more frequently in theoretical discussions of behavior variability. During these years, the drive concept was closely identified with the work of a group of psychologists who, for the most part, had been together at Yale University. Even in its contemporary form, the concept is most

---

[1] Bracketed numbers refer to readings in Part Two.

clearly reflected in their writings: Mowrer, 1939; Miller and Dollard, 1941; Hull, 1943, 1952; Spence, 1944, 1956; Dollard and Miller, 1950; Brown, 1953b, 1961.

Individual formulations of behavior variability differed significantly among the contemporary drive theorists, and even for the same theorist, from time to time. Collectively, however, their position remained quite similar to that espoused by early proponents of the drive concept. Operational definitions of the primary or innate drives included conditions of deprivation relating, for example, to food, water, and sex, and also intense external stimulation, such as electric shock, extreme heat or cold, intense light, and loud noise. In turn, these defining conditions were assumed to produce a drive state that (a) energized those responses that were innately associated with or previously conditioned to the stimuli impinging upon the animal at a given moment, and (b) provided a basis for the learning (reinforcement or strengthening) of new associations between the impinging stimuli and the responses that led to a reduction of the drive state. In addition, it was assumed that the drive-defining conditions produced characteristically different internal stimuli to which responses could be conditioned through the process of reinforcement.

Additional Refinements

Although the general formulation adopted by the contemporary drive theorists remained quite similar to that espoused by the early theorists, certain refinements, qualifying statements, and points of emphasis did emerge, along with an air of caution regarding the application of the model to all of behavior. First, it was stated rather explicitly that a drive state was not an observable, physical entity but only a theoretical construct that, through its ascribed functions, could serve to integrate the empirical relationships that had been or were to be obtained between the antecedent conditions in which the drive was defined and the behavioral consequents in which its functions were given expression. Thus, for Hull (1943, 1952) drive was a central state that was not directly observable; similarly, for Spence (1944, 1956), it was a construct that had no substantive reality but that, as a theoretical variable intervening between certain antecedent conditions and behavioral consequents, was convenient for purposes of integrating the facts within the relatively circumscribed area of investigation designated by these conditions and behaviors. For this reason, in part, the former notion that drives or motives related to the "organic needs" of the animal was eventually discarded (Dollard and Miller, 1950; Hull, 1952), even though it had been expressed in the earlier writings of some of the contemporary theorists (for example, Hull, 1943). It became evident, moreover, that the animal's "needs" did not bear any one-to-one relationship with its drives and their energizing or activating property. The animal might need, for example, to escape or avoid carbon monoxide in order to remain healthy, and even to survive, but the mere presence of this stimulus condition, undetectable as it is, did not energize behavior.

A second refinement pertained to the specification and interpretation of both the drive's functions and its defining or antecedent conditions. Because even those conditions of deprivation that were used to define the drive concept seemed to entail intense, persistent stimuli, such as the "parching" sensation associated with the lack of water or the "gnawing" of the stomach with the absence of food, Miller and Dollard (1941) posited the general, defining principle that "strong stimuli which impel action are drives." It was cautioned, nevertheless, that this general definition did not imply that all drives were strong stimuli. Other conditions of stimulation might exist by which the animal's responses could be energized; however, their discovery and isolation remained as a task for the behavioral scientist.

Similarly, qualifying statements were also made (for example, Dollard and Miller, 1950) in reference to the functions of a drive, especially as they were to be reflected in behavioral events. Although drives energized or impelled action, such a function did not necessarily imply that the motivated animal would show increased or more vigorous activity; only those responses that were innately associated with or previously conditioned to the stimuli impinging upon the organism at a particular moment would be energized. These responses might typically constitute the so-called random or restless activity of the motivated animal, but if, for example, the innate or learned response to a fear-provoking or pain-eliciting situation was one of cringing or "freezing," then these situations or similar ones would arouse that response, causing less rather than more activity. Another example might entail activating the response of *stopping* some vigorous task when one is affected by the "sore weight of fatigue" or, perhaps less abstractly, when a food-deprived animal is confronted with food. Theoretically, these responses of cringing or stopping or doing something less vigorous would be just as strongly energized as others, and this characteristic should be reflected in measures of them as, for example, in their frequency or length of occurrence.

The Concepts of Drive Reduction and Habit

A third development, and perhaps the most important was the emphasis placed on drive reduction as the theoretical mechanism of reinforcement—that is, the means by which a response became more strongly associated with a particular stimulus or set of stimuli and, thus, more prepotent when the animal was again confronted with these stimuli or a similar set. This concept of reinforcement was implicit in the writings of some of the early drive theorists (for example, Richter, 1922), but its formalization did not occur until later (for example, Dollard and Miller, 1950; Hull, 1952; Miller and Dollard, 1941). Moreover, with its formalization, it was made explicit that the reduction of a painfully strong or intense stimulus need not be the only form of reinforcement (for example, Dollard and Miller, 1950). Because strong stimuli served as drives, but not all drives were necessarily strong stimuli, reinforcement might also be occasioned through the reduction or termination of other drive-defining conditions. Thus, the drive-reduction or, more accurately, intense-stimulus-reduction theory of reinforcement was put forth as a working hypothesis—one that would serve both to explain some of the currently existing data and also to stimulate additional research or, as Miller has often commented personally, "to infuriate someone into performing really good experiments disproving it."

A fourth refinement within contemporary drive theory concerned the role played by drives in directing behavior. Although the early theorists had ascribed both energizing and directive properties to drives, contemporary theorists tended to argue for their separation (for example, Hull, 1943, 1952; and especially Brown, 1953b). General and specific behaviors could be energized by drives, but the directing or guiding of these behaviors was effected only through *habits*—that is, the innate, previously learned, or to-be-acquired associations that could exist between the animal's responses and the stimuli confronting the animal at a particular moment. Thus, a distinction was drawn between the energizing function of a *drive state* and the directing property of *drive stimuli,* both of which were defined in terms of the antecedent conditions of deprivation and intense stimulation. A similar thesis was advanced by Dollard and Miller (1950) with the distinction they drew between the "cue" properties of stimuli, to which responses could be conditioned and the intensity of these stimuli, which, if strong enough, impelled action.

Contemporay drive theorists also extended their formulation, as had the earlier theorists, to include secondary or learned drives. In addition, the concept of *secondary* or *learned rewards* was introduced and formalized (for example, Miller and Dollard, 1941). Through classical conditioning, new habits or stimulus-response associations could be acquired, whereby, in the absence of the defining conditions that produced the drive and those that served to reduce it, previously neutral stimuli or stimulus conditions could independently occasion either the drive reaction itself or that of drive reduction. Thus, if an animal were repeatedly confronted in some neutral stimulus situation, A, for example, with an aversive stimulus that it consistently terminated by escaping to some non-aversive stimulus situation, B, two conditioning effects would be achieved: not only would stimulus A serve in the absence of the aversive stimulus to elicit a drive state ("fear") which, in turn, energized the animal's existing habits and laid the basis for the learning of new ones, but in addition, stimulus B would produce a conditioned reduction of this drive state, thereby reinforcing any previously learned or to-be-learned response upon which stimulus B was contingent.

Theoretically, there was no limit to the number of secondary or learned drives and reinforcers that could be established on the basis of the primary ones. Nevertheless, the contemporary drive theorists were cautious not to overextend their model. To be useful in accounting for the varieties and complexities of behavior, both acquired drives and secondary reinforcers had to be empirically demonstrated. Thus, although attempts to demonstate a learned, fear drive, for example, were quite successful (for example, Miller, 1948, 1951), those relating to a learned drive based on hunger actually failed (for example, Myers and Miller [7]). For these and other reasons, relating primarily to the tendency of some investigators to equate the functions of drives and habits—that is, fail to distinguish between the properties of drive states and their associated stimuli— Brown (1953b) strongly admonished overenthusiastic supporters of the drive doctrine for their free usage of acquired drive terminology. To freely assume or postulate the existence of such acquired drives as a money-seeking drive or a prestige-seeking drive or an affection-seeking drive would be tantamount to the plight that had prevailed much earlier with unrestricted usage of the instinct concept.

CURRENT CONTROVERSY

Apparently, the adequacy of the drive concept, like that of its predecessor, instinct, was not to evade strenuous dispute. Even with the refinements, qualifying statements, and elaborations posed by the contemporary drive theorists (and, in part, because of them), other investigators were able to uncover grounds for criticizing the formulation. Hebb [13], for example, in studying the emotional reactions of chimpanzees, observed certain "spontaneous fears" that seemed not to result from the primary drives or their derivatives. Posing this problem for drive theory, he asked:

What is the drive that produces panic in the chimpanzee at the sight of a model of the human head; or fear in some animals, and vicious aggression in others, at the sight of the anesthetized body of a fellow chimpanzee? What about fear of snakes, or the young chimpanzee's terror at the sight of strangers? One can accept the idea that this is "anxiety," but the anxiety, if so, is not based on a prior association of the stimulus object with pain.[2]

Similar protests were also voiced in reference to the arousal of behaviors for which the presumed motive was not a secondary one but, in fact, primary or innate. For example, Nissen (1953) noted that, although sexually naive or virginal chimpanzees tended not to copulate during mating sessions, they engaged in sundry activities, such as scratching, cleaning, caressing, or generally grooming one another. These activities seemed completely independent of the operation of a sex motive, especially because they occurred in the absence of any copulatory activity. Moreover, the fact that these grooming behaviors occurred before the animals were sexually mature and even when a male was paired with another male or a female with another female argued strongly against their being elicited by any secondary or learned drive based on the primary one of sex.

In essence, the argument posed by both Nissen (1953) and Hebb [13] was that many complex acts and even simple ones are independent of the primary drives and their learned counterparts:

Observation of animals and people in "free," and even in highly "structured," situations indicates that much time and energy is taken up by brief, self-contained, often repetitive acts which are their own reason, which are autonomously motivated, and which are not to be interpreted as being small contributions to some remote, critically important aim. The organism scratches itself, stretches, shakes its head, grunts or chirps,

[2] D. O. Hebb, "Drives and the C.N.S. (Conceptual Nervous System)," *Psychological Review*, 1955, **62**, 245.

looks around, examines an irrelevant item of the environment, picks its nose or its teeth, rocks back and forth, shifts its position, twists a paper clip out of shape, cracks its knuckles, doodles, looks at a picture on the wall, and so on *ad infinitum*.[3]

To some of these "embarrassing" observations, the drive theorist could reply by noting, for example, that even such activities as scratching, or stretching, or picking one's nose or teeth, or shifting one's position seem instigated by annoyances (intense stimuli) that the animal tries to reduce, or that some of the behaviors might relate simply to spontaneous activity resulting from the metabolic functioning of the animal, or that the "spontaneous fears" of Hebb's chimpanzees could be due to the animals having previously experienced similarly strange, bizarre, or unexpected events in the face of painfully strong or intense stimuli, or that the general grooming of Nissen's sexually naive chimpanzees would not be expected to derive from a sex drive, because, in fact, these animals had never copulated and, thus, could not have been deprived of sex. Nevertheless, the significance of the other types of observations was well taken. The unending list of what Nissen (1954) referred to as "self-contained . . . autonomously motivated" acts reflected to a large extent that general class of behaviors, such as looking around, examining an irrelevant item of the environment, twisting a paper clip out of shape, cracking one's knuckles, and so forth, which came into focus in the early fifties under the labels of curiosity and exploration. And with preliminary analysis of these behaviors, drive theory seemed to fare even worse.

The Problem of Exploratory Behavior

Early studies by Harlow and his co-workers (for example, Harlow, 1950, 1953b; Harlow, Blazek, and McClearn, 1956) showed that mature monkeys would investigate and manipulate various mechanical puzzles in the absence of the primary drives, and that the same held true for infant monkeys that had always been fed by hand, a fact that seemed to call into question the operation of secondary or acquired drives, as well. More important, however, was the observation that investigation and manipulation of the puzzle devices apparently served to maintain or even increase the animal's total stimulation. This observation, together with the fact

[3] H. W. Nissen, "The Nature of the Drive as Innate Determinant of Behavioral Organization," in M. R. Jones (ed.), *Nebraska Symposium on Motivation* (Lincoln, Nebr.: University of Nebraska Press, 1954), 314.

that the monkeys actually learned to solve the mechanical puzzles, indicated that the process underlying the reinforcement or strengthening of the monkeys' responses entailed not the decrement or reduction in intense stimulation called for by contemporary drive theory but rather a maintenance or even an increase in stimulation. As a result, drive theorists were confronted with one of their more formidable challenges; the adequacy of both the drive concept and the hypothesis of reinforcement based on drive reduction was seriously questioned.

These challenges to contemporay theory were to be expected; the drive theorists had not offered their formulation as an all-inclusive, final account of behavior. Such a policy would have been rather foolhardy in view of some of the radical, theoretical changes that had occurred in the older, more developed sciences. Even in physics, that enduring concept of "force" succumbed under the weight of time and relativity theory. But herein lay the task: in the face of these challenging observations, to modify existing theory or to develop new, more adequate conceptualizations by which the "embarrassing" behavior patterns could be explained. On this point, both the drive theorists and their critics seemed in agreement, for even staunch antagonists had to conclude:

. . . the current criticisms of the drive doctrine do not so much show that it is "wrong," as they point to the desirability of devising alternative, competing frameworks for the study of motivation. It may be that an alternative approach can deal with behavioral data at least as well as the drive doctrine and may perhaps be as fruitful in stimulating research.[4]

[4] D. Bindra, *Motivation: A Systematic Reinterpretation* (New York: The Ronald Press Company, 1959), 16.

The Nature of Exploration

AS EARLY WORKERS IN THE FIELD OF EXPLORATORY BE-
havior, both Harlow [3] [1] (1953b) and Montgomery (1954) stressed
the import of considering all of the motivational processes of behavior. The "homeostatic" or "internal drives," which resulted from
conditions of deprivation and intense stimulation, represented only
part of these processes; just as important, if not more so, were those
processes underlying behaviors such as curiosity, exploration, and
play, behaviors that were presumably elicited by mild, external
sources of stimulation. Correspondingly, it was felt that analysis of
these "exteroceptively aroused" behaviors would greatly facilitate
an understanding of behavior variability in general, because a good
portion of infrahuman activity and much, if not all, of man's more
complex performances seemed to stem, not from the "intense affective states" to which the contemporary drive theorists had ascribed
behavior arousal but rather from nonemotional or mildly pleasurable
stimuli. If anything, the mainstream of man's activities seemed dis-
rupted or inhibited by "intense affective states."

On the basis of these considerations, and also observations of the
investigatory and manipulatory behaviors of both rodents and
primates, Montgomery [4] and especially Harlow (for example,
1953b) argued that the performances of these animals were primarily
dependent upon a number of "non-homeostatic" or "extroceptively
aroused" motives, or, more broadly, an *exploratory drive*. Interest-

[1] Bracketed numbers refer to readings in Part Two.

ingly enough, then, the theoretical development that initially took place in the context of exploration was not the development of a new concept but rather the extension of an old one. Nevertheless, the platform on which this extension was being propounded appeared somewhat unstable. The suggested extension of the drive concept stemmed, in part, from the apparent difficulties that the contemporary drive theorists had in accounting for exploration on the basis of the "homeostatic" or "interoceptive" drives relating to internal states of distress or imbalance. But these notions, which were advanced by the early drive proponents, had actually been discarded by the contemporary theorists. Moreover, in view of the emphasis that was placed by the contemporary theorists on intense, *external* stimuli as drive-defining conditions, the distinction drawn between interoceptively and exteroceptively aroused drive states seemed patently superficial. To make matters worse, the proposed conceptualization had its own problems.

Because the concept of an exploratory drive was to serve in both a summarizing and integrative capacity, it was imperative that it be both *meaningful* and *fruitful*, in the sense described previously (Chapter I). Unfortunately, the concept seemed loosely if not ill defined; reference was sometimes made to an exploratory drive in terms of observed variations in "exploration," and, then, these behavioral differences were explained by the drive. As a result, this new concept soon bore the brunt of a strenuous attack by both drive theorists and critics alike. Brown, the drive theorist who had earlier argued against free usage of acquired-drive terminology (Brown, 1953b), commented similarly with reference to usage of an exploratory drive:

. . . the presence of a drive to explore is sometimes inferred from, and at the same time used to explain, behavior of moving from one place to another, especially if there is no other apparent reason for the movement. The postulation of an exploratory drive in this way is quite circular, and therefore of questionable worth as a scientific explanation.[2]

Critics of drive theory went further, questioning the adequacy of the concept even as a descriptive or summarizing device:

In a few well-studied experimental situations, involving for the most part food deprivation, water deprivation, or electric shock as antecedent conditions, all of the ingredients of the operational definition are present

[2] J. S. Brown, *The Motivation of Behavior* (New York: McGraw-Hill Book Company, 1961), 334.

and "drive" can at least be used without ambiguity as a descriptive, or summarizing, concept. Its usefulness in this role breaks down, of course, when enthusiastic proponents extend usage of the term to situations in which only one of the defining relationships can be identified, thereby generating such ill-endowed mutants as "exploratory drive.". . .[3]

The essence of the arguments posed by both Brown (1961) and Estes (1958) is summarized rather well in a statement made by still another drive critic: "Where little is known about the conditions that control some behavior (e.g., exploratory behavior), the inference of a causal drive does little more than restate the facts to be explained."[4] Indeed, very little was known about curiosity and exploration when the concept of an exploratory drive first tumbled into the psychological literature in the early 1950's. During the ensuing years, however, research in the area began in earnest, and as a result, a wealth of findings was amassed. It would seem best that we review this recently formed empirical structure before giving additional consideration to the problems that plagued not only the conceptualization noted above but also other theoretical formulations that accompanied it.

AN EMPIRICAL ACCOUNT: DEFINITIONS AND DETERMINANTS

To describe the empirical (or theoretical) nature of some class of behaviors, the investigator typically proceeds by defining the behavior so that it may be studied and analyzed with respect to the conditions or factors that affect it. In the case of food- or water-seeking activities, for example, this task is relatively simple, because we may be guided in our definitions of these behaviors by certain, specific "goal" objects, and the responses that the animal makes to and for these objects. Thus, the study of food-seeking or appetitive behaviors entails observing and measuring the effects of particular conditions or factors on those responses that the food-deprived animal performs in order to obtain the food—*instrumental* responses, such as pressing a bar for food, running a straight alley, making a choice, and so on—and those responses that are elicited by the food

---

[3] W. K. Estes, "Comments on Dr. Bolles' Paper," in M. R. Jones (ed.), *Nebraska Symposium on Motivation* (Lincoln, Nebr.: University of Nebraska Press, 1958), 33 f.

[4] R. C. Bolles, "The Usefulness of the Drive Concept," in M. R. Jones (ed.), *Nebraska Symposium on Motivation* (Lincoln, Nebr.: University of Nebraska Press, 1958), 23.

object itself—*consummatory* responses, such as chewing, salivating, ingesting, or, in general, eating.

Other classes of behaviors for which there are no discernible goal objects, as in the case of escape or pain-terminating activities, can be defined, nevertheless, in terms of certain goal *conditions*—for example, those that have relatively little, if any, aversive-stimulus characteristics. Comparably, then, the study of escape behavior may entail observing and measuring those responses that are instrumental to the nonaversive condition and those "consummatory" responses—for example, "relief" or "relaxation"—occasioned by this goal condition. It seems evident that specification of different goal objects (or conditions) provides the basis by which we may distinguish and study specific classes of behavior—except when we are confronted with the study of exploration.

A Behavior Without a Definition

The task of defining curiosity and exploration seems difficult if not impossible, for there appears to be no goal object or condition to and for which the organism responds. We might consider that the organism explores in order to acquire new forms of stimulation and, thus, as a first attempt at definition, view curiosity and exploration as behaviors that have the sole function of altering the stimuli that impinge upon the organism. However, immediate reflection suggests that this definition is most unsatisfactory. The effect of changing the organism's stimulus field appears characteristic of all behaviors, food-seeking, pain-escaping, or otherwise. Moreover, each and every response may produce a perceptible change in the organism's stimulation through the kinesthetic or proprioceptive stimulus components of the response. Thus, with this initial definition of curiosity and exploration as behaviors that have the function of altering the impinging stimuli, we are faced with the fact that virtually all responses possess an exploratory function to some degree; and so it may be.

Actually, the problem of defining curiosity and exploratory behaviors has only been treated quite recently. Berlyne (1963) suggests that the essential point of difference between "exploratory" and other responses is that nonexploratory behaviors are "accompanied by biologically important effects on tissues other than the sense organs and the nervous system," a fact that presumably does not hold for exploration. Curiosity and exploration may refer, then, to a wide assortment of behavioral events that have "nothing very tangible to hold them together apart from our failure to recognize a specific biological function that can be associated with them." [5] Needless to say, "our failure" to recognize a specific biological function for exploratory behaviors does not guarantee or insure an absence of this function; nor does it provide us with much of a basis by which we may designate the goal of exploration and thereby study the responses to and for this goal.

Perhaps our best attempt at defining exploration can be made on the basis of the classification of exploratory behaviors suggested by Berlyne (1963), namely *intrinsic* versus *extrinsic* types of exploration. Food seeking and other classes of behavior for which there are clearly discernible and unique consequents—that is, goal objects or conditions—may be viewed as extrinsic types of exploration. The exploration involved in these behaviors relates to the animal's receipt and consumption of specific goal objects (or conditions), the presence of which is fostered by conditions of deprivation and intense stimulation. On the other hand, intrinsic types of exploration would refer, by exclusion, to those behaviors that seem unrelated to any goal object, or condition of reinforcement—behaviors that appear to be for their own purpose. These intrinsic types of exploration have reference, then, to the class of acts that Nissen (1954) labeled as "self-contained" and "autonomously motivated."

As unsatisfactory as this "definition" of exploration may be, it appears nevertheless to be the one that guided early workers in the area. Studying curiosity and exploration simply meant observing the activities of animals that were not or had not been subjected to conditions of deprivation or intense stimulation, or confronted with the goal objects that "satisfied" these conditions. Perhaps cognizant of the difficulties involved in defining the behavior that they were attempting to study, the early investigators limited their observations, almost exclusively, to the "intrinsic" exploratory activities of subhuman animals, primarily rodents and primates. With these animals, there seemed less chance that their exploratory performances would be influenced by specific, perhaps implicit, goals such as might be the case for humans involved in complex activities relating to recreation, entertainment, or play. In any case, a host of studies was conducted showing that, without any apparent motive, or condition of motivation or reinforcement as imposed by the ex-

[5] D. E. Berlyne, "Motivational Problems Raised by Exploratory and Epistemic Behavior," in S. Koch (ed.), *Psychology: A Study of a Science*, Vol. 5 (New York: McGraw-Hill Book Company, 1963), 288.

perimenter, animals would respond quite readily to stimulus objects and patterns of one form or another. And through the variety of measures and test procedures that were employed in these studies, consideration was given to the salient features, aspects, or properties of the stimuli that evoked the so-called "exploratory tendencies."

Response to Novelty, Change, and Complexity

Studies that employed choice procedures clearly demonstrated that animals would respond to *novel* stimuli or, more broadly, to a *change* in the complex of stimuli impinging upon them. For example, Kivy, Earl, and Walker (1956) permitted rats to investigate the choice-point region of a T maze, but prevented them from entering the goal arms by means of glass partitions. During this exposure period, both arms were of the same brightness—for example, black. Immediately following their exposure, however, the animals were again placed into the maze, but now with the partitions removed and one arm changed in brightness—for example, to white. Under these conditions, the animals reliably chose the changed or "novel" arm.

A more subtle response to novelty or change was demonstrated by Dember [6] and later replicated by Fowler (1958) and Woods and Jennings (1959). The procedure employed in these studies was similar to that used by Kivy *et al.* (1956): rats were exposed to the goal arms of a T or Y maze but prevented from entering them. With the initial exposure, one arm was white and the other black, but upon reexposure, when the animals were permitted a choice, *both* arms were of the same brightness—either black or white. Even though the animals were now forced to make a choice between two equally familiar brightnesses, they reliably chose the arm that had been changed. As such, these data demonstrated that, in addition to the animal's response to novelty, it would also respond to a change in the *pattern* of stimulation to which it had recently been exposed.

The results obtained with measures of the time that animals spent investigating—that is, sniffing or manipulating—various patterns or objects were in accord with those obtained from choice procedures. For example, Williams and Kuchta (1957) permitted rats to explore freely a black Y maze over a number of daily sessions. Subsequently, changes were introduced: in one experiment, one arm of the maze was changed to white; in another, unfamiliar stimulus objects were introduced into one arm. In both experiments, the animal spent more time investigating that arm in which the change had been introduced. Similar results, based on a measure of the time spent investigating, were also obtained for rats by both Berlyne (1950) and Berlyne and Slater (1957).

A response to novelty or change was also noted with "activity" measures of exploratory behavior, or the number of maze units traversed by the animal in a given period of time. Although these measures seemed somewhat insensitive in that it was questionable whether the animal traversing the greater number of maze units had a stronger "exploratory tendency" than one stopping at each unit to investigate it more thoroughly, a regularity of locomotor responses was reported. Rats in a checkerboard maze showed "*random* sequences of turns, but *ordered* sequences of locomotor responses, i.e., they tended to traverse that part of the maze occupied least recently." [6] Thus with this measure or test situation, the response to novelty or change was reflected in the animal's tendency to avoid that unit of the maze that was familiar to it or, conversely, to approach that unit that was novel or unfamiliar.

In addition to their response to novel or unfamiliar stimuli, animals also showed a preference for "complex" stimuli. Dember, Earl, and Paradise (1957) found that when rats were given access to two contiguous circular pathways differing in visual complexity—for example, a homogeneous black versus a striped black-white one—the animals tended to select the latter, more "complex" unit. In addition, shifts in preference for the alternatives were always toward the one providing greater complexity. Thus if the rat initially selected the more complex unit, it spent most of its allotted time investigating that unit; but if it initially selected the less complex alternative, it subsequently shifted its preference (as indicated by the time spent investigating) to the other, more complex alternative.

Similar results were also obtained in an extensive study by Berlyne (1955). His test situation consisted of a square enclosure in which both novel and familiar stimulus objects were introduced. Rats spent more time investigating that part of the environment providing numerous and complex stimuli and more time investigating novel rather than familiar stimuli.

[6] K. C. Montgomery, "The Relationship Between Exploratory Behavior and Spontaneous Alternation in the White Rat," *Journal of Comparative and Physiological Psychology*, 1951, 44, 589; and "Exploratory Behavior and Its Relation to Spontaneous Alternation in a Series of Maze Exposures," *Journal of Comparative and Physiological Psychology*, 1952, 45, 50–57.

Response Strength and Magnitude of Stimulus Change

The dependency of exploratory behavior upon novelty, change, and complexity suggests that the strength of this behavior should vary with the degree of novelty and complexity or the magnitude of the change in stimulation confronting the animal. To test this notion, the author (unpublished study) confined rats for a short duration in one arm of a Y maze and then permitted them a choice between the two alternatives, one of which was the exposure arm and the other of which differed in brightness, ranging from black through dark and light gray to white. Not only did the rats show a reliable preference for the arm to which they had not been exposed, but in addition, their preference for the unfamiliar arm was positively related to the magnitude of the brightness difference between the two alternatives.

A similar test was reported by Dember and Millbrook (1956). Rats were exposed in the choice-point region of a Y maze, but prevented from entering the goal arms, one of which was gray and the other a different brightness—for example, black. Following this initial exposure, the rats were permitted a choice between the two arms that were then of the same brightness, but both different in brightness from the initial exposure condition. Thus the rat was faced with making a choice between two changes, one greater than the other—for example, a gray to white change versus a black to white change. As in the above study, the animals reliably selected the arm providing the greater change.

The effect of degree of novelty or magnitude of stimulus change was also demonstrated with activity or locomotor measures of exploration. Montgomery [4] permitted different groups of rats to explore an H-type maze and then, several minutes later, another that differed in brightness, ranging from black through gray to white. The results of this study showed that exposure to the first situation produced a decrement in the amount of exploration of the second, and further, that this decrement was positively related to the degree of similarity between the two test situations. Thus the dependency of exploration on the degree of novelty, or the magnitude of change in stimulation, was indicated in two ways: with the general reduction or decrement in the amount of exploration of the second, basically similar situation, and with less of this reduction taking place in the second situation when it was more dissimilar in brightness to the first.

With several of the studies noted (for example, Berlyne, 1950,

1955; Montgomery, 1951a, 1952b, [4]), the relationship between strength of exploration and magnitude of stimulus change was investigated in still another way: simply by extending the animal's exposure to the novel or unfamiliar stimuli present. With this arrangement, the animal's exploration markedly declined over the time of its exposure to the novel stimuli or the unfamiliar maze situation, indicating that as these stimuli or situations were explored and presumably became less novel, offering less of a change in the animal's pattern of stimulation, the strength of the animal's exploratory response also declined. In line with these observations, it was also noted that when the animal was removed from the test situation, following extensive exposure to the novel stimuli therein, and then returned the next day, exploration recovered to its original strength. Presumably, as the investigated and thus familiar stimuli became novel or unfamiliar once again, through the animal's lack of exposure to them, exploration also recovered. Both of these effects —the decrement in exploration that resulted from extended exposure and the recovery of exploration that followed nonexposure to a novel situation—were also obtained over repeated, daily test sessions (for example, Berlyne, 1950, 1955).

Toward an Empirical Tenet

Collectively, the early studies on exploration achieved two ends: first, through the variety of measures and test procedures that they employed, the general and initially vague term of exploration was given specific reference to such behaviors as orienting or locomoting toward, investigating, sniffing, and manipulating particular objects or patterns; secondly, the findings of these studies demonstrated that an animal would explore a stimulus object or pattern to the extent that it was novel, unfamiliar, complex, or provided a change in the animal's present or recent pattern of stimulation. These findings are not limited in their generality by the fact that the specific investigations cited above used visual forms of stimulation primarily or dealt with rats as subjects. The effectiveness of changes in visual, auditory, and kinesthetic stimulation in eliciting and maintaining exploration in rhesus monkeys and chimpanzees was also studied and rather extensively (for example, Butler and Alexander, 1955; Butler and Harlow, 1954; Harlow, Blazek, and McClearn, 1956; Welker, 1956a, 1956b, 1956c). And, with these primate studies, comparable results were obtained. For example, the studies by Welker showed that the introduction of novel stimuli or stimulus objects effected increased responding (Welker, 1956b), and that behavior changes were more frequent in complex than in simple situations, with irregular objects or patterns being approached more frequently than symmetrical ones (Welker, 1956c).

Taken together, both the rodent and primate studies provide a common basis for the formulation of a simple, yet generally descriptive or summarizing tenet: the animal will respond to (that is, explore, in the sense described above) a change in the complex and/or pattern of stimuli presently or recently impinging upon it, and within limits, the strength of its exploratory response will be greater, the greater the extent or the magnitude of the change in stimulation. This empirical tenet (or law) describes a relationship that is of particular significance for theoretical accounts of exploration; however, before consideration can be given to this relationship and its significance, some comment must be offered on the form of its statement.

First, it should be recognized that the term *change* has broad and inclusive reference to the variables of novelty and unfamiliarity and, in addition, to that of complexity and even to other factors, such as *surprisingness, incongruity, asymmetry,* and so on, which have also been cited, but more recently, as effective determinants of exploration (see Berlyne, 1960). In other words, the effects of all of these variables or factors in eliciting exploration are subsumed, by definition, under a broad or generally descriptive response-to-change effect. As an aside, it should be noted that these factors may also be theoretically subsumed under the stimulus-change variable. For example, with a complex stimulus configuration, such as a striped black-white pattern, the animal encounters features of change by way of its commerce with the variety of stimulus elements comprising the pattern—that is, by the animal's visual scanning of first black, then white, then black, and so on. As such, the complex, asymmetrical, or incongruous configuration or pattern may be viewed as a composite of stimuli that provides numerous features of change.

A second consideration, relating to the empirical tenet, is the qualifying phrase *within limits* employed in stating a positive relationship between the magnitude or the extent of the change in stimulation and the strength of the exploratory response elicited by the change. Although this relationship derives from the finding that the exploration is more pronounced, the greater the dissimilarity between the presently or recently impinging stimuli and the novel stimulus introduced, it is not to be anticipated that far greater or more radical changes will increase exploration even more. We may expect, for example, that an animal in a darkened situation will explore a very weak source of light, and further, that the strength of its exploratory response will be greater with a mild or moderate brightness of light, but not if the light is too intense. The fact that bright lights and, similarly, loud noises elicit escape or withdrawal reactions provides, in part, the basis by which contemporary drive theorists posit intense external forms of stimulation as drive-defining conditions. Aside from the effect of too intense a stimulus, however, some findings also indicate that a change in stimulation that is "too" novel, in the sense of being strange, bizarre, or unexpected, may elicit fear and thereby reduce or even preclude exploration, at least as long as the fear persists. A good example of this effect would be the "spontaneous fears" that Hebb's [13] chimpanzees exhibited at the sight of a stranger, an anesthetized body of a fellow chimpanzee, or even a clay model of a human's head. These findings and those noted in regard to the effects of intense stimulation seem to require that reference be made to the factors or determinants of exploration as "mild" or "moderate" changes in stimulation.

THEORETICAL ACCOUNTS OF EXPLORATION

The significance of our empirical tenet becomes evident when note is given to the fact that the relationship that it describes, and that must be dealt with in accounting for exploration, is the same in *kind* as that underlying appetitive and escape behaviors. Just as the presentation of food elicits eating in a food-deprived animal, and intense stimulation such as strong electric shock elicits escape or withdrawal reactions, so similarly does a mild or moderate change in stimulation elicit exploration. Furthermore, the behavior involved in each of these relationships is stronger or more vigorous with increasing magnitudes or intensities of its eliciting stimulus. In other words, larger amounts of food elicit more chewing, salivating, and so on; more intense shock elicits more vigorous lurching, jumping about, withdrawing, and so on; and similarly, but within limits, a greater change in stimulation elicits more investigating, sniffing, manipulating, and so on. These points of similarity among appetitive, escape, and exploratory behaviors suggest that the contribution of the early studies on exploration related primarily to the isolation of another type of *unconditioned stimulus* (or UCS)—that is, one that could elicit the *unconditioned response* (or UCR) of exploration. It is, indeed, noteworthy that this relationship, between a change in stimulation and the orienting or "investigatory reflex" that it elicits, was first uncovered some quarter of a century earlier by Pavlov (1927).

On the basis of the analogous UCS–UCR relationships existing for appetitive, escape, and exploratory behaviors, it would seem that the process underlying the initiation or arousal of exploration should be comparable to that underlying the other behaviors, and further, that this motivational process for exploration should have similar kinds of defining conditions. But this presents a problem. For contemporary theorists, the initiation or arousal of escape behaviors is attributed to the intense stimulus—for example, strong electric shock —serving as the UCS; on the other hand, the arousal or activation of appetitive behaviors, such as eating, relates not to the UCS of food but rather to the condition of food deprivation. This problem of choosing the "appropriate" model seems not to have been explicitly recognized by the early investigators of exploration. Nevertheless, the variety of theoretical accounts that they offered were divided on exactly this basis; and thus two camps may be recognized.

The Concepts of Curiosity and Boredom

One group of theorists simply maintained that external forms of stimulation that were both mild and novel motivated the animal to explore and investigate these forms of stimulation. The animal became "curious" of the novel or unfamiliar stimuli and, hence, responded to them. This view, in which the novel stimulus (UCS) not only directs but also activates or energizes the behavior is clearly exemplified in Berlyne's (1950) early account of exploration: "When a novel stimulus affects an organism's receptors, there will occur a drive-stimulus-producing response . . . (which we shall call 'curiosity'). . . . As a curiosity arousing stimulus continues to affect an organism's receptors, curiosity will diminish." [7]

The theoretical accounts of exploration noted previously for both Montgomery [4] and Harlow (1953b) were very similar, if not identical, to that espoused by Berlyne (1950). Montgomery [4] simply hypothesized that ". . . a novel stimulus stiuation evokes in

---

[7] D. E. Berlyne, "Novelty and Curiosity as Determinants of Exploratory Behavior," *British Journal of Psychology*, 1950, 41, 79; "The Arousal and Satiation of Perceptual Curiosity in the Rat," *Journal of Comparative and Physiological Psychology*, 1955, 48, 238–241.

an organism an *exploratory drive. . . .*"[8] Moreover, like Berlyne, Montgomery assumed that the strength of the exploratory (or curiosity) drive would decrease with time of continuous exposure to the novel stimulus situation and then recover during a period of nonexposure. Harlow, on the other hand, in voicing an objection to the tendency of contemporary theorists to view all behaviors as dependent upon "homeostatic" drives, argued that a *manipulation motive* (Harlow, 1950) and a *visual exploration drive* (Harlow, 1953b) were but several of a class of externally elicited or "exteroceptively aroused" drives that impelled behaviors such as investigation, manipulation, and the like.

In contrast to proponents of the "curiosity" concept, other theorists maintained that animals became "satiated" or "bored" with stimuli to which they had been or were being exposed, and thus responded to other stimuli that were novel or unfamiliar. For these "boredom" theorists, then, it was the familiar or unchanging stimuli of the animal's present or recent surround that motivated exploration or the response to change; the novel or unfamiliar stimuli simply served as "cues" that directed this behavior. This viewpoint, in which the externally elicited drive of exploration is treated in a fashion analogous to that of hunger and thirst, was first given expression by Myers and Miller [7]. Stimuli that were homogeneous, unchanging, and therefore monotonous evoked a *boredom drive* that could be reduced by sensory variety. It was this conceptualization that served as the contemporary drive theorists' rebuttal to the criticisms that had been posed by both Harlow ([3], 1953b) and Montgomery (1954). Satiated with certain stimuli, the animal would respond to other, more novel stimuli, and thereby encounter additional stimulation, but this change in stimulation would reduce the drive that resulted from the stimuli with which the animal was satiated or bored.

Very similar to the notion of a boredom drive was the concept of *stimulus satiation* espoused by Glanzer [5]. Basic to Glanzer's highly formalized account of exploratory phenomena was the postulate that, "each moment an organism perceives a stimulus-object or stimulus-objects, A, there develops a quantity of stimulus satiation to A."[9] Because the assumption was made that stimulus satiation

[8] K. C. Montgomery, "Exploratory Behavior as a Function of 'Similarity' of Stimulus Situations," *Journal of Comparative and Physiological Psychology,* 1953, **46,** 129. Italics added.

[9] M. Glanzer, "Stimulus Satiation: An Explanation of Spontaneous Alternation and Related Phenomena," *Psychological Review,* 1953, **60,** 259. Italics omitted.

reduces the organism's tendency to make any response to A, those stimuli to which the organism had not been or was less satiated—that is, the novel or unfamiliar stimuli—elicited responses of approach and investigation. In view of the fact that this concept of satiation (or boredom) was of an opposed emphasis to that of curiosity, it is interesting to note that stimulus satiation was assumed (conversely) to increase with continued exposure to a stimulus object and to decrease or dissipate with nonexposure.

It should be made clear that, even though the early theorists stressed either boredom or curiosity as the motivational processes underlying exploration, an equally plausible account of this behavior might entail both concepts or, at least, certain aspects of each. Indeed, there was suggestion of such an admission within the curiosity camp. Montgomery (1951a) wrote of the rat tending "to avoid that place it has traversed last" and Berlyne (1950) spoke of the "urge to escape from monotony and boredom." In fact, quite recently, Berlyne (1960, 1963) has offered a theory of "optimal stimulation" or "arousal" in which the concepts of boredom and curiosity are viewed as the animal's drives to terminate or reduce conditions of high arousal potential, such as very monotonous or perceptually ambiguous ones. A similar theory based on the concept of optimal stimulation or arousal has also been posited by Fiske and Maddi (1961). These more recent formulations of exploration will be examined in Chapter IV; for the present, it is more than sufficient to treat the early conceptualizations of exploration and the problems that they engendered.

Logical Status of the Concepts

At the beginning of this chapter, note was given to the fact that both Harlow (1953b) and Montgomery [4] reacted to the inadequacies of contemporary theory not by proposing or developing new conceptualizations but simply by extending the existent concept of drive. Having reviewed the other theoretical accounts of exploration initially offered, we may note further that all, save one, of the "new" conceptualizations were, in fact, drive concepts. Only Glanzer's [5] concept of stimulus satiation was without a drive or energizing function; instead, it had a "decremental" or inhibitory property. Continued exposure to a given stimulus produced only a decrement in the animal's tendency to respond to that stimulus. In this sense, Glanzer's conceptualization adequately described a mechanism by which the animal would select a novel stimulus over a familiar one, but it failed to account for the arousal or occurrence of the behavior. The animal could have a *tendency* to respond to some novel stimulus because of satiation to some other, familiar stimulus, but this did not provide the means by which the animal would exhibit the tendency. As such, Glanzer's formulation represented only a partial treatment of the problems entailed in accounting for the variability of exploration.

It should be noted, however, that Glanzer actually molded his stimulus satiation concept after another prominent "decremental" notion, Hull's (1943) concept of *reactive inhibition,* or "fatigue." This concept also served in a decremental capacity in the sense that it reduced the potential of the reaction or response in which it was based; nevertheless, the concept was conceived and endowed with drive functions. It would appear, then, as Fowler (1963) has recently suggested, that drive or energizing properties may also be ascribed to the satiation concept. This issue aside, however, we may treat the early theoretical accounts of the *arousal* or motivation of exploration as relying solely on the drive concept, one which was defined by the curiosity theorists in terms of novel or unfamiliar stimuli, and by the boredom theorists in terms of the animal's exposure to familiar or unchanging stimuli. And with these defining conditions at hand, we may now consider the adequacy of the exploratory-drive concept and also those previously cited criticisms of it.

Contrary to the criticisms that were offered, the exploratory-drive concept (of either the boredom or curiosity variety) was not, in fact, circularly defined. The concept received expression in terms of a particular behavioral consequent—that is, exploration or the response to change—and *independent* definition in terms of specific antecedent conditions—that is, either novel or unfamiliar stimuli (curiosity notion) or familiar and unchanging stimuli (boredom notion). On the other hand, it is quite true that the postulation of this exploratory drive did little more than restate the fact that animals would respond to a change in stimulation. To say that novel (or familiar) stimuli produced a drive that, in turn, energized exploration was merely an elaboration of the fact that animals responded to a change in stimulation. This statement may seem to contradict the criticism that was offered of Glanzer's satiation concept, but the point can be made explicit.

To account for the variability of exploration, it is first necessary to specify a conceptual process by which both the direction and the arousal of this behavior can be explained. In its decremental form,

Glanzer's satiation concept accomplished the former but not the latter. In addition, and most important, it is necessary to demonstrate that the concept employed is, in fact, meaningful—that is, that the functions ascribed to the concept are adequately reflected in the behavioral events produced by the conditions that define the concept. As motivational or drive concepts, then, both the curiosity and boredom notions could be made meaningful only in terms of behavioral events that reflected the functions commonly attributed to drive-motivational notions. Hence, it had to be demonstrated that the exploratory drive could (a) energize those responses that were innately associated with or previously conditioned to the stimuli confronting the animal, and (b) provide a basis for the learning (reinforcement or strengthening) of new associations between the impinging stimuli and the responses that led to a reduction of this drive.

Viewed in terms of these criteria, the concept of an exploratory drive received little, if any, support from the early studies of exploration. By demonstrating that animals would respond to a mild or moderate change in stimulation, these studies indicated the need for a conceptual process by which the arousal or initiation of exploration could be explained. However, the findings from these studies could not provide independent support for the exploratory-drive concept, because this concept was posited on the basis of them. Fortunately, the concept was to receive independent verification with other findings that seemed to satisfy the criteria noted. Along with the previously cited investigations, there occurred, at about the same time, a sizable number of studies that demonstrated that animals would learn to perform responses that were *instrumental* to a change in stimulation. To put it simply, and perhaps more succinctly, these studies indicated that, aside from the animal's response *to* a change in stimulation, it would also learn to respond *for* the change.

Empirical Support: Response for Stimulus-Change Reinforcement

In the context of visual-locomotor exploration, Myers and Miller [7] found that rats satiated for food and water would learn to press a bar in a shuttle box in order to gain entry into a black compartment from a white one, or vice versa. On the other hand, animals that were not permitted to see into or enter the other compartment with their bar-press responses did not learn. Similarly, Chapman and Levy (1957) observed that visual changes in the goal box of a straight alley or runway would reinforce or increase rats' running speeds.

A number of investigations also demonstrated that rats would learn a bar-press response when it was followed either by weak light-onset (for example, Girdner, 1953; Hurwitz, 1956; Marx, Henderson, and Roberts, 1955; Robinson, 1959, 1961) or by weak light-offset (for example, Hefferline, 1950; Roberts, Marx, and Collier, 1958; Robinson, 1961). Moreover, with other studies (for example, Barnes and Baron, 1961b; Kish, 1955) it was shown that the number of trials or responses to extinction was generally greater, the greater the number of light-onset reinforcements presented during acquisition training.

The reinforcing effect of weak light-onset could not be dismissed on the basis of the possibility that it heightened the animal's activity, and thereby produced a greater frequency of "accidental" bar presses. In a study by Kling, Horowitz, and Delhagen (1956), two groups of rats were run in pairs: for the animals of one group, light-onset was contingent upon a bar-touch response, but for those of the other group, light-onset occurred whenever the animals of the former group responded and received the light. When the light stimulus was introduced after a period of operant responding, the bar-touch, light-contingent animals showed a significantly greater increment in response frequency than did those of the other group for which light-onset was not contingent upon the response.

Demonstrations of animals learning to perform for exploratory "rewards" were not limited to changes in visual stimulation. Kish and Antonitis (1956) found the operant, lever-pressing response of mice to be reinforced by microswitch clicks and relay noises, and Girdner (1953) obtained a similar effect for rats when bar pressing was followed by indifferent sound. Similarly, the results of a study by Barnes and Kish (1961) showed that various intensities and frequencies of sound would serve as adequate reinforcers for bar-pressing responses by mice.

The reinforcing effect of a change in stimulation was also demonstrated in selective learning tasks. In one of the earliest of these studies, Montgomery (1954) showed that female rats would learn to go to that arm of a Y maze that provided the opportunity to explore a Dashiell or checkerboard maze, and further, that these animals would successfully learn a reversal when the incentive was switched to the other arm. Subsequently, Montgomery and Segall (1955) demonstrated that rats would learn a black-white discrimination in a Y maze for exploration of a checkerboard maze. And in line with these findings, Forgays and Levin (1959) showed that rats would learn a discrimination habit in a double bar-press situation and then a reversal when weak light-onset served as the reinforcer.

Studies of the effect of exploratory incentives on the performance of monkeys yielded comparable results. As with rats, bar pressing by monkeys could be reinforced by a change in illumination, and irrespective of the direction of the change—that is, either an increase or a decrease in brightness (Moon and Lodahl, 1956). These animals would also learn a position discrimination when visual exploration served as the incentive (Butler, 1953) or when correct responses were followed by 15 seconds of sound emitted from a monkey colony (Butler, 1957a). In line with these observations, Harlow and McClearn (1954) reported that monkeys would show improvement in discrimination problems on the basis of manipulatory incentives, and as noted previously, the solution of complex mechanical puzzles could be learned by these animals for no other incentives than those provided by manipulation of the puzzle devices themselves (Harlow, 1950).

The reinforcing nature of a mild or moderate change in stimulation is clearly indicated in the results of the above class of studies: particular responses are progressively increased in strength over successive trials or days of trials, maintained with considerable strength, and then gradually extinguished with removal of the stimulus consequence or change employed as the reinforcer. That these changes in stimulation served to reinforce rather than simply elicit the response in question—that is, that the animals responded *for* rather than simply *to* the change—is evident in the fact that the responses observed in these studies were instrumental to the change in stimulation offered as an incentive.

Some Insights and Additional Problems

The findings of the "reinforcement" studies were significant in several respects. By showing that mild or moderate changes in stimulation could serve as conditions of reinforcement, they indicated that these changes in stimulation constituted the goal or incentive condition underlying exploration. With these findings, then, and also those previously noted on the response-to-change effect, a "definition" of exploration seemed complete. Comparable to the study of food-seeking or escape behaviors, a study of exploration entailed observing and measuring the effects of particular conditions or factors on those responses—for example, bar press, running, and so on—that were instrumental to this goal condition of a change in stimulation, and also those consummatory responses —that is, the exploratory responses of orienting, investigating, and so forth—that were elicited by this goal condition.

The above class of studies were also quite significant in view of the empirical support that they afforded the concept of an exploratory drive. By showing that a variety of responses—bar press, runway, choice, and so on—could be initiated, reinforced or strengthened, maintained, and then terminated, these findings seemed to satisfy both of the previously noted behavioral criteria by which drive concepts are typically assessed. But in doing so, they also demonstrated that the curiosity formulation was severely wanting. According to the curiosity theorists, the exploratory drive was elicited by the impingement of novel or unfamiliar stimuli on the organism's receptors. With the conditions employed in the reinforcement studies noted above, however, the novel or unfamiliar stimuli were not present during the instrumental-response sequence that led to them. That is, the animals began working—running, pressing the bar, and so on—for the novel stimuli prior to the introduction of these stimuli. Hence, as Brown (1953a, 1961) cogently argued, if novel or unfamiliar stimuli elicit the exploratory drive, this drive is not produced until *after* the animal has made the response the drive is supposed to be motivating.

There was still another paradox that plagued the curiosity formulation. Because the findings of the above studies demonstrated that particular responses could be reinforced by novel stimuli, or by a change in stimulation, the curiosity theorist was forced to ascribe both drive-eliciting and reinforcing properties to the *same* stimuli—namely, the novel stimuli for which the animal responded. But if these novel stimuli elicited the exploratory drive, then those responses that were reinforced by the novel stimuli led to an *increase* in drive rather than to its reduction or termination. Because of the defining condition that the curiosity theorists had posited for the concept of an exploratory drive, this paradox could not be reconciled with contemporary drive theory; thus it seemed to call for the development of a new conceptualization in which both increases and decreases in drive or arousal would be reinforcing. As a result, a basis was laid both for the final rejection of the curiosity conceptualization, as it had originally been formulated, and for the development of those theories of optimal stimulation or arousal that were noted above and to which fuller consideration will be given in Chapter IV.

As a final word, it should be made explicit that the above noted paradoxes, and the theoretical developments that they subsequently fostered, related not to the inadequacies of the boredom or satiation concept offered by the contemporary drive theorists but rather to the theoretical difficulties that confronted the curiosity conceptualization. The findings from the reinforcement studies served only to bolster the boredom formulation, and in this regard, it was somewhat ironic that these findings, which initially called into question the adequacy of contemporary drive theory, seemed only to be adequately explained by the extended formulation that the contemporary drive theorists had proposed.

CHAPTER III

Toward the Application of Contemporary Theory

ON THE BASIS OF THE DATA REVIEWED IN THE PREVIOUS chapter, in particular those findings relating to the reinforcing effect of stimulus change, it was concluded that the boredom conceptualization represented a productive extension of contemporary drive theory. In this respect, however, it should be noted that the conceptualization represented only a partial application of drive theory, for concomitant to its development, there occurred a major and quite related theoretical innovation within the drive framework, that of the *incentive-motivational concept* (Hull, 1952; Spence, 1956). Our purpose in the present chapter will be to consider this related theoretical innovation and to apply it to the exploratory-behavior context. As a result, we shall be concerned with the assessment of a formulation that incorporates the flavor of both the boredom and curiosity concepts, because in part it stems from early theorizing on the latter.

As noted previously, the curiosity concept was, in essence, a drive concept. Nevertheless, in the more extended discourse of the curiosity theorists, there occurred a frequent interchange of both drive and incentive concepts. Harlow (1953b), for example, in referring to a visual-exploration drive, spoke at the same time of the performance of his monkeys in visual-discrimination tasks as being *motivated* by visual incentives. Apparently, the significance of a theoretical distinction between drive and incentive-motivational concepts went unnoticed by the curiosity theorists, for this distinction provides not only a resolution of the paradoxes that plagued their conceptualization but, in addition, a basis for integrating the seemingly opposed concepts of curiosity and boredom.

A DRIVE-INCENTIVE FORMULATION

According to both Hull (1952) and Spence (1956), performances, such as bar pressing, running, or choosing, which are instrumental to a particular goal object or incentive, like food, will be motivated not only by the animal's drive—that is, condition of food deprivation—but also by the goal object or incentive itself. The manner in which the food incentive may exert a motivational effect on instrumental performances is quite intricate, but in short, this effect results from the animal learning to "anticipate" or "expect" the incentive. Because the particular mechanism that underlies the animal's *learned anticipation* of the food incentive is comparably intricate, its operation can best be illustrated with the following diagram.

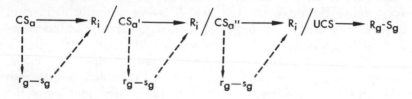

This diagram provides a symbolic representation of the stimulus-response associations that may occur in a "chain" or sequence of instrumental behavior, such as that exhibited in a straight alley or runway where, for example, a hungry animal learns to run for food. The diagram illustrates that, in reaction to the composite of external, physical stimuli at the start of the alley (CS_a), the animal begins to run (R_i), as a result encounters additional alley stimuli (CS_a), continues running (R_i) and so on, until it reaches the goal end of the alley, where it obtains the food (UCS) and engages in the goal response of eating (R_g). With its eating of the food, the animal also experiences the stimulation (S_g) that is characteristic of the goal response—for example, taste sensations and sensory feedback from chewing, salivating, and ingesting.

The motivation relating to the incentive or UCS of food in the above diagram is presumed to result indirectly from the classical conditioning of the goal response (R_g) to those alley stimuli (CS's) that the animal experiences prior to its receipt of food on each trial. With this conditioning, which may be of the trace, delay, or simultaneous variety, the goal response will occur (as indicated by r_g) when the animal is both near to and far removed from the goal; however, in becoming anticipatory—that is, in antedating the occurrence of the food—the goal response will have only a fractional form (hence, "little" R_g or simply r_g), because without food in the animal's mouth, salivation and chewing movements can occur, but not ingestion. With the occurrence, then, of this *fractional, anticipatory goal response* (r_g), and also *its* characteristic stimulation (s_g, sensory feedback from anticipatory salivation and chewing movements), the instrumental running response (R_i) will be affected in two ways. As a result of its close temporal association with s_g, R_i will become conditioned to s_g, and correspondingly, its strength will be directly affected by the amount or *intensity* of this stimulation. It is in this intricate manner that the incentive-motivational concept works like the familiar drive-motivational concept, energizing or intensifying instrumental response tendencies. However, unlike the drive concept, which is operationally defined in terms of the amount or length of food deprivation, the incentive-motivational concept is operationally defined in terms of the magnitude—for example, size, weight, or amount—of the food object, because it is this feature of the incentive that influences the strength and vigor of the goal response, its r_g–s_g component, and hence the strength and vigor of the instrumental response.

Curiosity as an Incentive-Motivational Construct

In the context of exploratory behavior, the curiosity construct may be conceptualized in a similar fashion. That is, "curiosity" may be viewed as the animal's "learned anticipation" of the novel or unfamiliar stimuli that it experiences upon performing some instrumental response. Correspondingly, the motivation stemming from curiosity, or the animal's anticipation will relate to the novel or unfamiliar stimuli serving as incentives. With this conceptualization, a basis is provided for the drive-incentive or boredom-curiosity formulation suggested previously. Specifically, drive motivation (boredom) may be defined in terms of the animal's length of exposure to or "familiarity" with a relatively unchanging stimulus condition, or conversely, in terms of the animal's length of deprivation of a change in stimulation. Incentive motivation (curiosity), on the other hand, may be defined in terms of the magnitude of the exploratory incentive—that is, the magnitude of the change in stimulation that the animal experiences upon performing some instrumental response for stimuli that are novel, unfamiliar, and so on.

It would be sufficient to treat "curiosity" as an incentive-motivational construct and simply describe its defining condition as above, without making specific reference to any underlying mechanism—for example, r_g-s_g. However, in order to complete satisfactorily the analogy being drawn between exploratory and appetitive motivation, specification of the goal response and its fractional, anticipatory component should also be required in the case of exploration. This might appear difficult, because a clearly definable goal object (UCS) and goal response (R_g), such as food and eating in the case of appetitive behavior, seem not to be had with exploration. But as was pointed out in the previous chapter, the functional relationships existing between a change in stimulation and the exploratory response that it elicits are quite analogous to those between the UCS of food and the UCR (or R_g) of eating. Furthermore, the findings reviewed in that chapter showed that a change in stimulation served as a goal or incentive condition in the sense that the animal learned to perform responses that were instrumental to this condition. On the basis of these considerations, it may be argued that the consummatory or goal response in the context of exploration is one and/or all of the components of seeing, looking, and orienting—that is, the exploration or response to change itself. Because the components of this type of goal activity can relate to changes in the sense organs, in the skeletal muscles controlling them, and/or in the general skeletal musculature, specific examples of such changes would include dilation of the pupil, photochemical activity, an opening of the eye, specific head turning and general movements toward the source of stimulation, a pricking up of the ears, sniffing, a rise in general muscle tonus, and so forth (see Berlyne, 1960).

It follows from our treatment of incentive motivation that the specific goal activities noted above may become conditioned to the stimuli temporarily preceding them and in a manner similar, if not identical, to the classical conditioning of consummatory responses, such as chewing, salivating, and so on. This contention is supported by the Russian literature, which, as reviewed by Berlyne (1960, 1963), has shown that, when one stimulus (a CS) repeatedly precedes another, the first will come to elicit *anticipatory* receptor adjustments—for example, orienting responses—appropriate to the second stimulus. This being the case, fractional components of this goal or orienting activity may occur in monotonous or perceptually restricted surrounds, antedating the occurrence of the novel or unfamiliar stimulus objects serving as incentives. Herein lie the means, then, by which the "bored" animal can also become "curious," can learn to anticipate the change in stimulation contingent upon some instrumental act. With this formulation, one may begin to speak more precisely of the motivational increments stemming from "curiosity" or the expectation of seeing, investigating, and so forth.

Response Strength and Amount of Stimulus-Change Deprivation

When the above interpretation was first presented (Fowler, 1959) at the Eastern Psychological Association meetings, relatively few studies especially pertinent to the formulation were available. Nevertheless, these studies, which differ by way of their parametric nature from those treated in Chapter II, were quite supporting of both the drive (boredom) and incentive (curiosity) constructs. In reviewing these studies, we shall consider first those that have reference to the boredom construct, on the basis of which it is posited that the strength of a response to or for a change in stimulation is a positive function of the organism's length of exposure to a relatively unchanging stimulus condition, or conversely, its length of deprivation of a change in stimulation.

In one of the earliest of these studies, conducted in the context of alternation behavior, Glanzer (1953b) found that when rats were exposed to one arm of a T maze and then permitted to choose between the arms, their tendency to alternate or select the unfamiliar arm was greater when their exposure to the other arm lasted 15 or 30 minutes than when it lasted for only one minute. Related to this finding is the general observation that rats' preference for either arm of a T or Y maze, prior to any exposure at all, is typically within the limits of chance expectancy (Dember and Fowler, 1958). Another study (Darchen, 1957), although not within the context of alternation behavior, offers similar results. Cockroaches were found to be more prompt in their investigation of a colored cube when it was introduced after the animals had 30 minutes exposure to an empty box than when they had only 15 minutes exposure to the box.

In Glanzer's (1953b) study, it is possible that the rats with the longer exposures were more highly motivated to avoid the *confines* of their surround rather than its "monotonous" stimulation; hence, they may have selected the unfamiliar alternative in search of less restriction. To assess independently the effect of length of exposure on alternation behavior, the author (unpublished study) confined different groups of rats for the same length of time to one arm of a T maze, but varied their length of exposure to the particular brightness of the arm, either black or white, by having the animals initially view inserts of a mid-gray brightness for different portions of their five-minute confinement. When the rats were then permitted to choose between the black and white arms, following either 0, 1, 2, or 4 minutes exposure to black, for example, their selection of the white arm was significantly greater the longer their exposure to black.

A positive relationship between the length of an animal's exposure to a particular stimulus condition and the strength of its *instrumental* response for stimulus change was also demonstrated; and in contexts where the possible effect of a confinement factor seemed precluded by the nature of the response measured. In a study by Butler [8],[1] for example, rhesus monkeys were individually confined in a chamber and deprived of varied visual experience for 0, 4, or 8 hours. When the animals were then permitted to make a panel-pushing response in order to view (through a small opening) the room outside of the chamber, the frequency of their responses was greater the longer their visual deprivation.

Similar findings have been obtained for rats, when a weak change in illumination serves as the incentive. Robinson (1957) has shown that illumination level during the animal's adaptation to a modified Skinner box is a significant determinant of the strength and reliability of its subsequent bar pressing for additional light stimulation. And in a perhaps more relevant study, Premack, Collier, and Roberts (1957) report that frequency of bar pressing for weak light-onset is positively related to light deprivation over 12-, 24-, and 48-hour periods. On the basis of their results, these authors suggest, in accord with the drive construct outlined above, that "the use of concepts such as novelty or curiosity to explain the reinforcing effects of puzzles, etc., is misleading. Rather, these effects are better treated as a *drive for stimulus change. . . ."*[2]

---

[1] Bracketed numbers refer to readings in Part Two.
[2] D. Premack, G. Collier, and C. L. Roberts, "Frequency of Light-Contingent Bar Pressing as a Function of the Amount of Deprivation of Light," *American Psychologist*, 1957, **12**, 411. Italics added.

Response Strength and Amount of Stimulus-Change Reinforcement

Supporting evidence for the drive-incentive formulation is also obtained in the case of the curiosity construct, which posits that, within limits, the strength of the animal's response for stimuli that are novel, unfamiliar, and so forth, will be positively related to the *magnitude* or *extent* of the change in stimulation afforded by these stimuli. In a study of the effects of various "incentive" conditions on the visual exploration of monkeys, Butler (1954) found that frequency of bar pressing was greater, in ascending order, with the following conditions: the monkey's viewing from a constant visual environment (a) an empty incentive chamber, (b) an array of foods, (c) a moving electric train, or (d) another caged monkey. Although it is difficult to assign ordinal values to these different "incentive" conditions, it would appear that the amount of stimulus change afforded by them increases in accord with their specified order.

More substantial evidence in support of the curiosity or incentive-motivational construct is obtained with parametric investigations bearing on the reinforcing properties of weak light-onset. Levin and Forgays [9] studied the effect of the intensity (or extent?) of this type of change in stimulation on an instrumental bar-press response by rats and found that, within the range of intensities employed, responding was greater the higher the intensity of light stimulation contingent upon the rat's response. (This relationship was actually nonmonotonic for younger rats, indicating that, perhaps for these younger animals, the highest light intensity was somewhat aversive.) Similar results have also been obtained by Stewart (1960); with a fixed-ratio schedule of reinforcement, and especially as the ratio increased, rates of bar pressing by rats were higher, the greater the intensity of weak light-onset employed.

Although the above studies have demonstrated a positive relationship between instrumental response strength and the magnitude of the change in stimulation provided as an incentive, one cannot be certain that it is the extent of the change that is reinforcing rather than the particular intensity of the stimulus consequence; both the extent of the change in and intensity of illumination are confounded. However, in view of those studies treated in Chapter II, which showed that such stimulus consequences as exposure to black subsequent to white and weak light-*offset* are also reinforcing, it would appear that the critical or effective variable is the extent of the change rather than the particular intensity or brightness. This conclusion is also supported by the results of more recent investigations. For example, Crowder and Crowder (1961) varied the duration of light-onset contingent upon bar pressing by female rats and obtained no differences among the several experimental groups, a fact that suggests that the reinforcing effect of light-onset relates to the change from darkness to light rather than from the light itself. Also relevant in this context is a study by Barnes and Baron [10]. Lever presses by different groups of mice were reinforced by the onset of different luminous patterns, namely circle, square, or X. In addition, a fourth group received a different one of these three patterns during each minute of the conditioning session. All groups showed increased rates of responding, with the multiple pattern group exceeding the circle and square groups but not the X group. In part, then, these data suggest that the magnitude of the reinforcing effect of light-onset is related to the amount of variation or change provided.

Finally to be noted is a study that bears on both the drive and incentive constructs. Zimbardo and Miller [11] placed rats in one compartment of a black-white shuttle box and then gave them the opportunity either immediately or after a two-minute delay to enter the other compartment. With training, the delayed animals, for which there presumably would be some satiation, showed faster running speeds, but the nondelayed animals did not. When the speed of delayed animals had reached a relatively stable level, the novelty of the apparatus was increased by the introduction of various unfamiliar objects into the compartments. Additional training under this increased incentive condition—that is, greater stimulus-change reinforcement—produced a substantial increment in the speeds exhibited by the delayed animals.

The results of the above studies are in close agreement with the proposed formulation and the functional S-R relationships that it posits. Nevertheless, it should be recognized that these findings do not fully attest to the meaningfulness of the boredom (drive) and curiosity (incentive) constructs employed. For example, with the studies relating to the boredom construct, relatively long periods of exposure (or deprivation of a change in stimulation) were employed. As such, the findings from these studies can only substantiate a concept of boredom that is operationally defined in terms of relatively long periods of exposure.

Some evidence of the meaningfulness of the boredom construct would seem to be obtained, relative to the effects of *short-term* exposure, from the studies noted above on alternation behavior, wherein the exposure periods varied over minutes rather than hours. However, with these studies, there is an additional problem; they do not satisfy the behavioral criteria by which a drive concept, like boredom, is typically assessed. For example, it cannot be concluded from these studies that the animal *learns* a response that is instrumental to the reduction of the drive (boredom) presumed to be operative, because subsequent to its exposure to one arm, the animal may only be responding *to* and not *for* the unfamiliar arm. In other words, the stimulus change provided by the unfamiliar or nonexperienced arm may not have reinforced, but simply elicited (directed), the choice behavior of approaching and investigating the unfamiliar arm.

A Current Program of Research and Some Tentative Conclusions

In view of the limitations of the above studies, the author initiated a program of research in 1961, which, being guided by the drive-incentive formulation, was generally designed to isolate those experimental operations and stimulus factors affecting the instrumental component of exploration. Because the proposed formulation stresses the importance of the relationship between (a) those conditions of exposure experienced by the animal prior to its exploration, and (b) the changed or "novel" stimulus conditions that the animal subsequently explores, in four of the five studies conducted to date, these conditions were structured, respectively, as enlarged start and goal compartments of a straight alley or runway. Thus the studies have been directed primarily to the effect on rats' runway performance of varied lengths of exposure to different intensities of visual stimulation (wall inserts painted different brightnesses) employed within the start and goal compartments.

Due to the paucity of relevant data on the effects of short-term exposure, this variable was investigated in the first study (Fowler, 1963), as well as in each of the others. Rats were constantly exposed, on each trial of a widely spaced training schedule, for 0, 1, 3, 7, or 15 minutes to the start compartment brightness—for example, black—prior to being permitted to run and be exposed briefly to the goal brightness—for example, white. (In each study, the end wall of the goal was the same brightness as the start compartment, making the brightness-change reinforcement contingent upon the rat's response of running to and looking inside the goal.) In addition to the effects of varied-start exposure, the second study assessed the effects of varied lengths of short-term exposure to the goal brightness; the third, the effects of different magnitudes of brightness-change reinforcement contingent upon the runway response (for example, black start to white, gray, or black goal); and the fourth, the effects of reversing, late in training, the lengths of start exposure and the amounts of brightness change at the goal that had been imposed upon different groups of rats earlier in their training. To assess the generality of the effects of the exposure and change variables, the fifth study investigated the learning by rats of a position habit in an E maze—that is a T maze with the goals being perpendicular extensions of the T arms and, thus, not visible at the choice point. In this study, the rats were exposed on each trial for 30 or 180 seconds to the start brightness (for example, black), prior to being permitted to make a choice and be exposed briefly to a goal that was either the same brightness as the start compartment (black) or a different brightness (white or gray).

In accord with the proposed formulation, the research has shown that (a) rats will learn to perform responses (runway or choice) which are instrumental to a simple change in brightness (for example, running from black to white), (b) response strength is greater the longer the exposure *initially* imposed on the animal— that is, in the start compartment, (c) conversely, response strength is weaker the longer the animal's required exposure to the novel surround or goal that it explores, (d) response strength is greater the larger the magnitude of brightness-change reinforcement contingent upon the response (for example, running from black to white as opposed to gray), and (e) response strength is relatively independent of the conditions of stimulus exposure and brightness change imposed upon the animal earlier in its training, a fact that argues strongly for the motivational or "energizing" nature of these variables. Collectively, the findings demonstrate that the exposure and change variables can affect performances in a manner comparable to conditions of appetitive motivation and reinforcement. As such, these data and also those from the parametric studies, previously reviewed, offer strong support for the operation, within the context of exploration, of both drive and incentive-motivational factors.

As supporting as the above data may be, it must be acknowledged that they are restricted to the particular behaviors, animals, and types of stimulation studied, and thus strongly suggestive but certainly not conclusive in any final sense. For this reason, additional studies of both the exposure and change variables will be required. Indeed, it would seem incumbent upon the exploratory-behavior theorist to provide the same intensive investigation of these drive and incentive variables as has been (and still continues to be) the case for the theorist interested in appetitive behaviors. Moreover, to complete the analogy drawn between appetitive and exploratory motivation, systematic studies of the effects of such relevant variables as the delay and/or schedule of stimulus-change reinforcement must also be undertaken. Finally, assessment must be made of the implications of the formulation for other, if not broader, issues and factors relating to exploration. In the remainder of this chapter, we shall touch upon a few of these related concerns.

RELATED FACTORS AND RELEVANT ISSUES

As noted previously, early investigators of exploration (for example, Montgomery [4]; Harlow, 1953b) simply postulated another drive in their attempt to account for the variability of this behavior. Thus their approach was to add one more to our list of so-called primary drives. With the present formulation, it is the intent of the author to imply quite the opposite approach, speaking not of primary drives but rather primary sources of drive (compare Brown, 1953b, 1961; Hull, 1943). Accordingly, the operations underlying the boredom or satiation construct outlined above and those relating to hunger, thirst, or pain are viewed merely as different sources of a general drive state. This "general" drive interpretation would seem to be a fruitful approach because of the extended integration of the number and kinds of empirical relationships that it permits— for example, those pertaining to appetitive, escape, and exploratory activities. Nevertheless, the meaningfulness of this interpretation and the relationships that it posits are open to and must rest upon empirical confirmation.

The Effect of Irrelevant Drive Sources

In that a prime function of the drive state is to energize those responses that are innately associated with or previously conditioned to the stimuli currently impinging upon the organism, it follows from our discussion above that the concurrent operation of both boredom and hunger- or thirst-producing conditions should energize an ongoing or dominant response pattern even more so than when any of these conditions is operative alone. This summation effect rests upon the provision, however, that the particular response tendencies that may be associated with either the external or characteristically different, internal stimuli relating to the different drive sources are not incompatible or antagonistic. When these response tendencies are incompatible, as, for example, when a hungry animal must choose between exploring some unfamiliar surround and eating the food located therein, the response competition should lead to an interference rather than a facilitation of exploration. This effect seems evident in the results of a study by Zimbardo and Montgomery (1957). Hungry rats and thirsty rats for which food and water were available in the compartments of a checkerboard maze showed less exploration than similarly motivated rats for which food and water were not available. Furthermore, with increasing hours of food or water deprivation, the time spent exploring by the rats that could eat or drink was progressively shorter. Similar results have also been reported by Chance and Mead (1955).

When the possible competing responses relating to the conditions of hunger and thirst are precluded, however, *presumably* by omission of the appropriate goal objects—food and water—exploration may then be facilitated. This effect was initially observed in the early study by Dashiell [1]. Nonetheless, in recent investigations where both food and water have been omitted, the particular effect of hunger and thirst would seem to be of considerable doubt. For example, Montgomery (1953c) found that food or water deprivation *reduced* the exploration of female rats in an enclosed Y maze, and Zimbardo and Montgomery (1957) obtained the same effect for both male and female rats in an enclosed checkerboard maze. On the other hand, Glickman and Jensen (1961) obtained some evidence of a facilitating effect of hunger and thirst on the Y-maze exploration of male rats; and, with an elevated, rectangular maze, Thompson (1953) found that food deprivation increased the exploration of male rats but not that of female rats.

The discrepant findings reported in these investigations would seem primarily due to the particular measure of exploration that was employed, namely the number of maze units traversed by the animal in a given period of time. As a sensitive or even valid indicator of the strength of exploration, this measure is severely wanting, and for two reasons: first, it is entirely uncertain that the animal traversing a greater number of maze units is exploring more than another animal stopping at each unit, perhaps, to investigate it thoroughly;

secondly, it is indeterminant whether the effect of the variables studied (hunger and thirst) are comparable for all of the components of the gross activity measured. In this latter regard, the results of a study by deLorge and Bolles (1961) are quite informative. Separating the several components of behavior in an "open field," these investigators found that investigatory and "window peeking" responses increased with food deprivation, whereas other components of open field behavior, such as locomotion, grooming, and cringing, were either unaffected or decreased with food deprivation. Moreover, these effects were found to be generally greater the longer the period of food deprivation.

Aside from the particular measure of exploration used, there is another factor that has contributed to the equivocal nature of the findings. In order to determine whether hunger- and thirst-producing conditions will additionally energize exploratory responses, it is incumbent upon the investigator to insure that exploration and not some other behavior, such as grooming or exercising, is the dominant response pattern. As Brown (1961) has cogently argued, "an increase in D [drive] does not activate or multiply approach tendencies alone, and reactions of exploring and manipulating would not be facilitated by intensified D unless these responses were, for other reasons, the dominant members of the response hierarchy."[3] Unfortunately, many investigators have failed to employ or even consider the experimental operations and stimulus factors that may be required to promote exploration.

According to the proposed drive-incentive formulation, facilitation of both the instrumental and consummatory components of exploration may be accomplished in either of two ways: (a) by providing the animal with sufficient exposure to a relatively homogeneous surround prior to its receipt of unfamiliar objects or its introduction to an unfamiliar area (that is, by heightening its boredom or satiation), and/or (b) by providing sufficient stimulus change (that is, sufficiently different or complex stimuli to and for which the animal may respond). This second factor seems to underlie, at least in part, the positive results of Thompson's study (1953). With an elevated maze and thus a more heterogeneous environment as provided by extramaze stimuli, Thompson's food-deprived animals generally showed more exploration than the nondeprived animals. In this regard, it is particularly noteworthy that Adlerstein and

---

[3] J. S. Brown, *The Motivation of Behavior* (New York: McGraw-Hill Book Company, 1961), 336.

Fehrer (1955) obtained comparable results for rats tested in an irregular maze that was structured so as to provide varied, extra-maze stimulation.

With the above two studies, the animals were placed directly into an "unfamiliar" situation, rather than first being exposed to the situation and then being permitted either to investigate stimulus objects subsequently introduced or to leave the exposed (familiar) surround in order to explore a different area. This latter type of arrangement, which relates more directly to the boredom construct outlined above and, thus, the other of the two conditions suggested as necessary for the demonstration of positive findings, has been employed in several studies. Fehrer (1956), for example, kept hungry and food-satiated rats in one compartment of an apparatus for 24 hours before permitting them to leave this area to explore an adjacent novel area. Other hungry and food-satiated rats were placed directly into the apparatus without having had the opportunity to experience the "familiar" area. No difference in the amount of exploration, as reflected by several measures, was found between the latter two groups, but with the groups permitted to leave the familiar situation, the food-deprived animals showed significantly more exploration; they explored the unfamiliar area sooner, more often, and for a longer period of time. As will be recalled, Zimbardo and Miller [11] obtained comparable results when they placed hungry and food-satiated rats into one compartment of a shuttle box and then gave them the opportunity to enter the other compartment either immediately or after a two-minute delay. The results of a recent investigation by Richards and Leslie (1962) are also relevant in this context. These investigators found that when rats in a T maze were permitted to choose between novel and familiar tactile stimuli (familiar through previous exposures), rats of both sexes that were hungry or thirsty chose the novel stimulus alternative significantly more often than others that had been maintained on an ad libitum schedule of food and water.

Evidence for the facilitating effect of irrelevant sources of drive on exploratory behaviors also derives from investigations of rats responding for weak light-onset. Although Hurvitz and De (1958) report a failure to find an increment in performance resulting from the addition of hunger, studies by Forgays and Levin (1958) with food-deprived and food-satiated rats and by Clayton (1958) with water-deprived and water-satiated rats have shown significantly more bar pressing by the deprived animals. Moreover, Davis (1958) reports that the frequency of response for weak light-onset is positively related to the length of food deprivation (0, 2, and 23½ hours) imposed upon rats. In a different context, Miles (1962) obtained the same effect for cats permitted to manipulate various hanging objects.

Collectively, the findings of this class of studies demonstrate that an irrelevant source of drive can additionally energize both the instrumental and consummatory components of exploration. And in accord with the proposed formulation, this summation effect becomes evident when complex or heterogeneous test environments are employed, and/or when the animals are initially exposed to a relatively homogeneous surround and are then permitted to investigate unfamiliar objects or to leave the familiar surround and explore an unfamiliar area.

The Temporal Course of Exploration

In contrast to the seemingly discrepant findings on the effect of irrelevant drive sources, one of the more reliable findings from studies on exploration is that, within a single test session entailing extended exposure to the unfamiliar stimuli present, animals show a marked decline over time in their investigation of these stimuli (Adlerstein and Fehrer, 1955; Berlyne, 1955; Glanzer, 1961; Montgomery, 1951a, 1952b, [4]; Thompson, 1953; Thompson and Solomon, 1954; Welker, 1956b, c). This intrasession decline in exploration is also evident with repeated test sessions (for example, Berlyne, 1950, 1955; Glanzer, 1961).

Theoretically, the observed decrement in exploration within a trial or test session is not surprising. Comparable to the animal that eats less as its hunger is depleted, the bored and/or curious animal should explore less with exposure to unfamiliar stimuli because its motivation is also being permitted to dissipate. Moreover, with continued exposure to the unfamiliar stimuli, the animal should satiate to these stimuli such that they become less "novel" and hence less potent eliciters or directors of exploration. From these considerations, it may also be deduced that exposure to certain stimulus objects prior to a test session will produce a decrement in the time that the animal spends investigating these objects during the test. The effect of preexposure has not been generally studied, but Berlyne (1955) reports that stimulus objects evoke less exploration when the animal has been exposed to them five minutes prior to testing.

In contrast to the temporal course of exploration within a trial or test session, a decrement in the amount of exploration or response to change *over* trials—that is, from one trial to the next—is not necessarily to be expected. The satiation accruing to the unfamiliar stimuli in one trial may dissipate partially or even completely during the interval between that trial and the next, for example, through the animal's extraneous activity with other, presumably different stimuli. Hence, amount of exploration from one trial to the next should be influenced by the length of the intertrial interval: with long intervals, the satiation accruing in any one session may dissipate completely, with the result that amount of exploration over sessions remains relatively constant; with short intervals, on the other hand, some residual satiation may be present on a subsequent trial to produce a decrement in exploration. Accordingly, studies that have employed short intervals, for example, 10 minutes, show a large decrement in exploration over sessions (Berlyne, 1950, 1955, and Berlyne and Slater, 1957, for example), whereas, those employing intervals as long as 24 hours or more show a marked constancy in amount of exploration over sessions (for example, Berlyne, 1955; Butler and Alexander, 1955; Montgomery, 1952b, [4]) or, at most, a relatively slight and gradual decline (for example, Berlyne and Slater, 1957; Zimbardo and Montgomery, 1957). This latter decremental effect suggests that the temporal course of exploration over trials is not solely a function of the intertrial interval.

Other factors suggested by the drive-incentive formulation as significant determinants of the temporal course of exploration include (a) the length of the test trial or session itself, and (b) the degree of complexity of the test situation. With very long test sessions, permitting extensive satiation to the stimuli present, an intertrial interval of 24 hours or more may be insufficient for complete dissipation of the satiation accrued. This being the case, residual effects on subsequent trials would produce a decrement in amount of exploration. Further, this decrement would be pronounced with extensive exposure to a relatively simple or homogeneous test situation, but diminished with a complex or heterogeneous arrangement. The animal's commerce with the variety of stimulus elements comprising the complex situation should facilitate a more gradual accumulation of satiation to the situation or pattern as a whole, because exposure to one element of the complex pattern permits nonexposure and therefore dissipation of the satiation accrued to another, previously experienced element. Thus for experimental arrangements involving the same intra- and intertrial intervals, but different degrees of complexity, intra- and intertrial decrements in exploration should be more gradual or perhaps nonexistent the greater the complexity of the test situation. It is also conceivable that experimental arrangements involving short, daily exposures to large and/or complex stimulus situations will produce a gradual increment in the amount of exploration over sessions. The animal may satiate to an initial portion or area of the complex test environment and then, because of some residual satiation on a subsequent trial, explore this area only briefly prior to moving on to additional areas. Although noted quite infrequently, this incremental effect has been obtained in studies employing conditions similar to those described above (Glanzer, 1961; Montgomery, 1952b).

The Efficacy of Exploratory Rewards

In that the above findings generally show that exploration undergoes a marked decrement with continued exposure to an unfamiliar stimulus pattern, and then recovers during a period of nonexposure to the pattern, these effects may be described *quite loosely* as the "extinction" and "spontaneous recovery" of exploration. As such, the above findings have been interpreted by some investigators as demonstrating that the reinforcement or reward value of a change in stimulation will subsequently pall. And on the basis of this interpretation, it is further argued that the use of incentive-motivational constructs to explain both appetitive and exploratory behaviors is quite incongruous:

. . . although expectancy-produced drive [incentive motivation based on anticipatory goal responses to food] becomes stronger as a function of the number of encounters with a rewarding object, curiosity drive is weakened by the same variable. Repeated experiences with food that is assumed to be drive reducing strengthen the expectancy mechanism; but repeated exposures to a novel stimulus, which in a comparable manner reduces the curiosity drive, weaken the power of the stimulus to arouse the drive. Conversely, anticipatory goal responses are extinguished when the rewarding object is omitted, while curiosity is extinguished when the rewarding object is kept in the situation.[4]

At least two factors contribute to the apparent incongruity. The first relates to the looseness with which the curiosity concept has been employed in previous accounts of exploration, resulting for example in the simultaneous ascription of both drive and reinforcing

[4] *Ibid.*, 335 f.

properties to novel stimuli. The inadequacies of this position—in particular, the paradoxes that it generates—were described earlier and need not be discussed further. The second factor relates to the failure of some writers to distinguish between experimental arrangements involving the consummatory or goal response to stimulus change—that is, the exploratory response elicited by the novel stimuli—and those situations involving response *for* change, behaviors such as bar pressing, running, and so on, which are instrumental to stimulus-change reinforcement.

The distinction between the instrumental response for change and the consummatory response to that change is essential for the following reasons. First, it is the instrumental response for which the anticipatory goal-response mechanism works; indeed, it would appear unlikely that the characteristic stimulation (s_g) of the anticipatory *goal* response (r_g) serves to intensify the goal response itself! Secondly, it is the instrumental response that is reinforced by the occurrence of the novel stimulus serving as the UCS; the goal or exploratory response, on the other hand, is elicited by the UCS. Hence, any assessment of both the efficacy of exploratory rewards and the adequacy of explanations based upon anticipatory-response mechanisms must have reference to the instrumental component of exploration and not to its consummatory component. Most appropriate in this context, then, are the findings of the parametric studies and the program of research considered earlier, and also that class of studies (reviewed in Chapter II) that demonstrated that animals would learn to respond for a change in stimulation. It will be recalled that "the reinforcing nature of a mild or moderate change in stimulation is clearly indicated in the above class of studies: particular responses are progressively increased in strength over successive trials or days of trials, maintained with considerable strength, and then gradually extinguished with removal of the stimulus consequence or change employed as the reinforcer." (Chapter II, page 37.)

By the very nature of the novel stimulus that serves as the reinforcer, however, both the magnitude and temporal extent of the change in stimulation that it provides should be critically dependent upon the particular distribution of training trials used to study its reinforcing effect. As with the consummatory response to change, then, a decrement in the strength of the instrumental response may also be observed (for example, Girdner, 1953; Kling, Horowitz, and Delhagen, 1956) when a relatively short temporal distribution of trials or sessions (or responses within a session in the case of the free-responding—for example, bar-press—situation) is employed. With this schedule of training, repeated massed exposures to the novel stimulus serving as the reinforcer should deplete its "novelty," thereby reducing the extent of the change in stimulation that it affords, and consequently, the magnitude of stimulus-change reinforcement contingent upon the instrumental response. This effect may even be sufficiently pronounced so as to preclude the learning of instrumental behaviors. Thus in the Myers and Miller [7] study, cited earlier, rats learned to press a bar to gain entry into a black compartment from a white one, or vice versa, but only when the trials were widely distributed; animals with highly massed trials exhibited little if any learning. These same results have also been obtained in a recent study by Forgays and Levin (1961).

Aside from the effects of a massed training schedule, the data leave little doubt that the strength of the instrumental response *for* stimulus change increases over daily trials or sessions, whereas the strength of the exploratory or consummatory response *to* the change remains relatively constant. Hence, with reference to the instrumental component of exploration, there can similarly be little doubt regarding the efficacy of exploratory rewards or of the appropriateness of explanations based on anticipatory-response mechanisms. The data are in agreement with the view that curiosity, redefined as an incentive-motivational construct, may become stronger as a function of the animal's encounters with the goal object, that repeated reinforced trials may strengthen the anticipatory responding that underlies this incentive-motivational effect, and conversely, that the anticipatory responding may be extinguished when the reinforcement is omitted.

Curiosity and Common Sense

As is emphasized with the above, the proposed formulation treats curiosity as a *learned*, anticipatory reaction to the changes in stimulation contingent upon some instrumental act. Accordingly, curiosity is not present when the animal initially encounters a novel or unfamiliar surround, but only on subsequent occasions or trials, and only as a result of the animal learning to anticipate the unfamiliar stimuli. This conceptualization of curiosity contrasts strikingly with that provided by "common sense" and, as such, requires some comment.

The "common sense" point of view, as voiced by the early curiosity theorists, suggests that curiosity is present with the animal's *initial* receipt of the novel stimuli; curiosity is not a learned reaction but rather an innate one elicited by these stimuli. Casual observations of a tamed animal placed for the first time in a completely novel surround would certainly seem to support such a contention. The animal readily explores the novel stimuli, apparently without the aid of satiation or boredom and certainly without the motivation stemming from any *learned* anticipation of these stimuli. Hence, to the extent that exploration-eliciting stimuli are, in fact, novel—that is, on an absolute basis—explanations of "curiosity" behavior that are based on the learning of object or condition-specific anticipatory reactions would seem patently inappropriate. Nevertheless, the type of observation noted is not antagonistic to the present formulation.

First, it must be recognized that the animal's test environment can only be novel or unfamiliar to the extent that it differs (affords a change) from the stimuli to which the animal has been *exposed* prior to testing. Thus, aside from the fact that animals are typically maintained in a somewhat sensorily depleted laboratory setting, exposure to any stimulus condition prior to the animal's introduction to novel stimuli should serve to promote satiation and thereby to energize the variety of exploratory reactions that may be elicited by (directed to) the change in stimulation afforded by these novel stimuli. Secondly, and just as important, is the possibility that the animal's initial approach and investigation of novel or unfamiliar stimuli may reflect, as Brown (1953a) has argued, not any innate reaction of curiosity or wonderment but instead, and quite simply, *generalized* response tendencies that were acquired on past occasions to other, similar stimuli. This interpretation may be elaborated upon within the proposed formulation.

Although reference is made to the animal's acquisition of an object or condition-specific anticipatory reaction, it should not be overlooked that the animal's previous history may be replete with an immense variety of previously conditioned, anticipatory reactions of orientation, approach, and/or investigation, one for each novel or unfamiliar event or object experienced. Indeed, it may well be that, as a result of the animal's previous encounters with an immense variety of unfamiliar and changing stimuli (literally, one at every turn), an anticipatory investigatory reaction becomes conditioned generally, comparable to a learning-to-learn phenomenon. The basis for this conditioning effect would be the ever-present internal stimuli associated with the animal's satiation (exposure) to one stimulus condition prior to its receipt of a different—that is, novel or unfamiliar—one. Thus through the action of a generally conditioned r_g or, as Brown (1953a) suggests, through the action of generalized anticipatory reactions (quite possibly conditioned to the cues of satiation, also), the animal in its initial encounter with a new and completely different surround may be replete with generalized incentive motivation. And this generalized source of motivation could well be sufficient for the energizing of approach and investigatory reactions and even, in fact, that vague sense of wonderment or anticipation which, by common sense, comes under the label "curiosity."

CHAPTER IV

Some Recent Developments
and Future Considerations

ASIDE FROM THE ADEQUACY OF THE CURIOSITY OR
incentive-motivational construct proposed in the previous chapter,
the boredom or drive-motivational concept, as originally espoused
by Myers and Miller [7] [1] would seem to have gained a firm
empirical basis, one that attests to its adequacy both as a
meaningful and *fruitful* concept (see Chapter I). One would think
that the evidence in support of this exploratory-drive concept would
be sufficient, then, to promote at least its consideration, if not acceptance. Actually, just the opposite has been the case. Not only did
the concept come under sharp criticism in the early 1950's, when it
was formally introduced into the mainstream of psychological theorizing, but even in recent years its treatment has been no less than
severe. Thus Koch (1961) tells us:

. . . one can only wince at the current tendency to talk about such things
as "curiosity drives," "exploratory drives," "sensory drives," "perceptual
drives," etc. as if the "activities" which are held to "satisfy" each of the
"drives" (if indeed they are distinct) were just so much undifferentiated
neutral pap that came by the yard.[2]

The remarks of others would seem to be a bit more constructive.
For example, White (1959) questions the adequacy of the exploratory-drive concept specifically on the following grounds: first, on

¹ Bracketed numbers refer to readings in Part Two.
² S. Koch, "Psychological Science Versus the Science-Humanism Antinomy,"
American Psychologist, 1961, **16**, 633.

the basis of its bearing no discernable relationship to a tissue need; secondly, on the absence of any consummatory response or "climax" to the behavior that the exploratory drive presumably motivates; and thirdly, on the difficulty of relating the reinforcement involved with exploration to the reduction of a need.

Although White's (1959) criticisms seem quite cogent, their close examination reveals that they are no more constructive than Koch's (1961). Considering them in order, we may recall from Chapter I, and thus note first, that one of the theoretical refinements offered by the contemporary drive theorists in the forties and fifties (for example, Spence, 1944, 1952) was their explicit treatment of drive as a theoretical construct that had no substantive reality (for example, tissue basis) but that was convenient for purposes of integrating the facts within the relatively circumscribed area of investigation designated by the conditions or operations defining the construct. Secondly, we may reiterate a point argued in both Chapters II and III: the functional relationships existing between a novel stimulus and the exploratory response that it elicits appear analogous in every respect to those between the UCS of food and the UCR or consummatory response of eating; hence, in the context of exploration, the consummatory behavior (or "climax") is one and/or all of the components of seeing, looking, and orienting; it is the exploration or response to change itself. And finally, as noted in Chapter III, the reinforcement relating to this behavior, at least its instrumental component, is the change in stimulation afforded by the novel stimulus serving as a UCS; correspondingly, the drive (rather than need) reduction underlying this reinforcement effect is the reduction of the animal's satiation to those stimuli that it experiences prior to its receipt of the novel stimulus.

One may certainly question why the above types of criticisms have been offered, when the data appear so supporting of the exploratory-drive concept. The answer appears to lie with either the unacknowledged or unrecognized fact that these criticisms are not general ones; they relate not to the satiation or boredom conceptualization of the exploratory drive but rather to the early curiosity conceptualization. As will be recalled, the inadequacies of this latter position, in which both drive-eliciting and reinforcing properties are ascribed to novel stimuli, are reflected in two paradoxes: (a) the exploratory drive is not produced until after the animal performs the instrumental response the drive is supposed to be motivating, and (b) instrumental responses that are reinforced by novel stimuli lead to an *increase* in drive rather than to its reduction or termination.

This second paradox provides, in part, the basis for the second and third points of White's (1959) criticism and, more important, the foundation for a theoretical camp that has only recently emerged, one that we shall consider directly. However, at this point, we should pause long enough to consider a relatively simple, but nevertheless important, aspect of psychological theorizing.

Obviously, a concept can only be assessed through its operational or defining condition. However, when more than one of these defining conditions exists, the paradoxes observed may relate not to the inadequacy of the concept and its ascribed functions, but instead to the inadequacy of *one* of the defining conditions suggested for the concept; and so it seems to have been with the concept of an exploratory drive, at least as it was defined by the early curiosity theorists. Apparently many investigators still fail to recognize the significance of this distinction, for even today it is generally held that the second paradox cited above actually reflects the inadequacy of the drive concept and, correspondingly, that of the drive-reduction hypothesis. It is no wonder then that, when this seemingly inevitable conclusion first presented itself, many investigators were led to seek out a theoretical innovation, one which would relieve the waning drive concept of all its burdens and thereby replace it.

THE CONCEPT OF OPTIMAL STIMULATION OR AROUSAL

The makings for the new conceptualization of *optimal stimulation* or *arousal* appeared in the mid-fifties and on two fronts. Citing primarily the behavioral data that we have reviewed, in particular the paradox that much learning appears to occur under conditions of increasing drive, Leuba [12] argued as follows:

Tension [drive] reduction would not seem to be a general or the only principle of learning. It may be only one aspect of a more general principle, a principle which might be called one of optimal stimulation: the organism tends to learn those reactions which will produce an optimal level of total stimulation . . . *reactions which, when overall stimulation is low, are accompanied by increasing stimulation; and when overall stimulation is high, those which are accompanied by decreasing stimulation.*[3]

At the same time, Hebb [13] argued in a similar vein and for similar reasons, but primarily in reference to physiological data

[3] C. Leuba, "Toward Some Integration of Learning Theories: The Concept of Optimal Stimulation," *Psychological Reports*, 1955, 1, 28f.

(for example, Lindsley, 1951; Moruzzi and Magoun, 1949) that drew attention to the diffuse projection system of the brain stem as an "arousal" or "activating" system by which all sensory excitations could reach the cortex. To paraphrase Hebb, when sensory input or bombardment of the arousal system is low, and therefore when arousal itself is low, responses that produce increased stimulation and hence greater arousal will be repeated (presumably reinforced and strengthened). On the other hand, very high or intense sensory bombardment, producing high arousal, should serve to repel the behavior that leads to this intense stimulation, for example, by facilitating conflicting or alternative responses. "Thus there will be an optimal level of arousal for effective behavior. . . ." [4]

The view expressed by both Leuba [12] and Hebb [13] formed the basis, then, for a new kind of "drive" concept: both decreases *and increases* in drive (arousal) could be reinforcing (or motivating, for that matter) depending upon the organism's momentary level of total stimulation and arousal. Hence, with this new conceptualization, which is reminiscent of Cannon's (1932) early doctrine of homeostasis, the "paradoxical" finding that animals would explore or seek out increased stimulation no longer posed a problem. The attractiveness of such a position was not to go unnoticed, and soon it formed the basis for independent but similar conceptual frameworks that were advanced by both Berlyne (1960, 1963) and Fiske and Maddi (1961). We shall treat each of these recent formulations, starting first with Fiske and Maddi's (1961), primarily because of the more formalized nature of their theory.

The substance of Fiske and Maddi's theory is contained in the form of eight propositions that may be paraphrased and summarized as follows:

Propositions 1–3: The organism's momentary level of activation (or arousal), A.L., is directly related to the combined impact—that is, intensity, novelty, and meaningfulness—of all the stimuli, both external and internal, impinging upon the organism at a given moment. (A.L. is presumed to relate to the excitatory state of the diffuse projection system of the brain stem referred to by Hebb [13]. The "novelty" of a stimulus is the extent to which the stimulus provides variation from the organism's previous stimulation; its "meaningfulness" has reference to the organism's perception of its

---

[4] D. O. Hebb, "Drives and the C.N.S. (Conceptual Nervous System)," *Psychological Review*, 1955, 62, 250.

significance, as, for example, reading the word *fire* in a newspaper as opposed to hearing it shouted in a crowded theater.)

Propositions 4–5: *In any given task, there is an optimal A.L. for effective performance; the organism will behave so as to maintain this optimal A.L.* (Accordingly, "effective" performance is an inverted U-shaped function of A.L. or, from propositions 1–3, total stimulus impact. When total stimulus impact is "too" low, the organism will attempt to increase stimulus impact; and vice versa.)

Propositions 6–7: *There is a normal A.L. that varies with the organism's sleep–wakefulness cycle; in the absence of specific tasks, the organism behaves so as to maintain the A.L. characteristic of the particular time of the sleep–wakefulness cycle.* (A.L. is presumed to be lowest during sleep, higher during the beginning and end of wakefulness, and highest during maximal or complete wakefulness.)

Proposition 8: *When A.L. differs markedly from the normal level or the optimal level for a specific task, the organism will experience negative affect; positive affect will be experienced when A.L. is modified so that it approaches the normal or optimal level.* (Positive affect is viewed as being comparable to reinforcement; negative affect, as comparable to heightened motivation.)

It should be evident that the Fiske and Maddi (1961) theory is quite comprehensive; indeed, it has reference to all of behavior and the extent to which such behavior will be "effective." Because our concern, however, is primarily with curiosity and exploration, we shall limit an evaluation of the theory to these behaviors, and in so doing, we may consider the level to which the concept of optimal stimulation or arousal can rise (or fall) as an explanatory construct.

The Rise and Fall of Arousal—As a Concept

The Fiske and Maddi (1961) formulation would seem to fare quite well, accounting for variations in both the instrumental and consummatory components of exploration. For example, exploration or response *to* change may be deduced from propositions 1–3, 6–7: under conditions of low arousal (minimal stimulus variation, as is presumably the case with exploration), the organism engages in behaviors, such as orienting, investigating, and/or manipulating, which increase total stimulus impact and thereby sustain its normal A.L. Confronted, on the other hand, with conditions of "extreme" novelty and thus high arousal, as presumably was the case for Hebb's [13] chimpanzees viewing a stranger or the model of a human head, the animal engages in impact-decreasing behaviors—for example, withdrawal or flight—aimed at lowering its A.L. With the addition of proposition 8, the reinforcement or strengthening of behaviors—bar-press, running, and so on—which are instrumental to a moderate change in stimulation may also be explained. These behaviors, also occuring presumably under low arousal, provide for the organism's experiencing of variation (novelty), heightened arousal, and hence positive affect. Furthermore, the strength of these instrumental responses should be greater with longer exposures to relatively homogeneous surrounds and with larger magnitudes of stimulus variation or novelty contingent upon them, because greater positive affect is afforded, either directly or indirectly, by both of these conditions. With an explanation of these general phenomena of exploration at hand, let us now consider certain, specific aspects of the behavior.

As noted in the previous chapter, exploration undergoes a marked decrement when the animal is confronted for an extended duration with a novel stimulus or surround. Presumably, this is due to a diminution in the novelty or unfamiliarity of the stimulus and, correspondingly, to its inability to maintain increased impact and, hence, heightened arousal. With its initial presentation, however, the then novel stimulus did afford increased impact and heightened arousal *and also positive affect*. Thus it would seem to follow from the Fiske and Maddi proposition set that, with lengthy periods of nonexposure to the "novel" stimulus—for example, intertrial intervals of 24 hours —repeated exposures to this stimulus should provide. repeated occasions of positive affect (reinforcement), and thereby lead to an *increase* in the amount of exploration obtained over test sessions. Contrary to this expectation, the data show that exploration or response to change remains relatively constant over repeated test sessions or even tends to decrease; comparatively few studies have ever reported an increase in the amount of exploration over test sessions.

The same paradox presents itself even more strikingly in the context of alternation behavior. After the animal's initial exploration, for example, of the black arm of a T maze, it selects the unfamiliar —for example, white—arm presumably to sustain its normal level of impact and arousal. But the animal's initial exploration—that is, of the *then* novel black arm—should afford positive affect and thereby permit a strengthening of the tendency to investigate that arm, rather than the tendency to alternate. To make matters worse, several alternation studies (for example, Fowler, Blond, and Dember, 1959; Rothkopf and Zeaman, 1952; Zeaman and House, 1951) have employed food reinforcement on the first trial that, if anything, provides for greater positive affect, because food for the hungry animal enables it to sustain its normal level of impact and arousal. Nevertheless, these studies have shown that the alternation tendency persists and further that, up to a point and prior to the animal's choice of arms, repeated food-reinforced trials to the same arm of the T maze only heighten the alternation tendency! In fact, alternation on the first few choice trials has only been counteracted completely when the additional reinforcement, extrinsic to exploration, is in the form of shock reduction, and of a considerable magnitude (Fowler, Fowler, and Dember, 1959). These "positively affective" difficulties are not half so bad in view of other considerations.

With all of the food-reinforcement studies noted above (as well as with other alternation studies and even some general exploratory studies), the animals performed under food deprivation, a condition of intense, interoceptive stimulation and, thus, *high* arousal. Nevertheless, these animals, and even those performing under low intensities of *shock* in the Fowler, Fowler, and Dember (1959) study, continued to alternate, presumably because they were under *low* arousal. Now which is it? High arousal, low arousal, or some intermediate value? (In the latter case, which seems to be the logical deduction, the animal should be at or near an optimal level of arousal and thus quite content so long as it continues to explore *familiar* stimuli!) These same embarassments are also evident in the results of studies that have investigated the effects on exploration of irrelevant drive sources. Although, as noted previously, some of these studies obtained less exploration when the animals were hungry or thirsty, by and large, most of them have reported increased exploration, especially when heterogeneous test environments are employed and/or when the animals are initially exposed to a homogeneous surround and are then permitted to explore unfamiliar areas or objects. But these differences should pose no problem; the findings may easily be explained by the *a posteriori* assertion of the animal's level of arousal. If the animal explores more, arousal must have been "too" low (even under the intense interoceptive stimuli resulting from food or water deprivation); on the other hand, if the animal explores less, then arousal must have been "too" high. The deciding question, however, is, which *will* it be? Interestingly enough, within the confines of these specific cases, the concept of optimal stimulation or arousal affords us the basis for explaining "everything" and predicting "nothing." Such a predicament is strange, indeed—unless, of course, the converse of our first proposition is true.

Reprise

The conceptual framework recently espoused by Berlyne (1960, 1963) is quite similar to Fiske and Maddi's (1961): both formulations describe the animal's behavior as being directed to the maintenance of an optimal or intermediate level of stimulus impact. Nevertheless, these formulations differ significantly with respect to their underlying assumptions and thus with respect to their predictive and explanatory utility. Whereas Fiske and Maddi propose that the animal behaves so as to maintain (through increments and decrements) an intermediate or optimal level of arousal, arousal being directly related to stimulus impact, Berlyne suggests that the animal performs in order to *reduce* arousal, arousal being simply a U-shaped function of stimulus impact. In other words, for Berlyne, arousal is high not only under stimulus conditions that are very novel or unfamilar but also under those conditions in which the stimuli are very familiar or monotonous. The basis for the assumption of high arousal with the animal's exposure to familiar or monotonous stimulation stems primarily from studies that show that for human subjects, a condition of sensory deprivation—that is, an extended period of minimal stimulus variation—occasions a rise in those physiological measures, for example, muscular, circulatory, and EEG activity, which are typically taken as indices of arousal. More important, however, is the fact that this assumption and the additional one, that the animal behaves so as to reduce arousal, provide the makings of a formulation in which the concept of arousal is not only equated with that of drive but in its traditional sense. And to this end, Berlyne (1963) has argued rather extensively.

Berlyne's conceptualization fares considerably better than that espoused by Fiske and Maddi (1961), but not simply by reason of the fact that the arousal concept is equated with the drive concept; rather, the conceptualization fares better because it precludes the inconsistencies noted for the Fiske and Maddi formulation. For example, by positing exposure to constant and unvarying stimulation as a condition of high arousal (or drive), Berlyne's interpretation affords an unambiguous prediction as to the effect on exploration of irrelevant drive sources. Since these conditions, such as food or water deprivation, are also productive of high arousal, their energizing or activating effect should summate with that of stimulus exposure (or stimulus-change deprivation) to produce the increased exploration obtained in those studies where the possible competing responses relating to the irrelevant drive sources have been precluded. Even the perplexing alternation-food reinforcement problem may be resolved with the assumption that both deprivation of stimulus change and of food are drive or arousal-producing conditions. Summating, the effects of these drive conditions should additionally energize the *initially dominant* alternation tendency, dominant because the novel stimuli of the unfamiliar arm are visible at the choice point and can elicit the exploratory response *to* them, whereas with the food reinforcement typically in a recessed cup at the end of the familiar arm and thus not visible, the animal must receive sufficient training to learn where to respond *for* the food. However, this additional training, entailing successive exposures to the familiar arm containing the food, will also serve to heighten the animal's satiation to that arm, thereby temporarily protracting, if not increasing, the dominance of the alternation tendency (see Fowler, Blond, and Dember, 1959).

The predictive and explanatory utility of designating stimulus exposure as a condition of high drive or arousal would seem, then, not to be denied. Nevertheless, Berlyne finds himself not completely committed to this boredom-drive concept, primarily because "in experiments on investigatory behavior in animals, the stimuli consequent on an investigatory response often have some reward value even when there is no prior period of *stimulus deprivation*." [5] For this reason, and apparently his failure to recognize that the relevant variable underlying boredom or satiation may not be stimulus deprivation but rather stimulus exposure (or, conversely, stimulus-*change* deprivation), Berlyne suggests that exploratory performances may also be motivated by a curiosity drive. It is here that his formulation runs aground, for this conceptualization is essentially that which he espoused as one of the early curiosity theorists, and as such, it is subject to the limitations previously noted for the concept. Because these limitations had reference to the instrumental component of exploration, it is conceivable that the concept of a curiosity drive might be applicable to the consummatory component of exploration

[5] D. E. Berlyne, "Motivational Problems Raised by Exploratory and Epistemic Behavior," in S. Koch (ed.), *Psychology: A Study of a Science*, Vol. 5 (New York: McGraw-Hill Book Company, 1963), 305. Italics added.

—that is, the response to change. One could argue, then, as Berlyne has, that novel, unexpected, and/or perceptually ambiguous stimuli first raise and then reduce the drive, the two processes of drive induction and then reduction (reinforcement) taking place in immediate succession. Unfortunately, there are two difficulties inherent in such a position: first, for the conceptualization to be meaningful and thus assessable, reference must be made to the two processes in contexts that are clearly separable and definable as such in terms of specific operations, but this would seem virtually impossible; secondly, by assigning drive-inducing properties to novel, unexpected, or ambiguous stimuli, there appears to be no clearly discernible basis for predicting exploration, because it logically follows that the animal may reduce its curiosity drive simply by turning away from these stimuli rather than by exploring them. In this context, it may also be noted that the concept of a curiosity drive becomes superfluous when one posits a boredom or satiation drive (at least one that is defined in terms of stimulus exposure rather than deprivation); the latter is logically applicable to every unfamiliar or unexpected stimulus complex because of the change in stimulation that the complex affords relative to the animal's previous stimulation.

As a whole, Berlyne's formulation (as well as Fiske and Maddi's) would seem suspect for additional reasons. For example, one may question the truth of the assumption that stimulus novelty and stimulus intensity represent independent but compatible dimensions of stimulus impact. This assumption, together with that positing arousal as a U-shaped function of stimulus impact, commits Berlyne to the rather dubious hypothesis that an animal will be highly motivated when exposed to a stimulus condition that is neither too novel nor too familiar and yet of very low intensity. Aside from these criticisms and those noted above in regard to the concept of a curiosity drive, Berlyne's formulation is instructive because of the convergence of theoretical ideas that it reflects. Initially proposed as a new and alternative conceptualization to the drive formulation, the concept of arousal turns out to be nothing more than that which it was supposed to replace. Indeed, with a view toward the theoretical difficulties encountered by Fiske and Maddi's conceptualization of arousal, and the resolution of these difficulties by Berlyne's equating of arousal with drive, we are left with the distinct impression that only through this old and worn concept of drive can our new one gain its salvation.

INFORMATION-THEORETIC CONCEPTS

Together with the intensification and proliferation of research and theory on exploration in the early 1950's, there emerged another but entirely different kind of conceptual framework, that of *information theory* (see Miller and Frick, 1949). Until recently, the relevance of information theory to the study of exploration went unnoticed, perhaps because of its very nature, for contrary to other theories, this one did not provide a set of propositions by which explanations or predictions of behavior could be derived; instead, it provided techniques for quantifying the organization of events as perceived by the animal. Nevertheless, this new way of quantifying events could suggest a new way of conceptualizing their effect on behavior, and such was soon to be the case with exploration.

The relationship between information theory and the stimulus events that affect curiosity and exploratory behaviors becomes evident when one considers the meaning of the term *information*. This term does not have reference to *knowledge* or *understanding*, or other commonly employed synonyms, but instead to a *reduction of entropy or uncertainty* in the organism (see Shannon and Weaver, 1949). This special meaning of the term is not so perplexing when we consider that the organism gains absolutely no "information" if it is certain of the sequence of events that it will experience—for example, events that are redundant, repetitive, and completely organized (or as we might say in the context of exploration) unchanging and completely familiar. On the other hand, the organism gains considerable information when it experiences a sequence of events of which it is uncertain—for example, events that are varying, disorganized, or random in nature and order, or (again, as we might say) changing and unfamiliar. In the context of information theory, then, when the animal explores a novel surround, or unfamiliar pattern or object, it reduces its uncertainty of the sequence of stimulus events or elements that it experiences, and thus it gains information; and the more change or variation provided, the more information it gains.

Following a lead by Attneave (1954) on the relevance of information theory to visual perception, Berlyne [14] proceeded to assess the effect of visual stimuli that differed in their degree of relative uncertainty (for example, complexity) on human "perceptual curiosity." College students were placed in a darkened room and then were permitted to make as many key-pressing responses as desired for very brief exposures to different kinds of visual patterns ranging from simple geometric to animate forms. This first study of information-theoretic variables showed that frequency of responses for the visual patterns increased progressively over the course of training (indicative of a learning effect) and varied directly with the degree of complexity, asymmetry, and irregularity of the patterns, or in other words, with the amount of information provided. Hence, the application of information theory to the study of human exploration prompted the discovery and isolation of a class of variables that were found to be both potent eliciters of visual exploration and reinforcers of such instrumental behaviors as the key-press response made by college students.

Information Deprivation and Information Reinforcement

Recently, Jones and his associates (Jones, 1961; Jones, Wilkinson, and Braden, 1961) initiated a program of research that was designed to assess the relationship between information-theoretic concepts and the motivational propositions of S-R reinforcement theory. Reasoning that the motivational determinants of information-acquiring or exploratory behaviors might well be comparable to those underlying appetitive or food-seeking behaviors, for example, Jones *et al.* (1961) subjected college students to different lengths of *information deprivation,* a condition of maximum certainty of stimulation. To produce this unvarying stimulus condition, the subjects (in two experiments) were isolated for 10 or 12 hours in a lightproof chamber with audition greatly restricted and then, after 0, 1, or 5 hours, they were permitted to press a button that caused a patterned series of faint light flashes, varying in the randomness of their order (that is, in amount of information), to appear on the ceiling. The results of these two experiments showed that frequency of response for the light flashes was positively related both to the length of the subject's period of information deprivation and to the amount of its information reinforcement. Hence, these findings indicated that information served as an incentive or goal condition and information deprivation as the drive condition underlying behaviors directed to this type of incentive.

To assess further the interpretation that information deprivation functioned as a drive variable, the energizing effect of which should summate with that provided by an irrelevant drive source, Jones (1961) then subjected three groups of college students to information deprivation, but with one group also being deprived of food and another receiving occasional shocks throughout the experimental session. In accord with the summation hypothesis, both the food-deprived and shocked subjects showed higher proportions of response for information reinforcement during the first half of the experimental session.

The findings of Jones' research are significant for several reasons. First, they demonstrate that a drive-incentive formulation of curiosity and exploratory behaviors may also develop from the relatively independent framework provided by information theory. Secondly, and together with Berlyne's [14] findings, they highlight the necessity of treating exploratory or response-to-change phenomena within a broad framework, one inclusive not only of relatively simple changes (as provided by novel or unfamiliar stimuli) but also of the more complex kind relating to information-theoretic variables. And finally, through their bearing on curiosity and exploration in humans, they serve to illustrate both the extent and continuity of the research that has developed over the past decade from the early studies of rodent and primate exploration. From this vantage point, we may begin to take stock of the developments that have accumulated.

EPILOGUE: THE SIGNIFICANCE OF EXPLORATION

With a view toward the "mechanics" or "workings" of exploration, it would seem from our review of the literature that we are justified in promoting two principal tenets: whether through high drive or high arousal, the organism is motivated by exposure to homogeneous, simple, restricted, and/or redundant stimulation; correspondingly, it will respond to and learn to work for stimulation that reduces its drive or arousal—that is, stimulation that is novel, unfamiliar, complex, and/or changing. If we are to summarize these two tenets in a few words or with a single picture, then that picture is one of the organism *needing, seeking, and processing information,* not in the sense of receiving signals or stimulus input, but in the full theoretical sense of the word.

The recency of work on exploration has required that our analysis of the behavior deal primarily with the performance of subhuman animals; in particular, rodents and primates. However, this seems not to limit the extent of our view. With the currently emerging findings on human exploration, indeed, even with the vagaries of our own behavior, we obtain a similar picture of the organism:

It is bored by the certainties of any humdrum job or routine entertainment. It seeks out the single moving spot on the landscape or the tiny squeak in the engine. It plays the slot machine to exhaustion, hoping for the rare and unpredictable payoff when the three lemons turn up. What it seeks in the variable light signals, and what it processes and responds to on all levels, is information—the changing, the novel, the surprising, and the uncertain.[6]

This total view of the animal, responding to and for information on "all levels" of functioning, neural and behavioral as Platt (1961) argues, seems not unduly overdrawn. Consider our initial difficulty in defining exploration, a difficulty that arose out of the fact that "virtually all responses possess an exploratory function to some degree." This observation, that exploration is a fundamental characteristic of the organism in all of its actions, would seem to reflect the significance and meaning, and the worth of our study, of the behavior. For within this framework, even those "basic" functionings of the animal begin to take on new significance

Hunger, for example, can be considered as a source of intense, persistent, little-changing, and very familiar stimulation; as such, it is dealt with by the animal in the same manner as any other monotonous stimulation. That is, the animal learns and/or performs those responses which are instrumental in removing this unchanging, intense stimulation or in providing new stimulation. In the case of persistent stimulation of external origin, e.g., the familiar maze arm, the animal, given the opportunity, seeks novel stimulation, e.g., by entering the other arm. In the case of hunger stimulation, the source of which the animal carries about with it, the most appropriate instrumental response is eating.[7]

A similar interpretation seems to obtain with sexual behaviors. For example, recent work by Fisher (1962; see also Fowler and Whalen, 1961) indicates that the male rat ceases to copulate after extensive mating not because it is physically or "sexually" exhausted but, instead, because it is satiated with its female partner. When this partner (which serves as the incentive or goal object) is changed or varied, the mating is renewed, and with full and continuing vigor. These findings suggest, through the significance that they impart to both the exposure and change variables, that the initiation

[6] J. R. Platt, "Beauty: Pattern and Change," in D. W. Fiske and S. R. Maddi (eds.), *Functions of Varied Experience* (Homewood, Ill.: Dorsey Publishing Company, 1961), 410.

[7] H. Fowler, Joyce Blond, W. N. Dember, "Alternation Behavior and Learning: The Influence of Reinforcement Magnitude, Number, and Contingency," *Journal of Comparative and Physiological Psychology*, 1959, **52**, 613.

and maintenance of sexual activities, even the preliminary sex play and grooming activities of Nissen's (1953) virginal chimpanzees or the reinforcing effects of copulatory behavior for male rats not permitted to ejaculate (Sheffield, Wulff, and Backer, 1951), relate not to that obscure concept of a sex drive, but instead to the constancy of the animal's exposure and existence and to the variation and change that is provided by sex play in all its forms from grooming and petting to copulation with or without the ejaculatory climax.

Even our own patterns of sexual activity, in all of their variety, may reflect this search for and processing of information. The vicarious actions and accompanying "thrills" of the curious adolescent, the inquiring pursuits and more formal patterns of courtship displayed by the teenager, even the satiations and cravings and "fanciful delights" of the experienced adult, with all of these we seem to view the human organism in its patterned and regulated strivings for variation and change. However, such "crass" activities need not shape or limit our view. Idle thought and occasional daydream, formal entertainment and light amusement, problem solution and invention, play and sports, knowledge and education, art and humor, all of these subject-events and their associated activities serve man well and reflect the nature of his functioning. And with these forms of "epistemic" curiosity on the one hand and, for lack of a better label, "playful" exploration on the other, our view is again of man in his need, his search for, and his processing of information.

The formal span of the psychologist's attention does not comprise at present so vast a panorama of subjects, but from his study of exploration he begins to consider and, in part, to understand these complex behaviors, and even those relatively "simple" ones such as twisting a paper clip out of shape, doodling, cracking one's knuckles, and so forth, which Nissen (1954) noted. Indeed, he even seems to acquire some insight into his own functioning.

The Exploratory Behavior of the Behavioral Scientist

As a scientific investigator, the psychologist is also involved in a search for and processing of information; however, in this context, the term *information* relates to his knowledge of the workings and orderings of the universe, in particular, those "laws of nature" that are applicable to behavior. Because these laws, both by definition and presumption, do not change or vary, the psychologist's task must entail a search for and a processing of the theoretical *constancies* of behavior. But apparently the psychologist is no less subject to the dictates of exposure and change than any of the organisms that we have considered, for with his lengthy exposure (for the past 40 years) to drive theory and the drive-reduction hypothesis, his more recent actions have often been indicative of a striving not for the constancies of behavior but for variation itself. Such a point seems all too well documented in the case of exploration and the conceptual developments that the study of this behavior has promoted.

Our review of these developments has shown how, in reaction to the "inadequacies" of the drive theory of the forties, the early investigators of exploration proposed the "new" conceptualization of curiosity. But this concept had its own limitations, and soon a basis was laid both for the extension of contemporary drive theory and the development of the concept of optimal stimulation or arousal. In turn, this conceptualization has offered additional problems that seem only to be resolved by equating the arousal concept with that of drive. And then, from the independent framework provided by information theory, the drive concept presents itself once more. Thus with each step in this progression, we seem only to have moved closer to that initial formulation of behavior for which there was such jeopardy. This progression is particularly instructive, because it demonstrates how the findings that initially seem to contradict a general formulation like that of drive theory may then serve both to promote and support extended versions of the same formulation. The irony of such a development is sufficient for us to consider one final aspect of the nature of science, in particular, the manner in which former concepts are abandoned and new ones accepted.

A concept like that of drive may and, in due time, probably will be succeeded by concepts that have greater interpretive and predictive utility. But contrary to expectation, this concept or any other will not be displaced by discrepant or contradictory evidence, because the findings that appear to be in opposition to the concept may relate instead to our failure to recognize the relevance of one or more variables. In the context of exploration, one such variable seems to have been that of *stimulus exposure* (or, more specifically, length of stimulus exposure), for with recognition of its potential motivating function, contemporary drive theory may be extended and applied not only to exploratory phenomena but also to those other "simple" and complex behaviors considered above. All this, however, is really not so new. As early as the 1920's, drive proponents like Carr (1925) Moss (1924), and Richter (1922, 1927) espoused the view that *intense, persistent* forms of stimulation served both to energize the animal's behavior and to provide a basis for the learning of responses that led to a reduction of its drive. This view was partially formalized some 20 years later, when Miller and Dollard (1941) posited that the animal's level of drive and performance would be a function of the *intensity* of its stimulation. Now, after some 40 years and a decade or more of research on exploration, it would seem that we are in a position to recognize that other drive-eliciting dimension of the animal's stimulation, that of its persistence, or perhaps more simply, its *duration.*

PART TWO

The Selected Readings

Important Sources Included in Whole Or in Part

[1]

A Quantitative Demonstration of
Animal Drive

J. F. DASHIELL

Latter-day developments of psychology have emphasized more
and more the dynamic side, the analysis of the energizing and the
motivating of behavior, shown by the discussions of "emotion" and
of "instinct," and the current additions to psychological vocabulary
—"drives" and "mechanisms," "emotional facilitation," "substitute
satisfaction," "preparatory and consummatory reactions," etc.

Unfortunately, the elaboration of demonstrations for the clearer
and more concrete presentation of these new concepts to students
has lagged; and a very dearth of methods is at present available.
The reasons are multiple. It may be expected that sufficient simplification and standardization of pioneer research methods will only
follow at a distance the research work itself; but the very nature of
the processes above referred to, being for the most part peculiarly
intra-organic and sub-peripheral and often dependent upon wide-
spread and slow-changing conditions of the total organism, makes
their instrumentation and controlled demonstration decidedly more
difficult than in the case of the simpler sensory, motor, and language-
using functions.

In the interest of this general modification of technique for pedagogical purposes the writer offers an experience of his own. It was
an attempt to make concrete for elementary students the point that
an inner organic condition may serve as a drive to produce exploratory behavior of a fairly continuous sort that is terminated typically
only when a particular stimulus appears to arouse an end-reaction.
Animals are decidedly more satisfactory subjects for such work than
humans because their whole organic condition is easily controlled
for experimental purposes. And of the various drives hunger is the
most conveniently manipulated. The writer has, then, employed

SOURCE: J. F. Dashiell, "A Quantitative Demonstration of Animal Drive,"
Journal of Comparative Psychology, 1925, 5, 205–208. Reprinted by permission
of the Williams and Wilkins Company, Inc., and J. F. Dashiell.

white rats in two comparison groups, a "hungry" and a "fed" or control group.

A more troublesome part of a desirable demonstration than that of subject and drive control is that of the method of measuring the activity produced by the animal. The writer tried the revolving cage without success with white rats: the members of this species not climbing and whirling the drum as do squirrels, even sliding and tumbling when it is revolved from without. The idea of using a table placed delicately upon tambours as employed by Nicholls (1922) was given up after the technical difficulties of arranging it for large

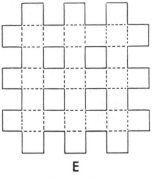

E

FIGURE 1.

class use became obvious. Recourse was had to a modified maze plan, with the idea of bringing out for quantitative observation the greater degree of exploratory behavior exhibited in the usual maze by the animal with the hunger incentive than that by an animal without this. The floor plan of the modified maze is presented in Figure 1. The whole floor was first lined off with dim lines 10 cm. apart in such a way as to produce square blocks of that dimension (represented by dotted lines in the figure). Outside partitions were then erected to form a completely enclosed space divided by other partitions into alley ways (partitions shown as continuous lines in the figure). The animal when introduced at E had several directions in which to turn and could proceed in an indefinite variety of ways. The marking off of the floor into blocks made possible a measurement of the subject's total locomotor activity sufficiently exact for pedagogical purposes. (Of course, students can often note the greater activity of the hungry animals simply by general observation, but for pedagogical reasons they should be trained to think always in quantitative terms.)

TABLE 1

Showing Number of Blocks Entered by Individuals of the Two Groups

"Fed"	*"Hungry"*
20	34
29	36
9	37
24	47
31	42
11	42
25	64
32	38
31	41
30	72
40	47
34	37
37	39
26	31
21	34
36	46
18	42
Totals 454	729
Averages 26.7	42.9

The above maze is simply planned and is easily constructed of wood floor with wood or metal partitions. The writer used a take-down form, with floor of cork composition, walls of black painted galvanized iron, and top of wire mesh. The convenience of this material has been elsewhere described (Stetson & Dashiell, 1919).

In the procedure, the instructor handled the animals, and the members of the laboratory section stood by with copies of the maze plan (easily run off in quantities with the gelatin type of duplicator) upon which they each traced in pencil the course followed by the rat. Rats from the "fed" and from the "hungry" groups were used alternately, each being given the same time in the enclosure, sixty seconds. After the laboratory work of the day each student inspected his tracings, counting the total number of blocks entered by each subject ("entered," if one forefoot was set down over the line), and tabulating these to determine relative group scores. A sample table of results recently obtained from a class demonstration is given in Table 1. A definite tendency of the hunger-driven animals to show more restless activity is exhibited. The difference would doubtless be much greater were it not that the mere being-placed-in-a-new-enclosure operates as something of a stimulus to set off exploratory reactions even in the non-hungry group. One who has handled white rats knows well enough that when these animals are returned to a renovated nest box they pay little or no attention to food placed there even though unfed for twenty-four hours, but give themselves up for a while to explorations over and through their new bedding. Whatever the finally assigned status for the "instinct of curiosity," it is undeniable that novelty in the environment is pretty sure to awaken "curious" behavior.

An attempt was made to cancel this novelty or curiosity-drive factor by putting the animals daily into the enclosure for two weeks before the above demonstration, but other difficulties here presented themselves inasmuch as it was almost impossible to prevent some sort of conditioning or associating of this enclosure-situation to feeding and other responses.

It goes without saying that quantitative variations of the above procedure can be made by testing animals of different degrees of hunger, somewhat as done by Moss (1924).

[2]

Spontaneous Alternation in Rats as an Indicator of the Persistence of Stimulus Effects

WAYNE DENNIS

In 1934 Wingfield and Dennis found that when the rat is presented with two or more equally long paths to food and when it is offered two or more choices of pathways within a relatively short period of time, the animal on any trial after the first tends to avoid the path most recently traversed and to diversify its course to the goal. This may be called a tendency toward variability of routes. In the simplest situation, namely two paths and two successive trials, this

SOURCE: Wayne Dennis, "Spontaneous Alternation in Rats as an Indicator of the Persistence of Stimulus Effects," *Journal of Comparative Psychology*, 1939, **28**, 305–312. Reprinted by permission of the Williams and Wilkins Company, Inc., and W. Dennis.

tendency results in a rather consistent alternation between the two pathways. Because most of our work has been done with two pathways, we shall speak of the rat's behavior as alternation, although it is realized that in a wider sense the phenomenon is one of variability.

Since our first publication, we have found that spontaneous alternation in rats was described briefly by Tolman (1925a). We therefore wish to make this acknowledgment of Tolman's priority. However, the phenomenon of spontaneous alternation seems to have played no part in Tolman's systematic account of rat behavior (1932).

It is well-known, of course, that alternation habits of various sorts occasionally appear when the animal faces a difficult discrimination problem. Hunter (1920) has said that "the tendency toward simple alternation and the tendency to alternate after success have appeared so constantly in all difficult problems with the T-box, that it seems safe to affirm that these are innate reaction tendencies of the rat." It may be remarked that under these same circumstances position habits also are formed. What determines the nature of the reaction in a difficult problem has not as yet been discovered. In our work, in which each of two paths leads to food, alternation has occurred in all animals and position habits have never appeared in a single subject.

Carr (1917, 1919), Hunter (1920, 1930, 1931), Loucks (1931), and others have trained animals in alternation habits. It may seem anomalous that a response which we have found to be spontaneous should require training. The work of these experimenters has differed from ours in this respect, that in their research the course of the rat was predetermined by the experimenter and any deviation from this route led to a blocking of certain pathways by the experimenter. Thus if the animal took the wrong pathway on any trial, it was then forced to traverse the correct one as well as the wrong one. In other words, on many trials *both* pathways were taken. It might be expected that this would upset any natural tendency to alternate on successive trials. The forced alternation technique does not permit the rat to alternate its choices at all times but only when the animal's choices coincide with the predetermined alternations imposed by the experimenter.

Subsequent to our first report of spontaneous alternation, the presence of the phenomenon has been checked in a variety of two-way maze situations. It has been found that spontaneous alternation is as marked on the exploratory trials as it is after hundreds of practice runs (Dennis, 1935; Dennis & Sollenberger, 1934). It has appeared in all the kinds of alternative-choice situations which we have constructed, and these have been quite varied. Under a large number of experimental conditions, the characteristic frequency of alternations has been roughly 80 per cent, whereas chance behavior would result in alternation in only 50 per cent of the opportunities.

The alternation phenomenon, we believe, has an important bearing upon several problems in animal psychology, but in the present instance we shall direct our evidence and our discussion chiefly to one problem. That is the question as to the extent to which the rat can carry over intraneurally the effects of the immediately preceding activity.

The retention of the effects of individual stimuli was first submitted to experimentation in the delayed reaction set-up (Hunter, 1913). Since that time other procedures have been used for the same purpose. These have been the forced alternation problem, the temporal maze, and the double alternation box. All of the methods have rather generally agreed in exhibiting a low ability on the part of the rat to be guided in its behavior by a stimulus applied a few seconds prior to the behavior test, so that the picture of rat behavior which has been built up is that of a reaction system dominated almost solely by stimuli which are immediately present.

The current methods of gathering evidence on this point are similar in this respect: that they impose a problem upon the animal without prior investigation of the animal's spontaneous reaction tendencies. In spontaneous alternation the animal, without training, responds at the time of a second choice in large measure on the basis of the reaction made at the time of the first choice. The external situation remains the same between first and second choices. The difference between the first and the second choices can be explained only on the basis of some change within the animal. This change must have been initiated at the time of the first trial, and must have persisted throughout the interval.[1]

In this sense, any alternation is in some degree a delayed alternation; that is, there must be an interval between trials, and the consequences of the first trial somehow bridge this interval.

[1] It may be suggested that on any trial after the first the rat is reacting to an olfactory trail laid down on the preceding trial. Control tests, involving the interchange of apparatus units, were made on this point in the study of Wingfield and Dennis. No evidence of such guidance was found. It should be noted that the animal would have to *avoid* the hypothetical trail.

It is not claimed that the spontaneous alternation technique is equivalent to the delayed reaction method. In the latter, the animal must respond to a previous cue which has been set by the experimenter whereas the former depends upon the rat's own previous behavior. In forced alternation problems, as in the delayed reaction problem, the rat in reality must respond in trials after the first to cues previously presented by the experimenter, for the only reliable cue on any trial after the first is some sort of "knowledge" as to which door was open and which was closed on the preceding trial.

Using spontaneous alternation as an indicator, we have been interested in finding some of the conditions under which the effects of the first choice in a two-way apparatus will persist so as to cause a reversal of choice in the second trial.

The animals used were two groups of rats, each group composed of twenty males of Wistar stock, between two and three months of age, and untrained at the beginning of the experiment. The general procedure, which was the same for the two groups, was as follows: the rat was placed twice in succession upon the apparatus and permitted at the end of each trial to take a very small quantity of a powdered diet ("Balra") which was found in a small pan nailed to the end of the goal section of the apparatus. The animal was then returned to its cage, and the next rat was chosen. The entire group of animals was run in approximately an hour, whereupon the first subject was given another pair of trials, etc. Each subject in the course of a day received six or seven pairs of trials, consecutive pairs being separated by approximately one hour. This plan of experimentation proved to be quite practicable, as will be shown by the results which follow.

The basic pattern of the apparatus was a hollow square of block elevated construction as shown in Figure 1. Each hollow square was two feet on a side; the starting block and the goal block each were one foot long, unless otherwise stated.

For Group A the goal block was varied in length in order to vary the interval between the two members of a pair of trials. The maximum length used was 38 feet which was the capacity of laboratory. This meant that at times the subject had to run 38 feet of straight pathway before receiving food and then had to be carried back to the starting point for the second trial.

In Group A, each rat was first given 24 pairs of trials on the simple unit, yielding 480 possible alternations. Of these 82 per cent were realized.

Next, 14 feet of goal pathway were added and 6 pairs of runs given. Then 24 feet of pathway were employed and 5 pairs of trials were conducted. Finally the goal path consisted of 38 feet of pathway and 14 pairs of runs were required of each animal. The per-

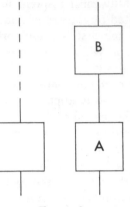

FIGURE 1.

centages of alternation for these trials were respectively 72, 78, and 76. In other words, the time required for running 38 feet of additional pathway plus the interval needed to carry the animal back to the starting point, did not appreciably affect the influence of the first choice upon the second. The interval between first and second choices was timed by a stop watch, and for the experiment with the 38 feet of additional straight-away the minimum time was 35 seconds; the median time was 105 seconds.

Group B began with a simple unit as did Group A. In 13 pairs of trials per animal, or 260 pairs of trials, the alternations were 81 per cent of the opportunities to alternate, or a percentage almost identical with the record of Group A.

Group B was then submitted to an arrangement of hollow-square units in tandem. The two-unit apparatus is shown in the right-hand part of Figure 1. On a two-unit apparatus, 34 pairs of trials were given each animal. On a three-unit arrangement, each animal was given 10 pairs of trials. Finally, on a 10-unit apparatus, 12 pairs of runs were given each subject.

We are most interested in the two-unit apparatus, for with it the number of trials was very large (680 possible alternations) and the evidence is clear.

In these trials, there was only a chance relationship between the choices on unit A and the choices on unit B. In other words, the behavior upon unit B was not influenced by the choice in unit A. Of records showing a left choice in unit A, only 50 per cent showed a left choice in unit B, and similarly those who made a right choice in unit A divided their choices equally between the right and left sides of unit B. One might have expected centrifugal swing to operate so as to throw animals toward the side of unit B which was opposite to that which they traversed in unit A. That centrifugal swing did not operate is probably due to the fact that the pathways were narrow (2 inches wide) and elevated. We are not acquainted with any evidence for the appearance of centrifugal swing on narrow elevated pathways.

The facts just presented show that spontaneous alternation is not the result of a generalized tendency to turn in a direction opposite to a choice which has just been made, for if such were the case the choices in unit B should have been opposite in direction from those in unit A.

The evidence shows that the alternation tendency is a tendency to *avoid a specific pathway* which has recently been traversed (on this point see also Wingfield and Dennis, 1934). In unit A and in unit B the second trip through the apparatus resulted in choices which were in the main contrary in direction in each unit to the choices made in the first trip, although as noted above, on either trip the choices in unit A and in unit B were independent of each other. As between first and second trials, the per cent of alternation was 75 for unit A and 72 for unit B.

These data show clearly that the result of the first trip through unit A is a tendency to avoid the same pathway when this particular unit is again traversed. Likewise the tendency which is aroused in unit B is specific to that unit. There is no general tendency to take an opposite direction regardless of the position of the choice point. There is no effect of the first choice in unit A upon the first choice in unit B nor of the first choice in unit B upon the second choice in unit A. However, the first choice in either unit affects a second choice in the same unit. In other words it would appear that the animal is able to retain at least for many seconds two distinct reaction tendencies each aroused by a specific stimulus pattern and each released by a recurrence of its appropriate stimulus pattern. This represents a degree of "immediate memory" or of "persistence of stimulus effects" not previously exhibited in the rat by delayed reaction techniques. It is similar to the multiple delayed reaction of some animals but there is this difference that the delayed reaction allows the completion of a reaction tendency which has been frustrated whereas in the present case the second reaction consists in taking the pathway which was avoided on the first trial. Apparently no frustration has occurred.

Naturally there is some limit to such an achievement. The breakdown occurs when 3 or more units are used. The alternation in the 3 units respectively was 67, 54, 52 per cent. The first is reliably better than chance performance, but the second and third are almost identical with chance expectations.

When 10 units were arranged in a series, the behavior on no unit was reliably different from chance expectation, but the per cent of alternation became rather consistently less from the early to the later units. The percentages were respectively as follows: 59, 55, 52, 61, 55, 47, 45, 45, 38, 36.

Summary and Discussion

Evidence has been presented which shows that a choice of pathways by the rat will influence a later choice at the same point even if an interval of more than a minute separates the two choices. The temporal limit of this influence was not determined.

A choice influences a second choice at the same spot in the apparatus, even though a choice elsewhere in the apparatus has intervened. However, a choice at one point in the present apparatus had no effect upon a subsequent choice in another section of the apparatus.

The situation in spontaneous alternation differs from forced delay problems in that the rat in spontaneous alternation shows evidence of some sort of retention of its spontaneous activity whereas in the forced delay problem the animal must retain the effects of a cue which has been given by the experimenter.

The phenomenon of spontaneous alternation shows that the rat, without training, may respond to a choice situation in part on the basis of its preceding activity. The rat's choice of pathway is not always determined by stimuli which are acting upon the sense organs at the moment but may be guided in part by events which preceded the choice by an interval at least one minute in length and perhaps by longer periods.

[3]

Mice, Monkeys, Men, and Motives [1]

HARRY F. HARLOW

Many of psychology's theoretical growing pains—or, in modern terminology, conditioned anxieties—stem from the behavioral revolution of Watson. The new psychology intuitively disposed of instincts and painlessly disposed of hedonism. But having completed this St. Bartholomew-type massacre, behavioristic motivation theory was left with an aching void, a nonhedonistic aching void, needless to say.

Before the advent of the Watsonian scourge the importance of external stimuli as motivating forces was well recognized. Psychologists will always remain indebted to Loeb's (1918) brilliant formulation of tropistic theory, which emphasized, and probably overemphasized, the powerful role of external stimulation as the primary motivating agency in animal behavior. Unfortunately, Loeb's premature efforts to reduce all behavior to overly simple mathematical formulation, his continuous acceptance of new tropistic constructs in an effort to account for any aberrant behavior not easily integrated into his original system, and his abortive attempt to encompass all behavior into a miniature theoretical system doubtless led many investigators to underestimate the value of his experimental contributions.

Thorndike (1911) was simultaneously giving proper emphasis to the role of external stimulation as a motivating force in learning and learned performances. Regrettably, these motivating processes were defined in terms of pain and pleasure, and it is probably best for us to dispense with such lax, ill-defined, subjective terms as pain, pleasure, anxiety, frustration, and hypotheses—particularly in descriptive and theoretical rodentology.

[1] This paper was presented September 3, 1951, as the presidential address of the Division of Experimental Psychology at the Chicago meetings of the American Psychological Association.

SOURCE: Harry F. Harlow, "Mice, Monkeys, Men, and Motives," *Psychological Review*, 1953, 60, 23–32. Reprinted by permission of the American Psychological Association and H. F. Harlow.

Instinct theory, for all its terminological limitations, put proper emphasis on the motivating power of external stimuli; for, as so brilliantly described by Watson in 1914, the instinctive response was elicited by "serial stimulation," much of which was serial external stimulation.

The almost countless researches on tropisms and instincts might well have been expanded to form a solid and adequate motivational theory for psychology—a theory with a proper emphasis on the role of the external stimulus and an emphasis on the importance of incentives as opposed to internal drives per se.

It is somewhat difficult to understand how this vast and valuable literature was to become so completely obscured and how the importance of the external stimulus as a motivating agent was to become lost. Pain-pleasure theory was discarded because the terminology had subjective, philosophical implications. Instinct theory fell into disfavor because psychologists rejected the dichotomized heredity-environment controversy and, also, because the term "instinct" had more than one meaning. Why tropistic theory disappeared remains a mystery, particularly inasmuch as most of the researches were carried out on subprimate animal forms.

Modern motivation theory apparently evolved from an over-popularization of certain experimental and theoretical materials. Jennings' (1906) demonstration that "physiological state" played a role in determining the behavior of the lower animal was given exaggerated importance and emphasis, thereby relegating the role of external stimulation to a secondary position as a force in motivation. The outstanding work in the area of motivation between 1920 and 1930 related to visceral drives and drive cycles and was popularized by Richter's (1927) idealized theoretical paper on "Animal Behavior and Internal Drives" and Cannon's (1932) *The Wisdom of the Body*.

When the self-conscious behavior theorists of the early thirties looked for a motivation theory to integrate with their developing learning constructs, it was only natural that they should choose the available tissue-tension hypotheses. Enthusiastically and uncritically the S–R theorists swallowed these theses whole. For fifteen years they have tried to digest them, and it is now time that these theses be subjected to critical examination, analysis, and evaluation. We do not question that these theses have fertilized the field of learning, but we do question that the plants that have developed are those that will survive the test of time.

It is my belief that the theory which describes learning as dependent upon drive reduction is false, that internal drive as such is a variable of little importance to learning, and that this small importance steadily decreases as we ascend the phyletic scale and as we investigate learning problems of progressive complexity. Finally, it is my position that drive-reduction theory orients learning psychologists to attack problems of limited importance and to ignore the fields of research that might lead us in some foreseeable future time to evolve a theoretical psychology of learning that transcends any single species or order.

There can be no doubt that the single-celled organisms such as the amoeba and the paramecium are motivated to action both by external and internal stimuli. The motivation by external stimulation gives rise to heliotropisms, chemotropisms, and rheotropisms. The motivation by internal stimulation produces characteristic physiological states which have, in turn, been described as chemotropisms. From a phylogenetic point of view, moreover, neither type of motive appears to be more basic or more fundamental than the other. Both types are found in the simplest known animals and function in interactive, rather than in dominant-subordinate, roles.

Studies of fetal responses in animals from opossum to man give no evidence suggesting that the motivation of physiological states precedes that of external incentives. Tactual, thermal, and even auditory and visual stimuli elicit complex patterns of behavior in the fetal guinea pig, although this animal has a placental circulation which should guarantee against thirst or hunger (Carmichael, 1934). The newborn opossum climbs up the belly of the female and into the pouch, apparently in response to external cues; if visceral motives play any essential role, it is yet to be described (Langworthy, 1928). The human fetus responds to external tactual and nociceptive stimuli at a developmental period preceding demonstrated hunger or thirst motivation. Certainly, there is no experimental literature to indicate that internal drives are ontogenetically more basic than exteroceptive motivating agencies.

Tactual stimulation, particularly of the cheeks and lips, elicits mouth, head, and neck responses in the human neonate, and there are no data demonstrating that these responses are conditioned, or even dependent, upon physiological drive states. Hunger appears to lower the threshold for these responses to tactual stimuli. Indeed, the main role of the primary drive seems to be one of altering the threshold for precurrent responses. Differentiated sucking response patterns have been demonstrated to quantitatively varied thermal and chemical stimuli in the infant only hours of age (Jensen, 1932), and there is, again, no reason to believe that the differentiation could have resulted from antecedent tissue-tension reduction states. Taste and temperature sensations induced by the temperature and chemical composition of the liquids seem adequate to account for the responses.

There is neither phylogenetic nor ontogenetic evidence that drive states elicit more fundamental and basic response patterns than do external stimuli; nor is there basis for the belief that precurrent responses are more dependent upon consummatory responses than are consummatory responses dependent upon precurrent responses. There is no evidence that the differentiation of the innate precurrent responses is more greatly influenced by tissue-tension reduction than are the temporal ordering and intensity of consummatory responses influenced by conditions of external stimulation.

There are logical reasons why a drive-reduction theory of learning, a theory which emphasizes the role of internal, physiological-state motivation, is entirely untenable as a motivational theory of learning. The internal drives are cyclical and operate, certainly at any effective level of intensity, for only a brief fraction of any organism's waking life. The classical hunger drive physiologically defined ceases almost as soon as food—or nonfood—is ingested. This, as far as we know, is the only case in which a single swallow portends anything of importance. The temporal brevity of operation of the internal drive states obviously offers a minimal opportunity for conditioning and a maximal opportunity for extinction. The human being, at least in the continental United States, may go for days or even years without ever experiencing true hunger or thirst. If his complex conditioned responses were dependent upon primary drive reduction, one would expect him to regress rapidly to a state of tuitional oblivion. There are, of course, certain recurrent physiological drive states that are maintained in the adult. But the studies of Kinsey (1948) indicate that in the case of one of these there is an inverse correlation between presumed drive strength and scope and breadth of learning, and in spite of the alleged reading habits of the American public, it is hard to believe that the other is our major source of intellectual support. Any assumption that derived drives or motives can account for learning in the absence of primary drive reduction puts an undue emphasis on the strength and permanence of derived drives, at least in subhuman animals. Experimental studies to date indicate that most derived drives (Miller, 1951) and second-order conditioned responses (Pavlov, 1927) rapidly extinguish when the rewards which theoretically reduce the primary drives are withheld. The additional hypothesis of functional autonomy of motives, which could bridge the gap, is yet to be demonstrated experimentally.

The condition of strong drive is inimical to all but very limited aspects of learning—the learning of ways to reduce the internal tension. The hungry child screams, closes his eyes, and is apparently oblivious to most of his environment. During this state he eliminates response to those aspects of his environment around which all his important learned behaviors will be based. The hungry child is a most incurious child, but after he has eaten and become thoroughly sated, his curiosity and all the learned responses associated with his curiosity take place. If this learning is conditioned to an internal drive state, we must assume it is the resultant of backward conditioning. If we wish to hypothesize that backward conditioning is dominant over forward conditioning in the infant, it might be possible to reconcile fact with S–R theory. It would appear, however, that alternate theoretical possibilities should be explored before the infantile backward conditioning hypothesis is accepted.

Observations and experiments on monkeys convinced us that there was as much evidence to indicate that a strong drive state inhibits learning as to indicate that it facilitates learning. It was the speaker's feeling that monkeys learned most efficiently if they were given food before testing, and as a result, the speaker routinely fed his subjects before every training session. The rhesus monkey is equipped with enormous cheek pouches, and consequently many subjects would begin the educational process with a rich store of incentives crammed into the buccal cavity. When the monkey made a correct response, it would add a raisin to the buccal storehouse and swallow a little previously munched food. Following an incorrect response, the monkey would also swallow a little stored food. Thus, both correct and incorrect responses invariably resulted in S–R theory drive reduction. It is obvious that under these conditions the monkey cannot learn, but the present speaker developed an understandable skepticism of this hypothesis when the monkeys stubbornly persisted in learning, learning rapidly, and learning problems of great complexity. Because food was continuously available in the monkey's mouth, an explanation in terms of differential fractional anticipatory goal responses did not appear attractive. It would seem that the Lord was simply unaware of drive-reduction learning theory when he created, or permitted the gradual evolution of, the rhesus monkey.

The langurs are monkeys that belong to the only family of primates with sacculated stomachs. There would appear to be no mechanism better designed than the sacculated stomach to induce automatically prolonged delay of reinforcement defined in terms of homeostatic drive reduction. Langurs should, therefore, learn with great difficulty. But a team of Wisconsin students has discovered that the langurs in the San Diego Zoo learn at a high level of monkey efficiency. There is, of course, the alternative explanation that the inhibition of hunger contractions in multiple stomachs is more reinforcing than the inhibition of hunger contractions in one. Perhaps the quantification of the gastric variable will open up great new vistas of research.

Actually, the anatomical variable of diversity of alimentary mechanisms is essentially uncorrelated with learning to food incentives by monkeys and suggests that learning efficiency is far better related to tensions in the brain than in the belly.

Experimental test bears out the fact that learning performance by the monkey is unrelated to the theoretical intensity of the hunger drive. Meyer (1951) tested rhesus monkeys on discrimination-learning problems under conditions of maintenance-food deprivation of 1.5, 18.5, and 22.5 hours and found no significant differences in learning or performance. Subsequently, he tested the same monkeys on discrimination-reversal learning following 1, 23, and 47 hours of maintenance-food deprivation and, again, found no significant differences in learning or in performance as measured by activity, direction of activity, or rate of responding. There was some evidence, not statistically significant, that the most famished subjects were a bit overeager and that intense drive exerted a mildly inhibitory effect on learning efficiency.

Meyer's data are in complete accord with those presented by Birch (1945), who tested six young chimpanzees after 2, 6, 12, 24, and 48 hr. of food deprivation and found no significant differences in proficiency of performance on six patterned string problems. Observational evidence led Birch to conclude that intense food deprivation adversely affected problem solution because it led the chimpanzee to concentrate on the goal to the relative exclusion of the other factors.

It may be stated unequivocally that, regardless of any relationship that may be found for other animals, there are no data indicating that intensity of drive state and the presumably correlated amount of drive reduction are positively related to learning efficiency in primates.

In point of fact there is no reason to believe that the rodentological data will prove to differ significantly from those of monkey, chimpanzee, and man. Strassburger (1950) has recently demonstrated that differences in food deprivation from 5 hours to 47 hours do not differentially affect the habit strength of the bar-pressing response as measured by subsequent resistance to extinction. Recently, Sheffield and Roby (1950) have demonstrated learning in rats in the absence of primary drive reduction. Hungry rats learned to choose a maze path leading to a saccharin solution, a nonnutritive substance, in preference to a path leading to water. No study could better illustrate the predominant role of the external incentive-type stimulus on the learning function. These data suggest that, following the example of the monkey, even the rats are abandoning the sinking ship of reinforcement theory.

The effect of intensity of drive state on learning doubtless varies as we ascend the phyletic scale and certainly varies, probably to the point of almost complete reversal, as we pass from simple to complex problems, a point emphasized some years ago in a theoretical article by Maslow (1943). Intensity of nociceptive stimulation may be positively related to speed of formation of conditioned avoidance responses in the monkey, but the use of intense nociceptive stimulation prevents the monkey from solving any problem of moderate complexity. This fact is consistent with a principle that was formulated and demonstrated experimentally many years ago as the Yerkes-Dodson law (1908). There is, of course, no reference to the Yerkes-Dodson law by any drive-reduction theorist.

We do not mean to imply that drive state and drive-state reduction are unrelated to learning; we wish merely to emphasize that they are relatively unimportant variables. Our primary quarrel with drive-reduction theory is that it tends to focus more and more attention on problems of less and less importance. A strong case can be made for the proposition that the importance of the psychological problems studied during the last fifteen years has decreased as a negatively accelerated function approaching an asymptote of complete indifference. Nothing better illustrates this point than the kinds of apparatus currently used in "learning" research. We have the single-unit T-maze, the straight runway, the double-compartment grill box, and the Skinner box. The single-unit T-maze is an ideal apparatus for studying the visual capacities of a nocturnal animal; the straight runway enables one to measure quantitatively the speed and rate of running from one dead end to another; the double-compartment grill box is without doubt the most efficient torture chamber which is still legal; and the Skinner box enables one to demonstrate discrimination learning in a greater number of trials than is required by any other method. But the apparatus, though inefficient, give rise to data which can be splendidly quantified. The kinds of learning problems which can be efficiently measured in these apparatus represent a challenge only to the decorticate animal. It is a constant source of bewilderment to me that the neobehaviorists who so frequently belittle physiological psychology should choose apparatus which, in effect, experimentally decorticate their subjects.

The Skinner box is a splendid apparatus for demonstrating that the rate of performance of a learned response is positively related to the period of food deprivation. We have confirmed this for the monkey by studying rate of response on a modified Skinner box following 1, 23, and 47 hr. of food deprivation. Increasing length of food deprivation is clearly and positively related to increased rate of response. This functional relationship between drive states and responses does not hold, as we have already seen, for the monkey's behavior in discrimination learning or in acquisition of any more complex problem. The data, however, like rat data, are in complete accord with Crozier's (1929) finding that the acuteness of the radial angle of tropistic movements in the slug Limax is positively related to intensity of the photic stimulation. We believe there is generalization in this finding, and we believe the generalization to be that the results from the investigation of simple behavior may be very informative about even simpler behavior but very seldom are they informative about behavior of greater complexity. I do not want to discourage anyone from the pursuit of the psychological Holy Grail by the use of the Skinner box, but as far as I am concerned, there will be no moaning of farewell when we have passed the pressing of the bar.

In the course of human events many psychologists have children, and these children always behave in accord with the theoretical position of their parents. For purposes of scientific objectivity the boys are always referred to as "Johnny" and the girls as "Mary." For some eleven months I have been observing the behavior of

Mary X. Perhaps the most striking characteristic of this particular primate has been the power and persistence of her curiosity-investigatory motives. At an early age Mary X demonstrated a positive valence to parental thygmotatic stimulation. My original interpretation of these tactualthermal erotic responses as indicating parental affection was dissolved by the discovery that when Mary X was held in any position depriving her of visual exploration of the environment, she screamed; when held in a position favorable to visual exploration of the important environment, which did not include the parent, she responded positively. With the parent and position held constant and visual exploration denied by snapping off the electric light, the positive responses changed to negative, and they returned to positive when the light was again restored. This behavior was observed in Mary X, who, like any good Watson child, showed no "innate fear of the dark."

The frustrations of Mary X appeared to be in large part the results of physical inability to achieve curiosity-investigatory goals. In her second month, frustrations resulted from inability to hold up her head indefinitely while lying prone in her crib or on a mat and the consequent loss of visual curiosity goals. Each time she had to lower her head to rest, she cried lustily. At nine weeks attempts to explore (and destroy) objects anterior resulted in wriggling backward away from the lure and elicited violent negative responses. Once she negotiated forward locomotion, exploration set in, in earnest, and, much to her parents' frustration, shows no sign of diminishing.

Can anyone seriously believe that the insatiable curiosity-investigatory motivation of the child is a second-order or derived drive conditioned upon hunger or sex or any other internal drive? The S–R theorist and the Freudian psychoanalyst imply that such behaviors are based on primary drives. An informal survey of neo-behaviorists who are also fathers (or mothers) reveals that all have observed the intensity and omnipresence of the curiosity-investigatory motive in their own children. None of them seriously believes that the behavior derives from a second-order drive. After describing their children's behavior, often with a surprising enthusiasm and frequently with the support of photographic records, they trudge off to their laboratories to study, under conditions of solitary confinement, the intellectual processes of rodents. Such attitudes, perfectly in keeping with drive-reduction theory, no doubt account for the fact that there are no experimental or even systematic observational studies of curiosity-investigatory-type external-incentive motives in children.

A key to the real learning theory of any animal species is knowledge of the nature and organization of the unlearned patterns of response. The differences in the intellectual capabilities of cockroach, rat, monkey, chimpanzee, and man are as much a function of the differences in the inherent patterns of response and the differences in the inherent motivational forces as they are a function of sheer learning power. The differences in these inherent patterns of response and in the motivational forces will, I am certain, prove to be differential responsiveness to external stimulus patterns. Furthermore, I am certain that the variables which are of true, as opposed to psychophilosophical, importance are not constant from learning problem to learning problem even for the same animal order, and they are vastly diverse as we pass from one animal order to another.

Convinced that the key to human learning is not the conditioned response but, rather, motivation aroused by external stimuli, the speaker has initiated researches on curiosity-manipulation behavior as related to learning in monkeys (Davis, Settlage, & Harlow, 1950; Harlow, 1950; Harlow, Harlow, & Meyer, 1950). The justification for the use of monkeys is that we have more monkeys than children. Furthermore, the field is so unexplored that a systematic investigation anywhere in the phyletic scale should prove of methodological value. The rhesus monkey is actually a very incurious and nonmanipulative animal compared with the anthropoid apes, which are, in turn, very incurious nonmanipulative animals compared with man. It is certainly more than coincidence that the strength and range of curiosity-manipulative motivation and position within the primate order are closely related.

We have presented three studies which demonstrate that monkeys can and do learn to solve mechanical puzzles when no motivation is provided other than presence of the puzzle. Furthermore, we have presented data to show that once mastered, the sequence of manipulations involved in solving these puzzles is carried out relatively flawlessly and extremely persistently. We have presented what we believe is incontrovertible evidence against a second-order drive interpretation of this learning.

A fourth study was carried out recently by Gately at the Wisconsin laboratories. Gately directly compared the behavior of two groups of four monkeys presented with banks of four identical mechanical puzzles, each utilizing three restraining devices. All four food- plus puzzle-rewarded monkeys solved the four identical puzzles, and only one of the four monkeys motivated by curiosity alone solved all the puzzles. This one monkey, however, learned as rapidly and as efficiently as any of the food-rewarded monkeys. But I wish to stress an extremely important observation made by Gately and supported by quantitative records. When the food-rewarded monkeys had solved a puzzle, they abandoned it. When the nonfood-rewarded animals had solved the puzzle, they frequently continued their explorations and manipulations. Indeed, one reason for the nonfood-rewarded monkeys' failure to achieve the experimenter's concept of solution lay in the fact that the monkey became fixated in exploration and manipulation of limited puzzle or puzzle-device components. From this point of view, hunger-reduction incentives may be regarded as motivation-destroying, not motivation-supporting, agents.

Twenty years ago at the Vilas Park Zoo, in Madison, we observed an adult orangutan given two blocks of wood, one with a round hole, one with a square hole, and two plungers, one round and one square. Intellectual curiosity alone led it to work on these tasks, often for many minutes at a time, and to solve the problem of inserting the round plunger in both holes. The orangutan never solved the problem of inserting the square peg into the round hole, but inasmuch as it passed away with perforated ulcers a month after the problem was presented, we can honestly say that it died trying. And in defense of this orangutan, let it be stated that it died working on more complex problems than are investigated by most present-day learning theorists.

Schiller [2] has reported that chimpanzees solve multiple-box–stacking problems without benefit of food rewards, and he has presented observational evidence that the joining of sticks resulted from manipulative play responses.

The Cebus monkey has only one claim to intellectual fame—an ability to solve instrumental problems that rivals the much publicized ability of the anthropoid apes (Harlow, 1951; Klüver, 1933). It can be no accident that the Cebus monkey, inferior to the rhesus on conventional learning tasks, demonstrates far more spontaneous instrumental-manipulative responses than any old-world form. The complex, innate external-stimulus motives are variables doubtlessly as important as, or more important than, tissue tensions, stimulus

[2] Personal communication.

generalization, excitatory potential, or secondary reinforcement. It is the oscillation of sticks, not cortical neurons, that enables the Cebus monkey to solve instrumental problems.

No matter how important may be the analysis of the curiosity-manipulative drives and the learning which is associated with them, we recognize the vast and infinite technical difficulties that are inherent in the attack on the solution of these problems—indeed, it may be many years before we can routinely order such experiments in terms of latin squares and factorial designs, the apparent *sine qua non* for publication in the *Journal of Experimental Psychology* and the *Journal of Comparative and Physiological Psychology*.

There is, however, another vast and important area of external-stimulus incentives important to learning which has been explored only superficially and which can, and should, be immediately and systematically attacked by rodentologists and primatologists alike. This is the area of food incentives—or, more broadly, visuo-chemo variables—approached from the point of view of their function as motivating agents per se. This function, as the speaker sees it, is primarily an affective one and only secondarily one of tissue-tension reduction. To dispel any fear of subjectivity, let us state that the affective tone of food incentives can probably be scaled by preference tests with an accuracy far exceeding any scaling of tissue tensions. Our illusion of the equal-step intervals of tissue tensions is the myth that length of the period of deprivation is precisely related to tissue-tension intensity, but the recent experiments by Koch and Daniel (1945) and Horenstein (1951) indicate that this is not true, thus beautifully confirming the physiological findings of thirty years ago.

Paired-comparison techniques with monkeys show beyond question that the primary incentive variables of both differential quantity and differential quality can be arranged on equal-step scales, and there is certainly no reason to believe that variation dependent upon subjects, time, or experience is greater than that dependent upon physiological hunger.

In defense of the rat and its protagonists, let it be stated that there are already many experiments on this lowly mammal which indicate that its curiosity-investigatory motives and responsiveness to incentive variables can be quantitatively measured and their significant relationship to learning demonstrated. The latent learning experiments of Buxton (1940), Haney (1931), Seward, Levy, and Handlon (1950), and others have successfully utilized the exploratory drive of the rat. Keller (1941) and Zeaman and House (1950) have utilized the rat's inherent aversion to light, or negative heliotropistic tendencies, to induce learning. Flynn and Jerome (1952) have shown that the rat's avoidance of light is an external-incentive motivation that may be utilized to obtain the solution of complex learned performances. For many rats it is a strong and very persistent form of motivation. The importance of incentive variables in rats has been emphasized and re-emphasized by Young (1949), and the influence of incentive variables on rat learning has been demonstrated by Young (1949), Zeaman (1949), Crespi (1942), and others. I am not for one moment disparaging the value of the rat as a subject for psychological investigation; there is very little wrong with the rat that cannot be overcome by the education of the experimenters.

It may be argued that if we accept the theses of this paper, we shall be returning to an outmoded psychology of tropisms, instincts, and hedonism. There is a great deal of truth to this charge. Such an approach might be a regression were it not for the fact that psychology now has adequate techniques of methodology and analysis to attack quantifiably these important and neglected areas. If we are ever to have a comprehensive theoretical psychology, we must attack the problems whose solution offers hope of insight into human behavior, and it is my belief that if we face our problems honestly and without regard to, or fear of, difficulty, the theoretical psychology of the future will catch up with, and eventually even surpass, common sense.

[4]

Exploratory Behavior as a Function of
"Similarity" of Stimulus Situations [1,2]

K. C. MONTGOMERY

The hypothesis of exploratory drive, developed by the writer
(Montgomery 1951a, 1951b, 1952b), states (a) that a novel stimulus
situation evokes in an organism an exploratory drive which motivates
exploratory behavior, and (b) that strength of exploratory drive, as
measured by amount of exploratory behavior, decreases with time
of continuous exposure to a given stimulus situation and recovers
during a period of nonexposure. This formulation, which has proved
useful in explaining certain cases of behavior variability such as
spontaneous alternation, emphasizes the role of external stimulation.
The dependence of exploratory behavior upon external stimuli
together with certain qualitative observations by the author suggested that a principle analogous to stimulus generalization operates
in exploratory behavior. Preliminary investigation appeared to confirm this hypothesis. On each of four consecutive days, nonmotivated
(for food or water) rats were permitted to explore two mazes in
immediate succession. For one group the second maze was identical
with the first; for a second group it differed in type of floor covering
and in brightness. The latter group exhibited significantly more
exploratory behavior in the second maze.[3]

The present experiment is a more detailed investigation of this
phenomenon. It is hypothesized (a) that the *decrement* in exploratory behavior produced by exposure to one stimulus situation
generalizes to other situations, and (b) that the magnitude of the
generalized decrement decreases as the similarity of the stimulus

[1] An abbreviated version of this paper was presented at the EPA meetings
in Atlantic City, N.J., in March, 1952.
[2] This research was conducted at Cornell University.
[3] Mr. Louis DiMarco ran the animals in the preliminary investigation.

SOURCE: K. C. Montgomery, "Exploratory Behavior as a Function of 'Simi-
larity' of Stimulus Situations," *Journal of Comparative and Physiological
Psychology*, 1953, 46, 129–133. Reprinted by permission of the American
Psychological Association.

situations decreases. Stated differently, as the difference between two consecutive stimulus situations increases, the amount of recovery of exploratory behavior in the second situation also increases. Similarity is varied in the present study by using mazes of three degrees of luminance.

METHOD

Subjects

Thirty-two female rats of the Wistar strain, about 100 days old and experimentally naive, were used as Ss.

Apparatus

The apparatus consisted of three enclosed mazes, identical except for brightness. One was painted flat black, one flat white, and one an intermediate flat gray, and their mean brightnesses were 0.18, 0.55, and 3.30 ft.-L, respectively. Each maze was constructed in the form of an H. Each arm of the H was 24 in. long, 4 in. wide, and 4 in. high (inside measurements), and was covered with hardware cloth. The mazes were placed close together on the floor of a 10-ft. square enclosure formed by black curtains. Illumination was provided by a single 60-w. bulb suspended 5½ ft. above the center of the floor of the enclosure. This setting provided relatively homogeneous extramaze stimulation. The E sat in one corner of the enclosure while observing the maze behavior.

Procedure

Before and during the three days of the experiment all animals were allowed free access to both food and water except during the 10 to 15 min. per day when they were actually in the maze. Four rats were assigned at random to each of eight groups. Each group received a different sequence of maze-exposures. Table 1 shows the experimental design.

On day 1 the animals were permitted to explore one maze freely for 5 min., then, after a 5-min. rest period, were allowed to explore a second maze for 5 min. The first maze was black for 12 rats, gray for 8, and white for 12; the second maze was black for 12 rats, gray for 8, and white for 12. Thus, the effect of maze luminance on amount of exploratory behavior can be determined.

On days 2 and 3 the design is somewhat more complicated. Groups I-A through IV-A were exposed to one maze for 10 min., then to a test maze for 5 min.; Groups I-B through IV-B were exposed to one maze for 5 min., then to a test maze for 10 min. The intermaze interval was about 10 sec. for all animals on both days. Thus, the influence of length of exposure to the first maze upon amount of exploratory behavior in the test mazes can be determined. Also, the change in maze luminance from the first to the test maze was varied systematically, in a counterbalanced order, among the groups. This makes it possible to evaluate the effect of exposure to a maze of each degree of luminance upon amount of exploratory behavior in test mazes of all three degrees of luminance.

On all days amount of exploratory behavior was measured by recording the total number of 12-in. sections explored during each minute of exposure. The criterion of a maze-section exploration was a full body-length entry, excluding the rat's tail.

TABLE 1

Experimental Design

Day	Exposure Time	Group							
		I-A		II-A		III-A		IV-A	
		a^*	b	a	b	a	b	a	b
1	5'	B	W	W	G	B	G	B	W
	5'	W	B	G	W	G	B	W	B
	10'	B	B	W	W	B	B	B	W
2–3	5'	W	W	G	G	G	G	B	W

Day	Exposure Time	Group							
		I-B		II-B		III-B		IV-B	
		a	b	a	b	a	b	a	b
1	5'	W	B	G	W	G	B	W	B
	5'	B	W	W	G	B	G	B	W
	5'	W	W	G	G	G	G	B	W
2–3	10'	B	B	W	W	B	B	B	W

* Each subgroup (a, b) contains two rats.

RESULTS

The data are analyzed to provide answers to five questions. First, does maze luminance bear any relation to amount of exploratory behavior? Figure 1 shows the average number of 12-in. sections explored plotted against minutes of exposure for the black, gray, and white mazes on day 1. Plots are presented for first exposure, for second exposure (after the 5-min. rest period), and for both exposures. There are no systematic differences attributable to maze luminance. Similar results obtain for days 2 and 3 when the first 5 min. of exposure are considered.

Second, are the groups homogeneous with respect to amount of exploratory behavior? Table 2 presents the mean number of 12-in. sections explored by each subgroup during the 10 min. of explora-

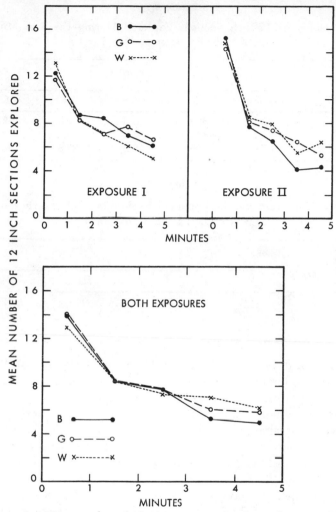

FIGURE 1.   Mean number of 12-in. sections explored as a function of time of exposure for each maze luminance on day 1.

tion on day 1. No systematic differences are apparent. Analysis of variance confirms the conclusion that there are no significant differences among groups in amount of exploratory behavior: the F ratio for groups is 0.22, a value that falls short of the .05 confidence level for 7 and 24 df.

Third, are there any day-to-day changes in amount of exploratory behavior? The mean number of 12-in. sections explored during the

TABLE 2

Mean Number of 12-Inch Sections Explored During the Ten Minutes of Maze Exposure on Day 1

Subgroup	Group				
	I	II	III	IV	Mean
A	82.2	83.8	75.0	88.0	82.2
B	89.2	82.0	84.0	79.5	83.7
Mean	85.8	82.9	79.5	83.8	83.0

TABLE 3

Mean Per Cent Decrement in Amount of Exploratory Behavior in the Test Maze for Days 2 and 3 Combined

Subgroup	Group			
	I	II	III	IV
A	−1	31	39	62
B	−3	24	36	59
Mean	−2	27	37	61

first 5 min. of days 1, 2, and 3 for all 32 rats is 41, 44, and 41. Thus, amount of exploratory behavior is a stable phenomenon over maze luminance, groups, and period of experimentation.

Fourth, is amount of exploratory behavior in the test maze a function of the amount of time spent in the first maze (5 min. vs. 10 min.)? Table 3 presents the mean per cent decrement in amount of exploratory behavior during the first 5 min. in the test maze as compared with the first 5 min. in the first maze for the various groups. The data for days 2 and 3 are combined. The A groups (10 min. in first maze and 5 min. in the test maze) show a slight tendency toward a greater decrement than the B groups. However, the results of an analysis of variance show that this tendency is not significant (see below).

The fifth question is the one posed by the experimental hypothesis: Is amount of exploratory behavior in the test maze a function of its difference in luminance from the first maze? Figure 2 summarizes the relevant data. It shows the mean number of 12-in. sections explored by each of the four major groups plotted against minutes of exposure for the first maze and for the test maze. The data for days 2 and 3 and for the subgroups within each major group are combined. In all cases only the first 5 min. of exposure to each maze is considered. Inspection of Figure 2 reveals (*a*) that no systematic differences among groups in amount of exploratory behavior occur during exposure to the first maze, and (*b*) that sys-

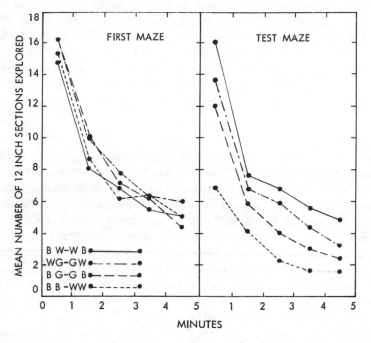

FIGURE 2. Mean number of 12-in. sections explored as a function of time of exposure to the first maze and to the test maze for each of the four major groups.

tematic differences do occur in the test maze. The BW-WB group shows the greatest amount of recovery in exploratory behavior in the test maze, the WG-GW group the next greatest amount, the BG-GB the next greatest amount, and the BB-WW group the least amount. A plot of per cent decrement in exploratory behavior in the test maze against differences in maze luminance in log units yields essentially a straight-line gradient. Thus, amount of exploratory behavior in the test maze is a function of its similarity to the first maze. Reference to Table 3 substantiates this conclusion.

Statistical analysis corroborates this and the preceding conclusion. The per cent decrement in amount of exploratory behavior in the test maze (first 5 min.) as compared with the first maze (first 5 min.)

was computed for each rat. These scores were transformed into angles according to the formula, Angle = arc sin $\sqrt{\text{percentage}}$, and were subjected to an analysis of variance. The experimental design permits a two-way factorial analysis, the two components of which are time spent in the first maze (5 vs. 10 min.) and degree of change in maze luminance from the first to the test maze. The F ratio for maze luminance is 43.7, a value significant at well beyond the .001 level for 3 and 24 df; the F's for time spent in the first maze and for interaction are 0.65 and 0.21, values which fall short of the .05 level. The greater per cent recovery for the WG-GW group as compared with the BG-GB group is attributable to the fact that the physical difference in maze luminance is greater in the former case.

Discussion

The major finding confirms the experimental hypothesis: The decrement in exploratory behavior produced by exposure to one maze does generalize to other mazes, decreasing in amount as maze similarity decreases. This result is interpreted as providing additional direct support for the hypothesis of exploratory drive. That is, it further emphasizes the importance of external stimulation as a controlling factor in exploratory behavior. It also points to the operation of a stimulus generalization principle in exploratory behavior: When the strength of the exploratory drive evoked by a given stimulus situation is reduced, the strength of the exploratory drive evoked by other similar stimulus situations is also reduced, the amount of reduction decreasing as the similarity of the situations decreases.

There are at least three other theoretical concepts that might be invoked to account for the present results. The first is Hull's (1943) construct of reactive inhibition. According to Hull's eighth postulate the performance of a response generates a certain amount of reactive inhibition—a negative drive—which mediates against the repetition of that response and which dissipates with time. This construct could account for the decrement in exploratory behavior produced by continuous exposure to a maze. However, because reactive inhibition is stated to be specific to specific responses, and because the behavior in the first and test mazes involves highly similar if not identical respones, reactive inhibition provides no basis for explaining the differential amounts of recovery of exploratory behavior in the test mazes.

Hull's (1943) concept of conditioned inhibition is more promising. Essentially, conditioned inhibition is a habit of resting, i.e., of not responding, which is conditioned to external stimuli. Hence, it would transfer from one stimulus situation to another in accordance with the principle of stimulus generalization. Although conditioned inhibition could account for the generalization effects from one maze to another that occur on any *one* experimental day in the present study, it leads to the prediction that the decrement in exploratory behavior developed in a maze on any one day would transfer to the next day. Unfortunately for this explanation, exploratory behavior in this and other short-term studies (Montgomery, 1952b) shows relatively complete "spontaneous recovery" over a 24-hr. rest period.

Sometimes exploratory behavior is explained by appealing to a "general activity drive" which supposedly is generated by internal organismic factors. There are at least two reasons why this concept is inadequate as an explanation of the present data. (*a*) It does not account for the rapid decrease in amount of exploratory behavior over short periods of time. In this and previous studies only one-fourth to one-third as much activity occurs during the fifth minute of maze exposure as during the first minute. (*b*) It provides no basis for predicting the differential amounts of recovery of exploratory behavior produced by the variable of maze luminance.

The fact that decrement in exploratory drive and its consequent exploratory behavior generalizes from one stimulus situation to other similar situations makes it possible to account for the gradual decline in exploratory behavior that occurs even in very large mazes. If a maze is relatively homogeneous, then the decrement in exploratory drive produced by exposure to any given segment generalizes to every other segment. The result is a cumulative decrease in the strength of exploratory drive. Thus, it is possible to explain the findings of Dennis and Sollenberger (1934) that rats run in large mazes comprised of homogeneous sections slow down in their activity and often stop exploring entirely. It should not be forgotten, however, that extramaze stimuli play an important role in exploratory behavior, particularly when elevated mazes are employed. Evidence on this point will be presented in a later paper.

Summary and Conclusions

Thirty-two albino rats were run in mazes of three degrees of luminance to test the hypothesis that the decrement in exploratory behavior produced by exposure to one stimulus situation generalizes to other similar situations. On the basis of the experimental results and the preceding discussion, the following conclusions are drawn:

(*a*) The experimental hypothesis is substantiated: The decrement in exploratory behavior produced by exposure to one stimulus situation generalizes to other situations, decreasing in magnitude as the similarity of the stimulus situations decreases. Hence, a principle analogous to stimulus generalization operates in exploratory behavior. (*b*) Exploratory behavior, of the kind studied in this experiment, is greatly dependent upon stimulation external to the organism. This provides additional support for the hypothesis of exploratory drive. (*c*) The concepts of "reactive inhibition," "conditioned inhibition," and "general activity drive" do not provide adequate bases for explaining the present results.

[5]

Stimulus Satiation: An Explanation of Spontaneous Alternation and Related Phenomena [1]

MURRAY GLANZER

In 1925 Tolman (1925a, p. 290) described a peculiar regularity in the behavior of rats that was later labeled spontaneous alternation.

A simple T maze was used, and it was arranged so that the animal could get back to the food box in identical fashion whether he chose the left or the right angle of the T. Either route met with success. . . . [There was] a very pronounced tendency toward continuous and regular alternation—left, right, left, right, or right, left, right, left. . . . It appeared, in short, that even where either side was equally "satisfactory"

[1] This paper is based upon a Ph.D. dissertation submitted in February 1952 to the department of psychology at the University of Michigan. The writer is indebted to the members of the committee and to Dr. Edward L. Walker, chairman of the committee, who gave invaluable aid in the preparation and editing of this paper.

SOURCE: Murray Glanzer, "Stimulus Satiation: An Explanation of Spontaneous Alternation and Related Phenomena," *Psychological Review*, 1953, **60**, 257–268. Reprinted by permission of the American Psychological Association and M. Glanzer.

there was in our rats a positive tendency left over toward variation of response . . . a positive tendency in and of itself.

Ten years after Tolman's report, spontaneous alternation received intensive study by Dennis and his coworkers. Although these early investigators did not incorporate their data into a formal theory, Dennis (1939) did imply that spontaneous alternation was in some way determined by the stimuli the subject faced. For example, the title of one article was "Spontaneous Alternation in Rats as an Indicator of the Persistence of Stimulus Effects," and, in discussion of his results, he wrote about "a tendency to avoid a specific pathway which has recently been traversed" (1939, p. 310). This formulation suggests a theory of spontaneous alternation in terms of the stimulus. The rat alternates from one alley (a set of stimuli) to the other (a different set of stimuli), going to Alley B because it has already experienced Alley A. The theory proposed in this paper develops and systematizes this basic approach.

In direct antithesis to a stimulus-oriented theory is one which interprets spontaneous alternation in terms of the response. In a response theory, the animal is viewed as alternating responses instead of alleys, i.e., making a right turn because it has already made a left turn. Many of the more recent investigations examined below have stemmed from this theoretical position.

A CRITIQUE OF RESPONSE THEORIES

Explanation of spontaneous alternation in terms of the response has been attempted by several Hull-influenced investigators: Heathers (1940) using the concept of performance decrement; and Solomon (1947) and Zeaman and House (1951) using the concept of reactive inhibition. According to both concepts, the occurrence of a response reduces temporarily the probability of its recurrence. The concepts were employed to explain both the fact of spontaneous alternation and the fact, predicted and demonstrated by Heathers (1940), that spontaneous alternation disappears as the interval between trials increases.

The concept of reactive inhibition, in addition, assigns an explicit role to the number of times the response is made and the amount of work required by the response. Thus, Zeaman and House (1951) predicted and found that giving animals forced trials to one of two alleys increased the tendency to alternate to the other; Solomon (1947) predicted and found some positive but not conclusive evidence that increased work resulted in increased spontaneous alternation.

Although these experiments seem to give considerable support to an explanation in terms of the response, a number of facts remain that resist explanation by this type of theory. Typical of these are the following:

1. Dennis (1939) found that rats did not show spontaneous alternation from unit to unit of a multiple-unit maze. That is, they did not go right-left-right-left within a single trial on a four-unit maze, but showed instead spontaneous alternation in their successive choices at a given choice point. They might go right-right-right-left on the first trial and left-left-left-right on the second trial. This finding is in direct contradiction to the prediction which should follow from a theory in terms of the response.

2. Jackson (1941) found that the difference between the two possible responses at the choice point did *not* affect the amount of spontaneous alternation. A Y maze with a small angle of separation, requiring a choice between two practically identical responses, elicited as much spontaneous alternation as a Y maze with a wide angle of separation. If the response were the key to spontaneous alternation, then differentiating the response should result in more alternation.

3. Zeaman and House (1951), using a procedure of ten forced trials followed by a free trial, and Walker,[2] using simply two free trials, found that rats showed spontaneous alternation with intervals greater than an hour between trials. These findings disagree with expectations on the basis of reactive inhibition which is ordinarily assumed to dissipate within a few minutes.[3]

4. Wingfield (1943) found that human subjects showed more spontaneous alternation in choice of lights that differed in color than of lights that were the same. Something in addition to consideration of the subject's responses seems to be demanded by this finding.

5. Dennis (1939) varied the amount of work for rats running a maze by increasing the length of the final section from zero to 38 ft. but found no change in the amount of spontaneous alternation. It would seem reasonable to expect that the reactive inhibition from

---

[2] Walker, E. L. Unpublished data.
[3] Reactive inhibition has to be assumed to disappear quickly in order that it meet its other theoretical commitments. (See Zeaman and House [1951].)

the added run of 38 ft. should dwarf the effects of reactive inhibition from the momentary act of turning right or left.

These difficulties suggest that it might be fruitful to turn to the construction of an explanation in terms of the stimulus. As already pointed out, Dennis (1939) anticipated this type of explanation. Recently Montgomery (1951a, 1952a, 1952b), on the basis of empirical findings of his own, has questioned the reactive-inhibition explanation of spontaneous alternation and proposes the concept of an exploratory tendency which is reduced by exposure to a pathway of the maze. Berlyne (1950) has presented a similar construct, a curiosity drive, designed to explain curiosity in rats. (Working toward a very different goal, that of incorporating perception and attention as "response" in Hullian theory, Berlyne (1951) has also sketched the outlines of a theory that displays some points of similarity to the formulation presented below.)

A THEORY IN TERMS OF THE STIMULUS

We shall assume that, with continued exposure to an *environment* —to the same *stimuli*—the organism becomes less active in that environment. With an eye to several experiments (Dennis, 1939; Heathers, 1940; Solomon, 1947; Zeaman & House, 1951), we assign a specific role to time in the disappearance of this boredom-like effect. Since, moreover, the explanation is in terms of the stimulus, it would be expected that "boredom" created in one situation would carry over to other similar environments and that the more similar two environments are, the greater the carryover.

Using these ideas to form the construct of stimulus satiation,[4] we shall follow Hull's procedure (1943) and present the basis of the theory in the form of a postulate.

This new postulate may not only enable us to circumvent the difficulties of the reactive-inhibition explanation but will also yield novel predictions. Furthermore, it may serve to interrelate and explain empirical results from a number of apparently unrelated areas.

The postulate reads as follows:

Each moment an organism perceives a stimulus-object or stimulus-objects, A, there develops a quantity of stimulus satiation to A.
   i. *The same amount of stimulus satiation develops in each successive moment. The total amount developed is, therefore, an increasing linear function of time.*

[4] This term is suggested by Karsten's work (1928).

ii. *There is loss of part of each quantity of stimulus satiation in each successive moment. The amount of stimulus satiation remaining from each quantity is a decreasing negative exponential function of time.*

iii. *Stimulus satiation developed to A will be generalized to other stimulus-objects B. The amount of generalized stimulus satiation is an inverse function of the discriminability of A and B.*

iv. *The various quantities of stimulus satiation combine additively.*

v. *Stimulus satiation reduces the organism's tendency to make any response to A.*

Definition 1. Generalization. When a change in behavior toward A results in a similar change in behavior toward B, all other things being equal, generalization has taken place from A to B.

Definition 2. Discriminability. The ease with which a subject can be induced to make a different response to A than to B, all other things being equal, is called the discriminability of A and B.

Two corollaries follow from the postulate:

Corollary I. As long as an organism remains perceiving A, the amount of stimulus satiation it has to A at a given moment (that is, the total amount developed [i] minus the total amount lost [ii]), is an increasing negative exponential function of time.

Corollary II. When an organism stops perceiving A, the amount of stimulus satiation it has to A at a given moment is a decreasing negative exponential function of time.

These corollaries are presented in Table 1 and Figure 1 with arbitrary values assigned to the functions.

Given the characteristics of various situations, the postulate yields a large number of deductions. A number of these for some basic types of situations are formulated and discussed below. For each deduction discussed, we will indicate whether or not it is crucial for the two theories, e.g., one in terms of the stimulus as against one in terms of the response, as well as state the nature of any existing evidence.

DEDUCTIONS FOR APPROACH RESPONSES IN A TWO-ALTERNATIVE SITUATION

Spontaneous Alternation

Let us start with a very simple situation. This situation is one in which S has evenly spaced, consecutive trials in an apparatus that contains two distinct areas, such as a single-unit T or Y maze. A trial starts with S's entrance into the apparatus and ends with its exit from the apparatus.

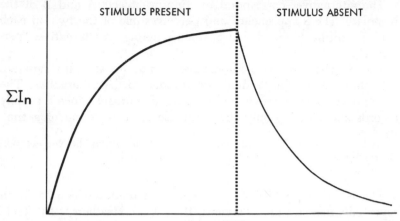

FIGURE 1. Total amount of stimulus satiation, ΣI_n, as a function of time and the presence or absence of the stimulus-object. The totals of the columns of Table 1 are represented by this figure.

TABLE 1

Corollaries I and II Illustrated by Obtaining Values for Stimulus Satiation, $I_n = 100 \, e^{-(n-1)}$ (Where n is the Number of Moments since the Appearance of the Stimulus)[*]

Stimulus Satiation Quantity	*Moments*							
	Stimulus Present				*Stimulus Absent*			
	1	*2*	*3*	*4*	*5*	*6*	*7*	*8*
I_1	100.0	36.8	13.5	5.0	1.8	.7	.3	.1
I_2		100.0	36.8	13.5	5.0	1.8	.7	.3
I_3			100.0	36.8	13.5	5.0	1.8	.7
I_4				100.0	36.8	13.5	5.0	1.8
ΣI_n	100.0	136.8	150.3	155.3	57.1	21.0	7.8	2.9

[*] Each row gives the history of a single quantity of stimulus satiation as it decreases with time. Each column gives the total amounts of stimulus satiation present during a single moment.

In order to complete a trial S has to enter one of the two areas or alleys. These areas should be initially more or less equally attractive to S. During the course of the experiment, furthermore, one area should not be made more or less attractive than the other by introducing reward or punishment. A situation that has these characteristics will be called a simple two-alternative situation.

The alternatives correspond to stimulus-objects A and B of the postulate. The S approaches and perceives one of the two on each trial. It will be assumed that S, upon entering an alternative, "perceives" it.

The S, perceiving one alternative, builds up stimulus satiation to it that reduces the tendency to respond to that alternative. The response considered here is the response of approach, since E usually records and requires only that response for completion of a trial.

Deduction 1. In the simple two-alternative situation, the subject will alternate choice of arms or alleys in successive trials.
Verified; not crucial.

This is the simple fact of spontaneous alternation which has been repeatedly demonstrated (Dennis, 1935, 1939; Heathers, 1940; Jackson, 1941; Solomon, 1947; Tolman, 1925a; Wingfield & Dennis, 1934; Zeaman & House, 1951).

Deduction 2. In the simple two-alternative situation, if there is an exchange between trials of stimulus-objects so that the cues that were on one side of the S now are on the other, and vice versa, S will alternate approach to stimulus-objects in successive trials. This will mean a *repetition* of responses rather than an alternation of responses (turns).
Verified; crucial.

This is a key deduction since it contrasts the stimulus satiation and reactive-inhibition explanation most sharply. Stimulus satiation theory predicts a reduction in alternation of response, whereas a theory in terms of the response predicts no decrease.

The author (Glanzer, 1953b) ran rats in a cross-shaped maze with two starting boxes (north and south), making it possible for the Ss to start from one starting box for one trial and from the opposite starting box for the next. When this was done, the position of the alleys relative to S was reversed: the alley that had been on its right during Trial 1 was on its left for Trial 2. By thus shifting stimuli, it could be determined whether the animals alternated responses as required by the reactive-inhibition explanation or alleys as required by the stimulus satiation explanation.

Twenty-six rats were given two immediately consecutive trials a day for eight days. On four of the days both trials were from the same starting box; on the other four days the trials were from opposite starting boxes. As predicted above, the animals tended to repeat (i.e., go right-right or left-left) rather than alternate their responses on the days that the cues were shifted. This indicates clearly that they were alternating alleys (stimuli) rather than turns (responses). A similar experiment has been described by Montgomery (1952a) who reports results consistent with these findings.

Deduction 3. In the simple two-alternative situation if an extended series of consecutive trials is given, the tendency toward spontaneous alternation will be at a maximum for the first pair of trials, and will decrease to a minimum in later trials. This decrease will be called cumulation-effect.

Tested but not clearly verified; not crucial.

In a series of consecutive trials in a two-alternative situation, if the first trial was to alternative A, then the second trial would be to alternative B (Deduction 1). There would be two stimulus satiation curves then: one for alternative A starting from the first trial, and continuing its rise through later trials to alternative A; the other for alternative B, starting from the second trial. Since, according to Corollary I, curves of stimulus satiation are negatively accelerated, the two curves would approach each other in the later trials. The difference in amount of stimulus satiation to the two alternatives would therefore decrease as illustrated in Figure 2, leading to the predicted decrease in spontaneous alternation.

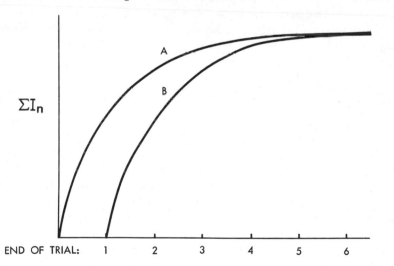

Figure 2. Total amount of stimulus satiation, ΣI_n, to two alternatives, A and B, in successive alternating trials. The curves, approaching their limits, cause a decrease in the difference (the distance between the curves) in the amount of stimulus satiation to the two alternatives. All odd-numbered trials are to A, even-numbered to B. Decreases occurring during intertrial intervals have not been drawn.

Although results from Wingfield and Dennis (1934), Heathers (1940) and the author (Glanzer, 1952) show the general trend toward decrease in spontaneous alternation from first to last trial in a series, the data also show reversals and considerable irregularity.

The inconclusive nature of these data may result from the very procedure indicated by Deduction 3. In this procedure the animal is free to choose either alternative each trial in the series. The *E* therefore soon loses control of the basic variable, the number and order of particular choices that precede a given trial.

In order to make an adequate test of the prediction, it may be necessary either to use a group of animals large enough to cancel individual differences in the pattern of choices or to change the procedure in order to control the pattern of choices throughout. Clearer results would be expected, then, for the following deduction.

Deduction 4. In the simple two-alternative situation, if a number of forced consecutive alternation trials is given, as the number of trials increases, the tendency toward spontaneous alternation decreases.
Not tested; not crucial.

Now we turn to consideration of the role of generalization. On the basis of part iii of the postulate, the prediction could be made that the more discriminable the alternatives, the greater the amount of spontaneous alternation. Discriminability can be varied by several methods. One is to eliminate or add cues that differentiate the two alternatives.

Deduction 5. In the simple two-alternative situation, as stimuli differentiating the alternatives are eliminated, spontaneous alternation will decrease.
Tested but not verified; crucial.

A study on this by the author (Glanzer, 1952) comparing spontaneous alternation in Y mazes with many and few differentiating cues yielded negative results. In that experiment, however, there may have been inadequate control of the differentiating cues, since only intramaze cues were varied.

Since discriminability is a function of the organism as well as the environment, the following deductions can also be derived.

Deduction 6. In the simple two-alternative situation, if the ability of the organism to discriminate is reduced, spontaneous alternation will decrease.

Of the conditions of the organism that may affect its ability to discriminate, two may be singled out on the basis of empirical studies. One is sense-organ damage and the other is brain-injury (Lashley, 1930). If these conditions may be considered to reduce discriminability, then the following more specific deductions may be made.[5]

Deduction 6*a*. In the simple two-alternative situation, the greater the extent of *S*'s sense-organ damage, the less the amount of spontaneous alternation.
Not tested; crucial.
Deduction 6*b*. In the simple two-alternative situation, the greater the extent of *S*'s brain damage, the less the amount of spontaneous alternation.
Verified; crucial.

Certain of Krechevsky's (1937a 1937b) results support this deduction. He found that brain-operated rats perseverated in choice of one of two paths much more than did normal rats. His situation described below was somewhat complicated but the basic two-alternative arrangement was employed.

Now we turn to the effects of time on spontaneous alternation.

Deduction 7. In the simple two-alternative situation, as the interval between trials increases, the amount of spontaneous alternation decreases.
Verified; not crucial.

This deduction follows simply from part ii of the postulate. It has been verified by Heathers (1940) who found that, as the time interval between trials increased from 15 sec. to 15 min., spontaneous alternation decreased from 86 to 50 per cent (chance). It is also verified by Zeaman and House (1951), who found a decrease over a period of 24 hr.

Deduction 8. In the simple two-alternative situation, the more highly differentiated the alternatives, the longer the time interval between trials necessary for the disappearance of spontaneous alternation.
Not tested; crucial.

This may, in part, explain the widely discrepant data that have been obtained concerning the effects of delay on spontaneous alternation. For example, Walker,[6] using a highly differentiated Y

[5] Strictly speaking, Deductions 6*a*, 6*b*, 15 hold only for situations in which there is empirical support for the stated relationship between brain or receptor injury and discriminability.
[6] See footnote 2.

maze, found spontaneous alternation with intervals longer than an hour. Montgomery (1951a), who took special care to keep his alternatives alike, found that spontaneous alternation disappeared with intervals as short as 90 sec.

Now we turn to an implication of Corollary I, that the longer the time the organism perceives a stimulus-object A, the greater the amount of stimulus satiation to A.

Deduction 9. In the simple two-alternative situation, if S is detained in one alternative, the amount of spontaneous alternation to the other alternative on the following trial will be greater, the longer the time of detention.

Not tested; crucial.

The apparent contradiction between Deduction 9 and Deduction 7 may be resolved in the following way. In Deduction 7, the concern is with "interval between trials," an interval spent *outside* the alternative chosen, whereas in Deduction 9, the concern is with a time interval spent within the alternative. These distinctions can be kept clear in the formulation of a new deduction in terms of the interval between choices.

Deduction 9a. In the simple two-alternative situation, with the time interval between choices constant, the greater the proportion of time between choices spent in the presence of the chosen alternative, the greater the amount of spontaneous alternation on the succeeding trial.

Deductions 7 and 9 can now be combined in the following.

Deduction 10. In the simple two-alternative situation, if S is delayed between choices and this delay occurs within the alternative last chosen, S will show more spontaneous alternation than under a condition of no delay. If, however, S is delayed between choices and this delay occurs outside the alternative last chosen, S will show less spontaneous alternation than under a condition of no delay.

Verified; crucial.

The author (Glanzer, 1953b) found that when rats were detained in the end box of the alternative chosen in the first run in a T maze, 96 per cent of the group showed spontaneous alternation on the following trial. When they were kept in other parts of the maze at the end of their first run, between 36 and 68 per cent of the group showed spontaneous alternation. When they were not detained, spontaneous alternation varied between 72 and 88 per cent.

Deduction 11. In the simple two-alternative situation, if S is given forced runs to one alternative, the greater the number of such forced trials, the greater the amount of spontaneous alternation on a subsequent free-choice trial.
Verified; not crucial.

This procedure is basically the same as that involved in Deduction 9. In Deduction 11 the animal builds up stimulus satiation during repeated visits to one alternative; in Deduction 9 it does so during a period of detention within the alternative. Zeaman and House, deriving their hypothesis from the reactive-inhibition postulate, verified Deduction 11.

The amount of spontaneous alternation obtained by each of the two procedures, by forced trials and by detention at the alternative, may now be compared to yield a clearly critical deduction.

Deduction 12. In the simple two-alternative situation, detention of S for a given period of time at the alternative last chosen will yield larger amounts of spontaneous alternation than will a series of forced trials to one alternative over the same period of time.
Not tested; crucial.

In the forced-trial procedure, as compared with the detention procedure, S, being taken from end box to starting box, spends a smaller proportion of the time within the alternative itself. Thus S has less time to develop stimulus satiation.

Variability (Preference for Variable Situations)

An important variation of the two-alternative situation is one in which the cues of one alternative are varied while the cues of the other are kept constant. This type of situation has been investigated in two studies of "variability." Krechevsky (1937a, 1937b) used a two-alternative maze, both arms of which contained a number of turns. One arm could be varied in pattern of turns from trial to trial. Both variable and constant arms were constructed so that there was an equal number of right and left turns within each arm.

Three different maze arrangements were used: a long varying versus a short constant path (Krechevsky, 1937a); a short varying versus a long constant path (Krechevsky, 1937b); a long constant versus a short constant path (Krechevsky, 1937b). In each of these Krechevsky ran two groups of rats, one group normal and the other brain-operated.

In such a situation, stimulus satiation to the varying alternative will be reduced by its division among the different forms of the varying alternative. Essentially, a situation exists in which the constant alternative A is opposed by a family of alternatives B_1, B_2, B_3, . . . B_n. Alternative A bears the weight of all of the stimulus satiation built up during an exposure to it; the family of alternatives B divides stimulus satiation among its variations.

Corollary III. If an alternative is varied from trial to trial, then less stimulus satiation will be built up to it than if no such variation occurs.
Deduction 13. In the simple two-alternative situation, if one of the alternatives is varied from trial to trial and the other is kept constant, then S will prefer the varied alternative.
Verified; crucial.

This is verified by Krechevsky (1937a, 1937b). Examination of the results for his normal animals shows that the predicted preference is strong enough to cause Ss to prefer the varied path even when it is the longer path.[7]

It follows that the division of stimulus satiation among the variations of the changing alternative depends on the degree of discriminability of the variations. As the variations become less and less discriminable, the condition of the constant alternative, i.e., of no change, is approached.

Corollary IV. If an alternative is varied from trial to trial, the more discriminable the variations the less the amount of stimulus satiation that will be present for the alternative.

There were indicated earlier two ways to reduce discriminability: reduction of the number of distinguishing cues of the perceived objects and impairment of the sensory or nervous systems of the Ss. Consideration of these methods leads to the following deductions.

Deduction 14. In the simple two-alternative situation, the preference for a varying alternative (as opposed to a constant alternative) will be greater, the greater the difference between variations.
Not tested; crucial.
Deduction 15. In the simple two-alternative situation, brain-injured Ss will show less preference for a varying alternative (as opposed to a constant alternative) than will normal Ss.
Verified; crucial.

[7] Krechevsky's findings cannot be explained in terms of reactive inhibition or any other theory in terms of the response since, as pointed out earlier, the mazes were designed so that each arm had the same number of right and left turns within it. The Ss would have, following each trial, an equal amount of reactive inhibition to right and left turning.

In Krechevsky's studies (1937a, 1937b) the normal animals preferred the varying alternative more strongly than did the operated animals.

Finally, it can be deduced that the greater the number of variations that share the stimulus satiation, the less the amount present to each.

Deduction 16. In the simple two-alternative situation, the greater the number of variations, the greater the preference for the varying alternative.
Not tested; crucial.

Deductions for the Multiple-Alternative Situation

We may now generalize the deductions to apply to situations with more than two alternatives. For example, let us apply the postulate to the behavior of S in the three-alternative situation. The S, after choosing one alternative, will build up stimulus satiation to it. Upon returning to the choice point for a second trial, S will probably choose a new alternative since responsiveness to the first choice has been reduced. If returned again to the choice point, S will probably choose the "unsatiated" third alternative.

Deduction 1′. In a simple multiple-alternative situation, S will choose many alternatives in a series of consecutive trials.
Definition 3. Many alternatives mean more alternatives than could reasonably be expected on the basis of chance.

Deduction 1′ is verified by the findings of Wingfield and Dennis (1934) on the number of different paths chosen by rats running four trials on a four-alternative maze.

Deduction 1 appears as simply a special case of Deduction 1′. In fact, a set of more general deductions can now be obtained in most cases merely by changing "two-alternative" to "multiple-alternative" and "spontaneous alternation" to "tendency to choose many alternatives." Each of the 16 earlier deductions becomes a special case of one of the new set of 16 deductions for multiple-alternative situations.

Consideration of situations involving more than two alternatives suggests a new variable, the number of alternatives, which can form the basis of several new deductions. One such deduction, of particular interest, concerns the cumulation effect of Deductions 3 and 5 and its counterpart in multiple-alternative situations, i.e., the decrease in the tendency to choose many alternatives in an extended series of trials.

Deduction 17'. If there are two simple multiple-alternative situations, and one of them has a greater number of alternatives than the other, then the cumulation effect will be smaller and will develop more slowly for the situation with a greater number of alternatives.

Cumulation effect depends on the summation of amounts of stimulus satiation from successive visits to the same alternative. In the two-alternative situation, S visits alternative A and then B, then A again, then B again, rapidly building up near-maximum amounts of stimulus satiation to both alternatives. According to Deduction 1', the S, in a three-alternative situation, visits A then B then C and then A again, B again, and C again. The time between successive visits to the same alternative is longer, thereby delaying the onset of maximum stimulus satiation for any single alternative. It will consequently take more time to reach the period when differences in the amounts of stimulus satiation present for the various alternatives approach zero.

DEDUCTIONS FOR "FREE" PROCEDURE

Deductions have been drawn thus far only for the procedure in which S makes a choice and then is returned by E to the starting point for the next trial. Another procedure, which we shall call the "free" procedure, is one that allows S to make as many choices as it will for a given period of time. The S makes a choice and then returns itself to the choice point for its next choice. When employed without rewards, this is the standard procedure in the study of "exploratory behavior." [8]

Exploratory behavior may now be derived from the stimulus satiation postulate. The deductions can be further generalized to cover this more complex procedure so that exploratory behavior, like spontaneous alternation, becomes a special case governed by the postulate. The word *choice* replaces the word *trial* in the deductions, since we are no longer concerned with a trial as defined earlier; and the procedure is no longer called "simple."

[8] The relationship between spontaneous alternation and exploratory behavior was pointed out by Tolman (1925a) who explained the former in terms of the latter. We, however, view both spontaneous alternation and exploratory behavior as manifestations of a single underlying factor.

Most of the deductions have not been tested in the "free" procedure. Those for which there are relevant data have been verified. For example, there is the following deduction involving cumulation effect.

Deduction 3". In the multiple-alternative situation, if an extended series of consecutive choices is given, as the number of such choices increases, the tendency to choose many alternatives decreases.

This has been verified by Dennis and Sollenberger (1934) and later by Montgomery (1952b). Both studies found that rats enter fewer and fewer alleys in successive periods of free exploration.
Another deduction for which there are data is the following:

Deduction 17". If there are two multiple-alternative situations and one of them has a greater number of alternatives than the other, then the cumulation effect will be smaller and develop more slowly for the situation with a greater number of alternatives.

This has also been verified by Dennis and Sollenberger (1934) and Montgomery (1952b). They found that larger mazes elicited more activity and continued to elicit activity over a longer period of time than did small mazes. Larger mazes are considered here to contain a greater number of alternatives.

POSSIBLE APPLICATIONS OF THE THEORY TO HUMAN SUBJECTS

Although most of the work in the areas under consideration has been carried out with rats as Ss, there is some evidence obtained from human Ss that is congruent with the postulate.

The closest analogue to the two-alternative situation that elicits spontaneous alternation in rats is found in a study by Wingfield (1943) who required college students to turn on one of a pair of lights. In a series of four trials the Ss not only spontaneously alternated the lights they chose to turn on (Deduction 1) but also showed more spontaneous alternation on the first pair than on the second pair of trials (Deduction 3) and more with lights of different hue than with lights of the same hue (Deduction 5).

Karsten's (1928) work on the phenomenon which she calls "satiation" (Sättigung) is of particular interest. She had her Ss perform repeatedly such tasks as drawing lines or tapping.[9] This activity

---

[9] Berlyne (1951) handles these data in the same way in his expansion of Hull's theory to include perceptual "responses."

produces repeated experience of certain stimulus-objects, e.g., lines drawn, and can therefore be considered a case covered by Deduction 13″. This deduction can be considered to predict Karsten's finding of the Ss' resistance to continuing the task as well as their variations from the prescribed activity.[10] The phenomenon of cosatiation (transfer of satiation symptoms to new and similar tasks) could also be predicted from part iii of the postulate.

A further finding by Karsten suggests the relevance of the postulate to the problem of fatigue. Symptoms of satiation, including the Ss' inability to move their arms, disappeared when the grouping of the lines being drawn was changed even though the required muscle movements remained the same. This recalls two things: part iii of the postulate and the recent emphasis on factors other than simple muscle states in understanding the phenomenon of fatigue (Bartley, 1951).

[6]

Response by the Rat to Environmental Change

WILLIAM N. DEMBER

Experiments by Montgomery (1952a), Glanzer (1953a), and Walker and associates (1955) have clearly shown the inadequacy of the concept of reactive inhibition for the explanation of T-maze alternation. Glanzer has offered as a substitute for reactive inhibition a theory based on the concept of "stimulus-satiation." The theory states that whenever an animal is exposed to a stimulus, there develops a quantity of satiation for that stimulus, resulting in a decreased tendency for the animal to respond positively to that stimulus upon subsequent presentation.

[10] The Ss' resistance also expressed itself in the form of inattentiveness and "fatigue." All of these symptoms could be predicted on the basis of Corollary I.

SOURCE: William N. Dember, "Response by the Rat to Environmental Change," *Journal of Comparative and Physiological Psychology*, 1956, **49**, 93–95. Reprinted by permission of the American Psychological Association and W. N. Dember.

An immediate implication of Glanzer's theory was tested by Walker, Dember, Earl, Fliege, and Karoly (1955). In one experiment, rats were placed in either a black or a white compartment for periods ranging from 30 sec. to 30 min. This exposure had no effect on the rat's choices when they were subsequently put in a T maze with one black and one white arm. In a second experiment, the exposure took place in either of the two goal boxes of the T maze. Again, this experience had no effect on the rats' behavior in an immediately following choice in the same apparatus.

Kivy, Earl, and Walker (1956) argued that while mere exposure per se was ineffective, it should be possible to produce "alternation" if the exposure were made in the context of the choice point. This hypothesis was tested and confirmed. Rats were introduced into the starting alley of a T maze, with the goal alleys blocked off at the choice point by means of two glass partitions. The rats could see into, but not enter, the goal arms. Exposure periods of 1, 15, and 30 min. were used. During this time the two arms were either both black or both white. For the test trial the glass partitions were removed and the color of one of the arms was changed, thus presenting the animal with a choice between a black and a white alley. For the 15- and 30-min. exposures the results were as predicted.

These data may be looked on as supporting a version of the satiation concept in which the relevance of *context* is emphasized. An alternative hypothesis is possible, however. Consider the rat that sees on its first exposure a black arm on the left and a black arm on the right. On the second trial the left arm is still black, but the right arm has been changed to white—a change certainly worth exploring. In the language of Berlyne (1950) and Thompson and Solomon (1954) the changed arm might represent "novelty" and would therefore invoke the "curiosity motive." Behaviorally, the animal would enter the changed arm.

In the Kivy, Earl, and Walker experiment the satiation and the novelty hypotheses are equally applicable. It is the purpose of this paper to describe an experiment for which only the latter hypothesis seems appropriate.

In the present experiment the stimulus configurations in the two trials of the Kivy, Earl, and Walker experiment are reversed. That is, on trial 1 the rat is presented with, but cannot enter, one white and one black arm. On trial 2, one of the arms is changed so that the rat now encounters two alleys, either both black or both white. On the basis of the novelty hypothesis it is predicted that the rat will enter the arm which has been changed. A simple satiation theory can make no prediction about the choice on the second trial, since the animal is equally "satiated" for both alternatives.

METHOD

Animals

Two groups of animals were used. Group I was composed of 12 male albino rats, approximately 180 days old, obtained from the Maguran Farms colony. About 90 days previous to the present experiment these rats had served in an alternation experiment involving neither reward nor punishment, and in which a different procedure, apparatus, experimenter, and experimental room were used. It is assumed that for the purpose of the present experiment the animals were naive. The rats were handled for several days prior to the experiment, and for two days were run hungry to food along a board between two chairs.

Group II consisted of 8 male albinos of the Maguran Farms strain, approximately 100 days old; these animals were experimentally naive. Their two days of pretraining involved placing them hungry on a large table on which food pellets had been scattered. They were allowed to explore and eat freely for about 30 min. each day.

During the experiment itself animals of both groups were satiated for food and water.

Apparatus

The T maze which was used has been described by Kivy, Earl, and Walker (1956). Its only special characteristics were the two glass partitions which could be inserted at the choice-point, and the fact that the color of each arm could be easily changed.

Procedure

As in the Kivy, Earl, and Walker experiment, four stimulus conditions were called for. On trial 1 the two arms could be arranged either black-left, white-right, or black-right, white-left. On trial 2 they could be either both black or both white. Three rats from Group I and two from Group II were randomly assigned to each of the four conditions. Only one exposure period, 15 min., was used.

Each rat was brought into the experimental room individually in a tin barrel, the maze having been suitably prepared prior to its entry. The rat was placed in the starting alley of the T maze and allowed to explore freely for 15 min., except, of course, that S could not enter the goal arms. At the end of the 15-min. period the rat was taken out of the maze and replaced in the tin barrel. The proper maze arm was changed and the glass partitions were removed. These manipulations took approximately 2 min. The rat was then reintroduced into the starting alley for the second trial.

RESULTS AND DISCUSSION

Ten of the 12 Group I rats made the predicted choice, as did 7 of the 8 rats in Group II. By the sign test, the combined results are significant at the .001 level of confidence.

The amount of actual "exposure" at the choice point is of some interest; these data are available for the animals of Group II, which spent an average of 3.45 min. with their heads in the area of the choice point. The one rat in this group that did not make the predicted response also had the briefest exposure, 117 sec.

These results support the hypothesis that *exploration of novel stimulation,* in the form of a change in the color of one maze arm, rather than simple stimulus-satiation, is the appropriate explanation of the Kivy, Earl, and Walker data. To explain the results of the typical alternation experiment, it would be necessary only to assume the maze arm last entered is, for some period afterward, the less novel.

Proponents of satiation theory might argue that satiation occurs only for a stimulus-in-a-place. Thus, an animal is satiated for black-on-the-left, not simply for black. With this assumption added to satiation theory, it is then possible to account for the present results. It should be pointed out, however, that such an assumption is incompatible with the logic of the original stimulus-satiation experiments (Glanzer, 1953a; Montgomery, 1952a; Walker, *et al.*, 1955), wherein stimulus and place must be assumed to be independent.

[7]
Evidence for Learning Motivated by "Exploration" [1]

ARLO K. MYERS and NEAL E. MILLER

(*Editor's note:* In its original form, this article reported two experiments. The first attempted to demonstrate that rats would acquire a *learned drive* based on hunger. Four groups of hungry rats were given 0, 10, 30, or 70 drive-acquisition trials in a black-white shuttle box— that is, they were started in the white compartment and trained both to touch the intervening door, to open it, and to run into the black compartment containing the food. Then, in a subsequent drive-acquisition test, when the four groups of rats were satiated with food and not rewarded for running, they were required to learn a new response of pressing a bar in order to gain entry into the black compartment. All of the groups learned this new response, but no reliable differences were obtained among them as a result of their different amounts of prior drive-acquisition training. Thus, although the first experiment did not provide any evidence for a learned drive based on hunger and food reward, it did show that the rats would learn to perform a response even when they were without any apparent motive or condition of reinforcement, such as hunger and food.)

EXPERIMENT II

The purpose of the second experiment was to determine some of the conditions that are necessary for the learning which was observed in the first experiment. In order to test the hypothesis that the extensive handling, taming, and feeding of the 0-trial group was responsible for their learning, all rats were given briefer taming while satiated and without any food reward. To test the hypothesis of preference for the black compartment (e.g., from light avoid-

[1] This investigation was supported by a research grant, M647, from the National Institute of Mental Health, of the National Institutes of Health, Public Health Service. The main findings were presented at the April 1954 meeting of the Eastern Psychological Association at New York.

SOURCE: Arlo K. Myers and Neal E. Miller, "Failure to Find a Learned Drive Based on Hunger; Evidence for Learning Motivated by 'Exploration,'" *Journal of Comparative and Physiological Psychology*, 1954, 47, 428–436. Reprinted by permission of American Psychological Association and A. K. Myers and N. E. Miller.

ance), the first group was run from white to black while the second one was run in the *opposite* direction. This symmetrical type of a control for obvious, or even latent, preference is believed to be a particularly important one for experiments purporting to demonstrate learning from a motivation such as exploratory behavior, curiosity, or activity drive. To determine whether the sight and sound of the door dropping is sufficient to produce learning or whether entering and inspecting the black compartment is necessary, a third group was run from the white compartment but with a white panel fastened securely in place just behind the door. To determine whether spaced practice was necessary, a fourth group was run with massed trials. So that the massing would be comparable to that used in Miller's (1947, 1948) experiments on fear, it was necessary to eliminate the 16 min. in the activity box and 8 min. in the detention cage. In order to control for these changes in procedure, a fifth group was run with spaced trials, but with the periods in the activity box and detention cage omitted.

Method

Subjects. The Ss were 50 naive male albino rats of the Sprague-Dawley strain, approximately 70 days old at the start of the experiment. All animals were maintained in individual cages on an ad lib. diet of water and Purina Laboratory Checkers.

Apparatus. The apparatus was identical with that used in Experiment I except for minor changes. For the animals running from the black compartment, pressure on its floor started the timer; touching a bar located in the same relative position as the one in the white compartment dropped the door and stopped the timer. In other words, the operations of running from white to black or black to white were similar.

Procedure. The animals were tamed by being handled once a day for five days when satiated *without* receiving any food reward. The first phase of Experiment I, hungry-reward training in the apparatus, was omitted. The animals were on ad lib. feeding throughout the experiment, and were fed wet mash for 48 min. before each training trial. Immediately after taming, the animals were divided into five groups of ten each, approximately equated for mean body weight, and randomly assigned to the following five experimental conditions:

1. A *white-to-black group* with a procedure duplicating that used in the second phase of the first experiment.

2. A *black-to-white group* run in exactly the same way but in the opposite direction. This was the only group started in the black compartment.

3. A *white panel group* run exactly like the first group except that when the door dropped, the animals were prevented from seeing or entering the black compartment by a white wooden panel immediately behind the door. To equate the effect of the time interval between bar

pressing and being picked up and placed in the detention cage, each member of this group was given a partner in the white-to-black group and was removed from the apparatus at the moment which would make S's interval on that trial equal to that of its just-previously-run partner.

4. *The massed group* received all 18 of their trials in a single afternoon with an intertrial interval averaging approximately 3 min. The ten animals in this group were randomly subdivided into three, four, and three animals, respectively, which were run on the first, middle, and last days of the experiment. To achieve the close massing, the activity box and detention cage were omitted from the procedure; the animals were returned immediately to their home cages (from which food and water had been temporarily removed) after each trial. In other respects, the procedure for the massed group was the same as that for the white-to-black group.

5. *The massed control group* was run without the activity box or detention cage to determine the effect of omitting these procedures. They were run exactly like the massed group except that their trials were distributed at the rate of one per day like those of the first three groups.

Results

All the latency scores were transformed into speed scores as described for Experiment I. The results are presented in Figure 1.

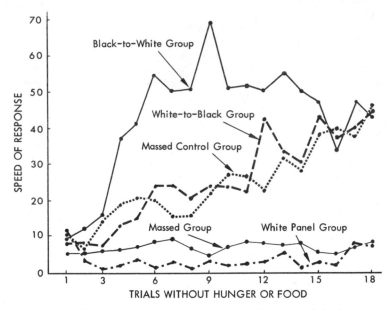

Figure 1. Effect of experimental conditions on learning of the bar-pressing response by groups trained without hunger drive or food reward. Speed of response = 100/time in sec.

The five groups start out at roughly the same level of performance; although the white panel and massed groups show little change throughout the 18 trials, the others show definite learning.

Each animal's scores were summed for the first six, middle six, and last six trials, and the resulting matrix of 150 scores for the 50 animals was subjected to analysis of variance to assess the over-all effects due to blocks of trials, groups, and groups × trials interaction. All three produced highly significant F's, with p in each case less than .01. Table 1 summarizes this analysis.

Then, for the mean of all 18 trials, separate t tests were computed comparing each group with every other one. Of these ten comparisons, all but two produced differences significant at the .01 level of confidence or beyond. The difference between the white-to-black and massed control groups and between the massed and white panel groups were not significant ($p = .79$ and .59, respectively).

Next, the significance of the *trend* for each group was analyzed by computing separate t tests among the three blocks of six trials. None of the comparisons among blocks of trials even approached significance for either the massed or white panel groups. The other three groups all showed an increase from the first to the third block of trials significant beyond the .01 level of confidence. These three groups also showed significant increases from the first to the second block, and from the second to the third block, with the exception of the black-to-white group, which showed a significant *decrement* from the second to the third block of trials.

TABLE 1

Analysis of Variance of Speed Scores in Experiment II

	Source of Variance	Mean Square	df	F	p
1.	Groups	2,716,275*	4	13.86	<.01
2.	Trials	865,061†	2	71.48	<.01
3.	Trials × Groups	221,908†	8	18.34	<.01
4.	Rats within groups	196,031	45		
5.	Rats within groups × Trials	12,102	90		

* Tested against 4.
† Tested against 5.

Since all groups started from nearly the same level of performance, the foregoing analysis gives a fairly complete picture of the differences among the five groups. As a further check, separate t

tests were computed on the differences between trends among the five groups. An examination of the resulting 30 comparisons simply confirms the impression one gets from an examination of Figure 1. There is little difference between the white-to-black and massed control groups or between the massed and white panel groups at any stage of training.

After pressing the bar, all the animals (except those prevented by the white panel) at least poked their heads into the other compartment and sniffed around. More of the animals going to the white entered all the way than of those going to the black. On the first trial, the difference between the black-to-white group and each of the others was significant beyond the .01 level.

For the first 18 trials during which a direct comparison is possible, there is little or no difference between the learning by the white-to-black group in Experiment II and by the 70-trial group (white-to-black) in Experiment I. Though the rats that had had 70 drive-acquisition trials before the test may show some slight superiority in early trials (presumably because their fear of the door's dropping has been extinguished), the mean speed for these animals averaged over all 18 trials is not significantly greater than that for the white-to-black group of Experiment II ($p = .38$).

Discussion

The main results of Experiment II were as follows: (a) Satiated and nonrewarded animals will learn the bar-pressing response either to open the door from the white to the black compartment or from the black to the white compartment. (b) Animals that pressed the bar (in the white compartment) to drop the door but were prevented from seeing or entering the other compartment did not learn. (c) Animals trained with massed instead of spaced trials (white-to-black) did not learn. (d) The failure of the massed group to learn was not due to the omission of the activity box and detention cage from their running procedure because the massed control group, which was given spaced trials with these procedures omitted, learned as well as the white-to-black group.

The fact that the black-to-white group learned faster than the white-to-black group suggests that a preference for the white compartment may be a source of some motivation and reward in the apparatus. However, the fact that both groups (running in opposite directions) learned shows that such a preference is not a necessary condition for learning. Apparently the fact that pressing the bar is followed by the chance to observe and enter a new compartment is sufficient to produce learning.

The fact that the white panel group did not learn shows that the cues produced by bar pressing and door dropping, or by being picked up and returned to the home cage via the detention cage, are not sufficient to produce learning; it suggests that the act of seeing or exploring the other compartment, or perhaps experiencing the change between the two compartments (irrespective of the direction of change), produces the reinforcement. But we cannot tell whether or not exposure to the new stimuli in the other compartment would produce learning even if the animals were prevented from entering or exploring.

Since dropping the door provided the animals with more space in which to move about, it might be argued that the reinforcement came from this greater opportunity to exercise or escape restriction. However, the white-to-black group did not seem to perform any worse than the massed control group which was run under identical conditions except for the omission of the activity box and detention cage. Presumably exercise in the activity box before each trial, as opposed to confinement in the small home cage, would have reduced the exercise drive and produced poorer performance in the white-to-black group. The fact that the massed controls were returned directly to their home cage, rather than to a detention cage, after each trial might also be expected to produce superior learning if return to the home cage were a significant part of the reinforcement. Thus, the lack of any appreciable difference between these two groups also serves as additional evidence against assigning an important role in these particular experiments to reinforcement from return to the home cage.

Guthrie's (1952) principles might be used to explain the learning shown by groups that had a chance to enter the other compartment and were run with distributed practice. Pressing the bar would be the last thing that the animal did before entering the other compartment, where the change in cues would protect S from unlearning the habit of pressing the bar by removing the opportunity to perform different responses to the original cues. But this explanation— at least in its simplest, most obvious form—would seem to apply equally well to the massed group which did *not* learn. If it is assumed that general changes in posture and other sources of interoceptive stimulation are more likely to occur during the longer interval, the task of the animals with distributed practice would be more difficult, since they would have to attach the response of pressing the bar to a greater variety of combinations of cues. Thus it seems that a simple form of Guthrie-type explanation is not able to account for the difference between the learning of the groups with massed and distributed practice.

The failure of the massed group to learn confirms the conclusion from Miller's (1947, 1948, 1951) previous studies that learning will not occur during *massed trials* in his apparatus unless specific procedures have been used to establish a learned drive, such as fear.

Though some inferiority of the massed group would be expected from the principle of reactive inhibition (Hull, 1943), the magnitude of the difference found in this experiment suggests that other factors may be operating. If learning were motivated by a relatively weak drive of exercise, exploration, or curiosity, it is possible that this motivation might be satiated or extinguished by the massed practice and not have enough chance to recover during the short time between trials. Montgomery (1951b, 1952b, 1953a) and Berlyne (1950) have shown that a rat's tendency to investigate a new stimulus object decreases rapidly with continued exposure and shows little recovery during a short interval of nonexposure but considerable recovery during a 24-hr. interval. Thus, the satiation of an exploratory drive during massed trials but recovery during spaced ones may account for the difference in the second experiment. If an exploratory tendency can produce learning like other drives such as hunger, and also show a similar pattern of satiation and recovery, these functional parallels to already known drives would help to justify its classification in the same category with them, namely as a drive.[2]

A considerable body of challenging experimental work interpreted in terms of "exploratory" and "manipulatory" drives has been reported by Harlow and his associates (1953b). Harlow believes that these drives differ from the better-studied ones, such as hunger, in that external stimuli, i.e., the ones explored, both elicit the drive and operate as reinforcement.

We, however, would not put a drive in a special category simply

[2] According to observations by Sharpless (1954a), novel stimuli elicit an "arousal reaction" presumably involving the brain-stem reticular formation. This "arousal reaction," indicated by characteristic changes in brain waves, shows fairly rapid extinction (presumably as the stimulus loses its novelty) and eventual recovery analogous to that described above. It is conceivable that this arousal reaction to novel stimuli is part of the mechanism of exploratory motivation.

because it is elicited by external stimuli. We prefer the drive-reduction hypothesis developed by Hull (1943) and Miller and Dollard (1941), which treats externally elicited drives (such as pain) in the same way as other drives. Furthermore, as Brown (1953b) has pointed out, in some of the Wisconsin studies on the "visual exploration drive" the novel stimuli to be explored are not present at the time the animal begins working to secure them. If the novel stimuli elicit the drive, this would mean that the drive is produced *after* the animal has performed the response the drive is supposed to be motivating.

If, as Harlow seems to imply, the same novel stimuli elicit an exploratory drive and *simultaneously* serve as an exploratory reward, a strict drive-reduction theory would be unable to deal with these phenomena. However, we believe it is possible that confinement produces anxiety, restraint is frustrating, or monotony arouses a drive of boredom. Indeed, the observation of small children who are required to sit absolutely still, the reports of prisoners subjected to solitary confinement, and the difficulty of Bexton, Heron, and Scott (1954) in retaining Ss in their experiment on the effects of decreased sensory variation would indicate that such conditions can produce strong motivation. Therefore, we suggest that drives produced by homogeneous or monotonous stimulation, enforced inaction, etc., may be reduced by sensory variety, freedom of action, etc., and that such drive reduction is the *reinforcement* involved in learning for "exploratory," "manipulatory," and "exercise" rewards. For the present, we choose the more parsimonious alternative of trying to analyze such concepts as exploratory drive along the same lines as conventional drives.

We also believe some writers have been too quick to assume that novel stimuli elicit a drive simply because such stimuli commonly elicit activity or exploration. This may well be a case of confusing the cue properties of a stimulus with possible drive properties. Exploration may be an innate response to novelty in some species, or it may occur because exploration has been reinforced in the presence of novel cues in the animal's past history. Activity is a poor measure of drive; some drives, such as fatigue or fear, may tend to decrease activity.

Irrespective of how the foregoing problems of theory and interpretation are handled, we agree that it is extremely important to develop techniques for studying significant sources of motivation which have previously been neglected. Such studies may lead to fundamental extensions or radical revisions of our present concepts. Certainly our present list of experimentally studied motives is far too short.

[8]
The Effect of Deprivation of Visual Incentives on Visual Exploration Motivation in Monkeys[1]

ROBERT A. BUTLER

The results of several experiments suggest that a curiosity motive is operative in the behavior of higher animals. For example, when monkeys are permitted to manipulate objects or explore the surrounding environment, these animals engage in this type of behavior for prolonged and repetitive test sessions (Butler & Harlow, 1954; Butler & Alexander, 1955; Harlow, 1950). Other researches have demonstrated that discrimination learning can be established when the only apparent reward is the opportunity to engage in manipulatory or exploratory behavior (Butler, 1953; Harlow & McClearn, 1954; Montgomery & Segall, 1955). There is also evidence that the motivational strength of exploratory behavior varies with differences in incentive conditions (Butler, 1954).

These studies were conducted to show that the behavioral manifestations of manipulatory and exploratory motives are, in many respects, similar to those usually associated with the biological drives. A frequently studied characteristic of biological drives is the relation between drive strength and duration of deprivation (Heron & Skinner, 1937; Warner, 1927, 1928; Yamaguchi, 1951). Indeed, food deprivation is used routinely to ensure that animals are sufficiently motivated to perform in various test situations for food re-

[1] The author wishes to express his appreciation to Dr. Murray Sidman, Walter Reed Army Institute of Research, Mr. Maurice Whitlock and Mr. John Jones, Audiology and Speech Center, Walter Reed Army Hospital, for their work in planning and constructing the apparatus used in this study.

SOURCE: Robert A. Butler, "The Effect of Deprivation of Visual Incentives on Visual Exploration Motivation in Monkeys," *Journal of Comparative and Physiological Psychology*, 1957, **50**, 177–179. Reprinted by permission of the American Psychological Association and R. A. Butler.

ward. Measurable physiological changes take place when food and water are denied, and, within certain limits, it is inferred that drive strength is directly proportional to the magnitude of these physiological changes. There are no a priori reasons why deprivation of incentives which elicit manipulation and exploration would cause an increase in the strength of these motives, since the physiological phenomena accompanying this kind of deprivation are by no means apparent. If, however, manipulation and exploration are important motivational mechanisms, it is reasonable to hypothesize that motivational strength would become greater when animals are deprived of the relevant rewards. The present experiment was designed to determine whether the responsiveness of monkeys to visual incentives would increase following restriction of visual exploratory experience.

Method

Subjects

Five rhesus monkeys (no. 301, 302, 304, 305, and 306), whose weights ranged from 6½ to 9 lb., participated in this experiment. All Ss had been tested previously on a visual exploration problem (Butler & Alexander, 1955), but they had received no training on any other type of problem.

Apparatus

Testing Box. During the deprivation and testing periods, the Ss were housed in an enclosed box 26 in. long, 16 in. wide, and 30 in. high. The box was constructed of 16-gauge aluminum. Metal bars, ⅜ in. in diameter and spaced 1⅛ in. apart, formed the floor of the box. Directly beneath the bars was a metal pan for the collection of urine and feces. The inside of the box was illuminated by a 25-w. lamp fixed to its top. Circulation of air inside the box was provided by an inner and outer series of ventilation holes ½ in. in diameter located along the top and bottom of each side of the box. The holes overlapped in such a way that animals could not see out. Monkeys were put into the testing box through a vertically sliding door at the rear of the box.

Centered on the front of the box was a window 3¼ in. square. Covering the window was a motor-operated door which opened outward. A sheet of Plexiglas ¹⁄₁₆ in. thick was inserted between the window and the door. One end of the Plexiglas was fixed securely to the front of the box while the other end could be pushed outward approximately ⅛ in. before contacting and activating a microswitch. The microswitch delivered an electric pulse to a relay which initiated the opening of the motor-operated door. By these means, monkeys could cause the door to open by pushing against the Plexiglas. During the deprivation periods a metal plate was fixed rigidly over the window in place of the Plexiglas sheet.

Control and Recording Unit. In an adjacent room a system of

relays and a program device were arranged to control the times when the door could be activated. In addition, a timer controlled the length of time the door would remain open. The number of responses against the Plexiglas and the number of times the door opened were recorded automatically on impulse counters. The rate of response was charted on the cumulative recorder.

Procedure

PRELIMINARY TRAINING.   Since all Ss had been previously trained to push directly against the door to receive visual reward, they quickly learned to push against the Plexiglas sheet inserted between the box and the door. During the beginning stages of preliminary training, the monkeys were reinforced for each response, i.e., the door opened and the animals were allowed to look outside the box. Then, in an attempt to devise a more sensitive measure of motivational strength, monkeys were trained under conditions of variable-interval reinforcement. Several schedules were employed until one was found under which monkeys produced a relatively constant rate of response throughout a 60-min. test session. With this reinforcement schedule, a maximum of either 0, 4, 8, 12, or 16 sec. occurred between the time the door closed and the time the door could be opened again by a response against the Plexiglas. These interreinforcement intervals were arranged so as to prevent the presence of temporal cues. For each reinforced response, the door remained opened for 12 sec. Preliminary training continued until the Ss were generating a relatively stable rate of response curve.

FORMAL TESTING.   Frequency of responses to visual incentives was measured for different durations of visual exploration deprivation. The monkeys were placed in the testing box with the metal plate covering the window. After a delay of either 0, 2, 4, or 8 hr., the Plexiglas sheet was quickly inserted in place of the metal plate, and testing was begun. The length of the actual test session was 1 hr. Testing was conducted in the room housing the monkey colony, and the front of the box faced the other animals. The monkeys were fed at approximately 7:30 A.M. and testing began at 4:00 P.M. The interior of the box was illuminated throughout the deprivation and testing sessions.

Presentation of the deprivation conditions followed a 4 by 4 Latin square with rows representing animals, columns representing test sessions and Latin letters representing deprivation conditions. Two animals were assigned to one row of the square, and each of the other three monkeys was assigned to a separate row. Only one monkey was tested on any day, and from four to six days elapsed before the animal was tested again. After the Ss had experienced every condition of deprivation, the entire formal testing procedure was repeated, thereby giving each animal a total of eight test sessions.

RESULTS

Mean frequency of responses for the various deprivation conditions was calculated. Friedman's chi-square test indicated that differences between conditions were significant at the .05 confidence level. As shown in Figure 1, mean response frequencies increased as the duration of deprivation was lengthened. The responsiveness of the Ss after 8 hr. of deprivation was only slightly greater than that recorded for the 4-hr. deprivation condition. Differences between

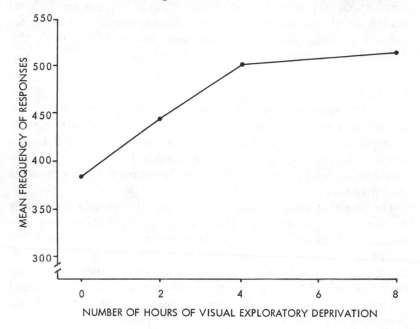

FIGURE 1. Mean frequency of responses as a function of duration of deprivation.

conditions, with respect to number of reinforcements attained, were also significant ($p < .05$) as measured by the Friedman chi-square test. Mean number of visual rewards was 141.0, 149.1, 155.5, and 157.2 for the 0-, 2-, 4-, and 8-hr. deprivation conditions, respectively. The response/reinforcement ratio tended to increase as the deprivation periods were lengthened, but this trend failed to reach significance at the .05 confidence level. Not all monkeys consistently responded more frequently with increased durations of deprivation. Monkey no. 301, however, was the only S whose mean frequency of responses was actually less for one of the deprivation conditions than it was when there was no deprivation.

Deprivation appeared to have had a disproportionate effect on visual exploration motivation at the beginning of the experiment.

Notwithstanding the length of the deprivation period, i.e., 2, 4, or 8 hr., four of the five animals responded most frequently on the first test session that necessitated visual corfinement than on any subsequent test session. Only one of these Ss received 8 hr. of deprivation on the first test day, one was tested after 4 hr. of deprivation, and two were tested after 2 hr. of deprivation. Following the initial test session under a deprivation condition, the magnitude of response frequencies was more in accordance with the duration of deprivation.

Discussion

A visual exploration motive is postulated to account for the performances observed in this experiment. These data indicate that the strength of visual exploration motivation can be increased by restricting the visual experience of the animals. Furthermore, motivational strength appeared to be positively correlated with duration of deprivation.

The fact that some Ss failed to demonstrate consistent increases in response frequency when the periods of deprivation were prolonged might be attributed to two factors: (*a*) day-to-day variability within the incentive condition, and (*b*) failure on the part of the Ss to adjust immediately to a test situation involving deprivation. Some degree of control over the incentive condition was exerted by testing animals at the same time each day. Previous research suggested that frequency of responses to visual incentives provided by a colony of monkeys varies with the amount of activity occurring in the colony (Butler & Alexander, 1955). Colony activity, in turn, fluctuates in accordance with feeding schedules and the time of day that routine laboratory tasks are being carried out in the vicinity of the animals. Although the time of day when the monkeys were tested remained constant, this type of precautionary measure served only as a partial control over the vagaries of colony activity. Regarding the lack of initial adjustment to the test situation, the inordinately high response frequencies on the first deprivation test session caused reversals between the number of responses and the length of deprivation.

Earlier studies have shown that visual exploratory behavior can be maintained at a relatively high level with little or no evidence of satiation. The data reported here demonstrate that the responsiveness of monkeys to visual incentives can indeed be increased when animals are prevented from engaging in visual exploratory behavior for various periods of time. The development of testing conditions which produce an orderly satiation function of visual exploration needs further research.

SUMMARY AND CONCLUSIONS

Five rhesus monkeys were deprived of a varied visual experience for 0, 2, 4, and 8 hr. The animals were then tested to determine whether their responses to visual incentives would be increased as the result of this deprivation. A variable-interval reinforcement schedule was used to test the motivational strength of the monkeys. Reinforcement consisted of a 12-sec. view of the monkey colony outside the test cage. The results showed that the number of responses to visual incentives approached a maximum after 4 hr. of deprivation. Differences between mean response frequencies for the various conditions were significant at the .05 confidence level. These data provide another demonstration of the similarities between behavior based on a proposed curiosity motive and behavior based on biological drives.

[9]
Learning as a Function of Sensory Stimulation of Various Intensities [1]

HARRY LEVIN and DONALD G. FORGAYS

Reinforcement is usually thought to occur when responses result in stimulus decrease to the organism (e.g., Hull, 1952). A number of recent studies indicate, however, that under certain conditions, an increase in external stimulation can also be reinforcing (e.g., Forgays & Levin, 1958; Kish, 1955; Marx, Henderson, & Roberts, 1955; Montgomery, 1952b). The present series of studies are designed to explicate certain of these conditions.

[1] These studies were supported in part by a grant from the Faculty Research Grants Committee of Cornell University and in part by a research grant from the National Science Foundation. We wish to thank Alan Goldman and Jay Perlman for their help with the investigations.

SOURCE: Harry Levin and Donald G. Forgays, "Learning as a Function of Sensory Stimulation of Various Intensities," *Journal of Comparative and Physiological Psychology*, 1959, 52, 195–201. Reprinted by permission of the American Psychological Association and H. Levin and D. G. Forgays.

In a previous study (Forgays & Levin, 1958), we investigated lever-press learning by food-deprived and food-satiated rats when 5 sec. of light was the reinforcing agent. In general, the food-deprived animals tended to respond at a higher rate than the food-satiated animals. The principal finding of the experiment, however, was that the lever-light paired groups responded significantly more frequently than their controls and exhibited typical acquisition and extinction behavior during the appropriate trials.

In the above study only a single light intensity was used as a reinforcing stimulus. The question arises as to the nature of the reinforcing effects of light stimulation of different intensities.

It is possible that both very bright and very dim lights will not be effective positive reinforcers. Extremely bright illuminations can be aversive stimuli because they are painful to the organism; low illuminations, on the other hand, may not be readily discriminable. In this regard Thomson (1955) reports that the reinforcing value of stimulus increase varies positively with the degree of change of the external stimulus. Marx *et al.* (1955), using a greater range of stimulus intensities than Thomson, report that the amount of reinforcement is related in a rectilinear fashion to light intensity up to 16 mL. but that stronger intensities of light are aversive stimuli. Whether intensities intervening between the extremes will differ in reinforcing value is an empirical question.

The present study was undertaken to investigate the effect of different intensities of light stimulation on the learning of a lever-pressing response. Since some of the findings in this study were not anticipated, the results were replicated in part and extended in a second investigation whose results are also presented here. Specifically, the first study reports differential reinforcing effects of various light intensities and an interaction of these effects with the age of the animals. The second experiment studies further the reinforcing properties of two of the same light intensities and investigates directly the age variable. Each study will be described separately, but their results will be discussed together.

Experiment I. Variation of Stimulus Intensity

Method

SUBJECTS.   The Ss were 32 albino rats of the Cornell University Psychology Laboratory strain. Seventeen were male and 15 were female; all were members of five litters born within a few days of each other. Eight animals were assigned to each of the four groups constituting the design. Males and females of each litter were distributed as equally as possible among the groups. Half the animals began acquisition trials when they were approximately 70 days of age; the remainder began 40 days later, when they were about 110 days old. All animals were experimentally naive prior to beginning this experiment.

APPARATUS. The apparatus consisted of a soundproofed, boxlike enclosure whose inside dimensions were 12 in. long, 10½ in. wide, and 12 in. tall. The interior walls were brown masonite (dull side exposed) covered with ½-in. hardware cloth. The floor was solid; the roof was hinged and was used as a door. The single object within the box was a solid bar lever 2 in. wide, extending ½ in. into the box through a wall at a point 5½ in. above the floor and 2 in. from the juncture of two walls. A section of the roof consisted of a circular pane of clear glass, 4 in. in diameter, above which a 40-w. bulb was mounted outside the box. The bulb was wired through a variable rheostat, allowing control of the intensity of light emitted. The box was placed in a lightproof and soundproofed room. A series of electrical relays was wired in such a way that lever pressure led to illumination of the bulb for 5 sec. Further pressure of the lever while the light was on had no effect on future appearance of the light; the light could only be reactivated after a time-delay relay closed, 5 sec. after the onset of light. The number of lever presses was recorded on an electrical counter. The latency of the first lever press in each trial was also recorded.

PROCEDURE. Each animal was placed singly in the dark box for 12 min. a day on 20 consecutive days. All animals were on an ad lib. food diet in their home cages; food was never obtained in the experimental box by any animal. The three experimental groups differed in the intensity of illumination delivered into the box following a lever press. For the high-intensity group, the illumination was 33.04 mL.; for the medium-intensity group, 1.76 mL.; for the low-intensity group, .01 mL. These brightness readings were taken at the light source with a General Electric Luckiesh-Taylor Brightness Meter. No illumination followed the lever presses of control animals. Thus, there were three experimental groups which differed in the intensity of illumination following lever presses and one control group, the animals of which received no light after pressing the lever.

The animals, it will be recalled, were run in two phases; when first run, the second group of animals was about 40 days older than the initial group. It became apparent that the younger and older animals were differently affected by the various illuminations which followed bar presses. We, therefore, included age as a classification in the analysis below.

Results

The two scores available for analysis are the number of lever presses for each 12-min. trial and the latency of the first response in each trial. For all 32 animals, the two measures correlate $-.87$, so that they are virtually interchangeable. Analysis of both the response and latency measures yield similar results, with only slight differences in probability statements.

From the way the data are grouped, there are, in effect, two observations for each animal: the sum of the responses for the first 10 days and the corresponding sum for the last 10 days.

The mean number of responses by animals in the various classifications is presented in Table 1, and the summary of the analysis of variance of these means is in Table 2.

TABLE 1

Mean Numbers of Responses

Condition	Younger Animals Trials			Older Animals Trials			Combined Groups Trials 1–20
	1–10	11–20	1–20	1–10	11–20	1–20	
High intensity	10.25	47.25	57.50	65.00	107.50	172.50	115.00
Medium intensity	67.75	118.50	186.25	56.25	74.50	130.75	158.50
Low intensity	66.75	90.50	157.25	22.75	40.50	63.25	110.25
Control	57.25	53.50	110.75	33.50	25.50	59.00	84.87

TABLE 2

Summary of the Analysis of Variance of the Response Data

Source	df	SS	MS	F	p
A. Between Subjects	(31)	113,619.11			
Intensity	3	11,214.92	3,738.31	1.20	N.S.
Age	1	1,859.76	1,859.76	0.60	N.S.
Age by Intensity	3	25,959.55	8,653.18	2.78	N.S.
Error	24	74,584.88	3,107.70		
B. Within Subjects	(32)	26,025.50			
Periods	1	7,943.27	7,943.27	15.96	<.001
Periods by Intensity	3	5,001.30	1,667.10	3.35	<.05
Periods by Age	1	346.89	346.89	0.70	N.S.
Periods by Age by Intensity	3	789.92	263.31	0.53	N.S.
Error	24	11,944.12	497.67		
Total	(63)	139,641.61			

Consider first the analysis of the total number of responses (Table 2, Part A). The interaction of intensity and age approaches significance ($p = .07$). The nature of this interaction is clarified in Figure

1. For the younger animals, the relationship between intensity of the reinforcing stimulus and response frequency is curvilinear. The brightest light is associated with the fewest number of lever presses, the medium light with the most responses, and the dimmest light and the no-light (control) conditions with the next fewest number of responses, in that order. With the older animals, there is a rectilinear relationship between light intensity and response level. In other words, the major difference between the two age groups is the manner in which the light of high intensity affects lever pressing.

Calculated according to Tukey's gap test, the least significant difference at the .10 level of confidence for mean number of responses within each group over the total of 20 trials is 67.46. As can be seen in Table 1, for the younger animals, the high-intensity group responded significantly less than either the medium- or low-intensity groups, and less even than the control gorup, but not significantly so. The medium intensity group responded more frequently than the control group. Among the older animals, the significant groupings are the high and medium, which are similar to each other but different from the low and control groups. The latter two do not differ.

The next section of the analysis of variance (Table 2, Part B) concerns the differences in the number of responses between the early and late experimental periods. Results show that all groups

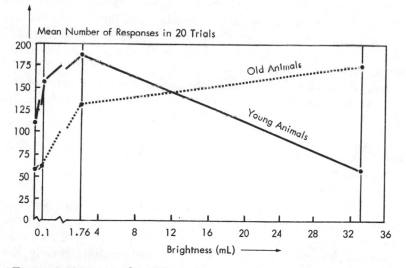

FIGURE 1. Mean numbers of responses according to age of animals and intensity of stimulus.

except the control group responded more frequently in the last ten trials than in the first ten trials ($p < .001$).

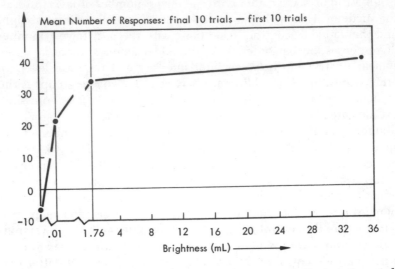

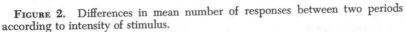

FIGURE 2.   Differences in mean number of responses between two periods according to intensity of stimulus.

In addition, the period by intensity interaction is significant at the .05 level of confidence. Figure 2 helps to clarify this interaction. Learning is most pronounced, that is, there is the greatest second-period increase under the high-intensity condition. Medium- and low-intensity reinforcers are next with respect to second-period increases. When there is no reinforcement, there is an actual decrease of response over periods.

Age of the animals does not relate to the reinforcing value of the various light intensities when period differences are taken as an index of learning.

EXPERIMENT II. VARIATION OF AGE AND EXPERIENCE OF ANIMALS AND STIMULUS INTENSITY

The results of the above study indicate that age is an important determinant of effects associated with stimulus intensity. Since the age variable appeared somewhat fortuitously in the reported study, a second investigation was undertaken to examine directly the effects of two intensities of light stimulation, the high and low illuminations of Experiment I, on lever-pressing response levels in animals of different ages. Specifically, we wish to see if the results of the above study can be replicated and further, to examine the effects of prior experience with a given light intensity upon present response levels in animals of different ages when lever pressing leads to the onset of that specific light intensity.

Method

SUBJECTS. The Ss were 54 albino rats of the Cornell University Psychology Laboratory strain. There were 30 males and 24 females all members of seven litters born within a few days of each other. Nine animals were assigned at random to each of six groups so that litters and sexes were equally represented over the groups. Two of the groups began experimental trials when they were approximately 32 days of age, two began when they were about 80 days of age, and the last two groups began when they were about 130 days of age. All animals were experimentally naive prior to initial running.

APPARATUS. The same apparatus was used here as in Experiment I above. Only two light intensities were employed—the high and the low illuminations (33.04 and .01 mL., respectively). The number of lever presses was recorded as above.

PROCEDURE. All animals were on an ad lib. food and water diet in their home cages. Each animal was placed singly in the dark box for 12 min. a day on 10 consecutive days for each series of trials to which the animal's group was exposed. As stated above, two groups of animals were run initially on a series of ten trials when they were 32 days of age; they received a second series of ten trials when they were 80 days of age, and a final series of ten trials when they were 130 days of age. Two groups were initially run when they were 80 days of age and received a second series when they were 130 days of age. Two groups received only a single series of ten trials, when they were 130 days of age. The animals in one of the groups in each of the three pairings received the brighter illumination for lever press, the other group's animals received the dimmer illumination for lever pressing. Thus, there were six groups of animals run in the sequence shown in Table 3.

TABLE 3

Experimental Design

Condition	Age at Start of Series		
	32 days	80 days	130 days
Bright light	Group 1	Group 1	Group 1
		Group 3	Group 3
			Group 5
Dim light	Group 2	Group 2	Group 2
		Group 4	Group 4
			Group 6

TABLE 4

Mean Numbers of Responses for the Various Conditions
and Significant *t*s Found (*p* < .05)

Light Intensity	Time of Testing (Days of Age)			Significant *t*s Between
	32	80	130	
High	23.67 (a)	82.22 (b)	79.44 (c)	a, b
		39.78 (d)	102.00 (e)	b, d
			94.00 (f)	d, e
Low	21.22 (g)	102.44 (h)	156.33 (i)	c, i
				d, j
		74.56 (j)	258.77 (k)	e, k
			147.67 (l)	g, h
				j, k

Results

We will present the results of Experiment II in two sections. First, we will present those results relevant to the effect of age, independent of specific prior experience (uncorrelated measures), upon response level for each light intensity. Next, we will outline those results pertaining to the effects of prior experience and light intensity upon response level within each of the two relevant age groups.

AGE EFFECTS INDEPENDENT OF EXPERIENCE.   The mean number of responses by animals of the various groups, selected *t* test results, and appropriate probability statements are presented in Table 4. Consider here the response figures given for animals initially run at 32, 80, or 130 days of age. These are the mean figures appropriate for the analysis of the effect of age and light intensity upon response level, independent of prior experience in the experimental situation. An analysis of variance of these means was conducted. A significant Between-Groups effect was found and thus broken down into its three components: age of animal, intensity of light, and the interaction of these two effects. The Age-of-Animals effect is significant at the .01 level of confidence. Reference to Table 4 reveals that in each comparison older animals respond at a higher rate than do the younger animals. This is true for both the high- and low-intensity light groups. The Light-Intensity effect and the Age-Intensity interaction are not significant.

EFFECTS OF PRIOR EXPERIENCE.   In the first part of this section we will be concerned with an analysis of the data only for the four groups of animals run at 80 days of age; then we will present the analysis of the data for the six groups of animals run at 130 days of age.

Eighty-day-old animals.   It will be recalled that of the four groups run at this age, two had had previous experience and two were introduced to the experimental situation for the first time. The mean number of responses for these four groups is presented in Table 4. An analysis of variance of these means was conducted. The significant Between-Groups effect which was found was further analyzed in terms of its three components: experience, light intensity, and the interaction of these two effects. The Experience effect is significant ($p < .05$). For both light intensities, the animals having had prior exposure at 32 days of age responded at higher levels than did the inexperienced animals. Analysis by t test for uncorrelated means reveals that this comparison is significant at the .02 level of confidence for the bright-light groups only, and is not significant for the dim-light groups.

The Light-Intensity effect is not significant ($p. < .10$). In general, however, animals receiving dim illumination for lever pressing respond at higher levels than do animals receiving bright illumination. Further analysis by t test indicates that this comparison is significant at the .05 level of confidence for the inexperienced groups only. Experienced animals receiving dim illumination for lever pressing do not respond at a significantly higher rate than do experienced animals receiving bright illumination.

The Experience-Intensity interaction effect is not significant.

One-hundred-thirty-day-old animals.   The mean number of responses for these six groups is presented in Table 4. An analysis of variance of these means was conducted. The significant Between-Groups effect which was found was further analyzed in terms of its three components: experience, light intensity, and the interaction of these two effects. The Experience effect is not significant ($p < .20$). The bright-light and the dim-light groups having had a single experience at 80 days of age (a single past experience) tend to respond at higher levels than do the remaining two relevant groups (animals with no prior experience and those with two prior exposures). Analysis by t test reveals that specific comparisons are not significant for the bright-light or the dim-light groups.

The effect of light intensity is significant at the .01 level of confidence. In general, animals receiving dim illumination for lever pressing respond at higher rates than do those receiving bright illumination. Further analysis by *t* test indicates that this comparison is significant only for those groups of animals which had prior exposure to the experimental situation. The Experience-Intensity interaction is not significant.

DISCUSSION

In a previous paper (Forgays & Levin, 1958), the writers reported that a sensory change following a response acted to reinforce that response. The results of Experiment I here replicate those of the previous study. In addition, as indicated in the present Experiments I and II, there appear to be systematic effects attributable to the age of the animal, his experience, and the intensity of the stimulus change.

The results of Experiment I indicate that intensity of stimulation is an important determinant of the lever-pressing response for light. The most interesting feature of this study is the unexpected finding that younger animals prefer the dim light while older animals prefer the bright. Replication and extension of these results is necessary.

In the second study reported here, age of animal was found again to be an important determinant of response level. In both studies inexperienced animals of 70 to 80 days of age respond at higher rates for the onset of dim illumination than for bright light.

In the first study older animals responded at higher rates for bright-light reception than for dim light. Results of the attempted replication in our second study for this age level are equivocal; older animals respond no differently for the two light intensities.

The effects of specific past experience were studied only in Experiment II and yield findings in addition to those discussed above based on the similarities of the two studies.

The design of Experiment II permits us to analyze the effects upon lever-pressing behavior of either one or two previous exposures to the experimental situation. Regardless of the age of the animals (80 or 130 days) or the intensity of the light stimulation, one prior exposure significantly increases the rate of response. An additional exposure has no further effect upon response rate. It appears that a ten-day testing period adapts the animal in some way to the experimental situation and that further testing (experience) does not change this adaptation as indexed by response level.

It is interesting from a developmental point of view to note the effects of experience and light intensity on 80-day-old animals. It will be recalled that in both experiments the bright light appears to be an aversive stimulus for these animals. Yet animals that have had experience with this same stimulus earlier in life prefer it no less than the dim light. Two reasons are suggested for this result: (*a*) the prior experience with the intense light has changed the adaptation level of the animals, or (*b*) the previous handling has made them less excitable and less likely to react with fear to an intense stimulus.

Why a given light intensity should be avoided by younger animals and preferred by older ones and why past experience with light intensities should change these preferences is not clear. Whether threshold changes to visual stimulation occur with increasing age and experience in the rat is not known to the writers. On the basis of such changes we would expect that the specific stimulus values which are positively and negatively reinforcing for young, naive animals would not be the same as those for older animals.

It might be suggested that the apparently differential reinforcing effects associated with variation of stimulus intensity are simply due to the increased activity which might be expected to result from an increase of sensory stimulation. On the basis of this point of view, however, there would be no reason to expect the increased response rates in the second half of the trials over the first half, as found in Experiment I. Response rate based solely on increased activity association with stimulus intensity should presumably stay at a constant level over trials as long as the stimulus intensity remains constant or, perhaps, should decrease over trials as a result of fatigue or adaptation. The increase which we report in Experiment I argues against this possibility.

Even more crucial evidence against the activity-intensity notion are the latency data which we mentioned briefly above in Experiment I. The latency (of first response for each trial) data provide the same results as do the response data presented. However, the latency measure is one which is taken before light stimulation occurs in any trial, and hence could not be the result of increased activity due to intensity of sensory stimulation except in the learned manner which we have suggested.

[10]
Stimulus Complexity and Sensory Reinforcement [1]

GERALD W. BARNES [2] and ALAN BARON

While there is no doubt that sensory reinforcement, e.g., response-contingent dim illumination, produces a radical increase in rate of responding (Antonitis & Barnes, 1961; Kish, 1955; Marx, Henderson, & Roberts, 1955), the basic nature of this effect is still not clear. Studies of light reinforcement have involved investigation of lever responding in a relatively homogeneous experimental environment, viz., a Skinner box situation, and discussion of the results has been centered around properties of the response-contingent light itself, e.g., intensity, onset, direction of change. Although the observed response-rate increases show conclusively that Ss do not behave so as to illuminate the environment continuously, it is nonetheless possible that the visual characteristics of the briefly illuminated environment are important in sensory reinforcement.

Some support for the hypothesis of a perceptual variable in response determination has been provided by Berlyne with rats (1955) and Welker with chimpanzees (1956b, 1956c) in reports of enhanced exploratory tendencies as complexity of the stimulus situation being explored was increased. By permitting unlimited exploration of three-dimensional stimulus objects, however, the experimental procedures of Berlyne and Welker confounded complexity of stimulation both within and between several sense modalities. Use of the simpler Skinner box situation to study the effects of stimulus complexity would appear to permit effective separation of the sense modalities excited by response-contingent stimulation. In the present study, perceptual consequences of response-contingent

[1] This research was supported in part by a grant-in-aid from the Wilson Coe Research Fund, University of Maine.
[2] Now at the University of Arkansas.

SOURCE: Gerald W. Barnes and Alan Baron, "Stimulus Complexity and Sensory Reinforcement," *Journal of Comparative and Physiological Psychology*, 1961, **54**, 466–469. Reprinted by permission of the American Psychological Association and G. W. Barnes and A. Baron.

stimulation were limited to the visual modality, and systematic variation in stimulus complexity was assured by using as sensory reinforcers luminous line drawings appearing on a dark screen just above the lever in a Skinner box.

METHOD

Subjects

Thirty experimentally naive male mice of the C57 Black Subline 6 strain were tested. The Ss were housed in a large communal living cage and allowed ad lib. access to food and water there.

Apparatus

Apparatus consisted of a ventilated Skinner-type box measuring 5¾ in. in all dimensions. At the vertical midline of one flat-black wall (the "lever wall") a T-shaped aluminum lever with a 2¾ in. arm protruded ⅜ in. into the box at a ¾-in. distance above floor level. A force of 2 gm. applied to the lever through a ⅛-in. downward arc operated a snap-action switch which in turn operated a ZDG-I 3-0 printing counter, Cramer .01-min. running time meters, and stimulus presentation equipment located in an adjoining room. Both data recording and stimulus presentation were automatically controlled.

A digital display unit (24 v. dc, Model No. 10229, manufactured by Industrial Electronic Engineers) was affixed, in the horizontal plane, to the outside of the ½-in. thick "lever wall" behind a circular hole 1¼ in. in diameter, whose center was 1¾ in. above floor level and ½ in. to the left of the vertical midline. The Lucite screen of the display cell was thus visible, just above the lever, from the interior of the box through the 1¼-in. hole. Three luminous stimulus patterns could be presented on the dark screen of the display cell: a filled circle 1⅛ in. in diameter; an open square with 1-in.-long, ⅛-in. sides; and a ½-in.-high X with 1-in.-long, ⅛-in.-thick arms. These particular stimuli were selected from the 12 stimuli available on the display cell because they seemed to be aligned circle, square, and X in order of increasing complexity. When a pattern appeared on the display-cell screen, illumination of the otherwise dark box interior was minimal; no other illumination of the box was provided at any time.

Procedure

The Ss were randomly assigned in equal numbers to five groups and tested in the apparatus during a single 54-min. experimental session following the basic light-conditioning procedure developed by Barnes and Kish (1958). Each 54-min. experimental session was divided into three periods, each of 18-min. duration. (a) During the first 18-min. period (operant level) bar depressions were not followed by presentation of a stimulus pattern for any S. (b) During the second 18-min. period (conditioning) members of the Circle, Square, and X groups received, conterminously with each bar depression, the appropriate stimulus pattern on the display-cell screen. The Ss in the Multiple group received all three stimulus patterns during conditioning, conterminously with each bar depression, a different pattern being available during each successive minute and each pattern being available for a total of 6 min. Order of presentation of the three stimulus patterns for the Multiple group was randomized with the restrictions that each pattern appear once during each 3-min. block of the conditioning period and that no pattern immediately succeed itself. Control group Ss received no response-contingent stimulus pattern during the conditioning period. (c) During the third 18-min. period (extinction) bar depressions did not produce stimulus patterns for any of the groups.

Results

Mean numbers of responses per minute during successive 6-min. intervals are displayed in Figure 1. Inspection indicates that the stimulus-pattern variable produced differences in responding during both the conditioning and extinction periods. Although the Multiple and X groups were apparently almost identical in response rates throughout the experimental session, alignment of the groups in order of increasing stimulus complexity is otherwise striking. Of the several available procedures for analyzing the apparent group differences, we have chosen analysis of "difference scores" as lending themselves to clearest interpretation. Accordingly, response frequencies (i.e., total numbers of responses emitted) during each of the three 18-min. periods were converted for each S into the difference scores $C - OL$ (conditioning minus operant level) and $E - OL$ (extinction minus operant level). Analysis of variance yielded an F of 16.06 ($p < .005$, df 4 and 25) for $C - OL$ scores and an F of 4.06 ($p < .02$, df 4 and 25) for $E - OL$ scores. Duncan's range test, with $\alpha = .05$, indicated that all $C - OL$ scores were significantly different except the Multiple-X difference. Duncan's test also indicated no differences in $E - OL$ scores between the Multiple and X groups or among the Control, Circle, and Square groups, although the difference between these two *sets* of groups did reach significance. Examination of Figure 1 indicates the $C - OL$ differences were due in part to slower rate deceleration during conditioning for the Multiple and X groups than for the Square and Circle groups. The $E - OL$ differences were evidently due to a prolonged acceleration in response rate over the last half of extinction for Multiple and X groups contrasted with the operant-level (or control group) rates rapidly reached by the Square and Circle

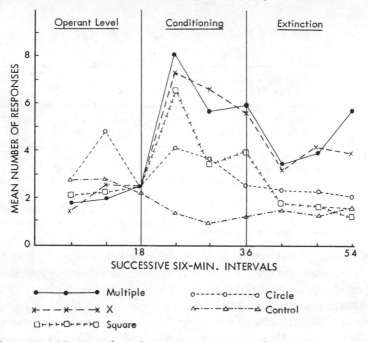

FIGURE 1. Mean number of responses per minute during successive 6-min. intervals over the entire 54-min. experimental session for each group.

groups. It should also be noted that the Multiple group emitted about the same average number of responses during intervals in which a square or an X was available as the corresponding "single stimulus" groups, but the average rate of the Multiple group over intervals in which a circle was available was roughly double that for the Circle group.

Mean total response times and mean average times per response (T) during each period are presented in Table 1. Analysis of total response times gave interpretations identical with those for response frequencies. Although analysis of the mean T data over the three periods indicated a significant period trend with both linear and quadratic components, the absence of other significant values of F, particularly for interaction, indicated no differences in T between groups at any period. Thus, T was not a useful measure in differentiating the groups studied.

An outstanding feature of the data was an abrupt change from prevailing operant-level response rate to a high, slowly decelerating rate as soon as the first reinforced response occurred. This transition

TABLE 1

Mean Total Response Times and *T*s* during Each
Experimental Period

Group	Mean Total Response Time (in 1/100 min.)			Mean T (in sec.)		
	Operant Level	Condi-tioning	Extinction	Operant Level	Condi-tioning	Extinction
Control	1.12	0.72	0.74	1.21	1.47	1.36
Circle	0.97	1.55	0.88	0.77	1.30	1.20
Square	0.98	2.11	0.84	1.26	1.41	1.18
X	0.88	3.26	1.78	1.25	1.78	1.54
Multiple	0.76	3.11	1.76	1.03	1.58	1.38

* *T* is the mean average time per response.

from operant-level rate to a high rate was immediate, with cumulative response curves for each S that received reinforcement showing an abrupt discontinuity at delivery of the first reinforcement. As an illustration, the average number of responses for all 24 reinforced Ss during the first minute following the first reinforced response was 7.8 times greater than the average number of responses in the immediately preceding minute for those Ss. No S showed less than a doubling in rate, and one S showed a 24-fold increase. Rates of the indicated orders of magnitude were maintained on the average over at least the first quarter of the conditioning period, with a deceleration then beginning toward terminal values somewhat in excess of terminal operant-level rates.

DISCUSSION

The immediate increase in response rate following delivery of the first reinforcement, and the subsequent slow decline in rate, observed in the present study were highly similar to rate changes observed in studies involving response-contingent dim illumination of the entire environment (Barnes & Baron, 1961b; Barnes & Kish, 1958). Luminous patterns and diffuse over-all illumination, then, are evidently representative of the same basic process. It should be further noted that the immediate conditioning effect accompanying the availability of either form of response-contingent illumination is remarkably similar to the immediate conditioning observed when response-contingent food reinforcement is first made available to highly pre-trained rats (Skinner, 1938).

There is, then, no doubt that conditioning occurred in all groups tested with response-contingent luminous patterns. Further, the data of the present experiment indicate that stimulus complexity was a powerful determinant of magnitude of the effects of sensory reinforcement. Marked differences in response rates, attributable to differences in the visual pattern presented as reinforcement, were observed during the conditioning period. In addition, the Multiple and X groups, exposed to the presumably most complex stimuli, emitted more responses during extinction than during operant level. The latter finding is noteworthy because in no previous study involving a continuous schedule of sensory reinforcement over an extended conditioning period has response frequency in an immediately subsequent extinction session exceeded operant-level frequency (e.g., Barnes & Baron, 1961b; Barnes & Kish, 1958). The results, then, show that increases in complexity of visual patterns are associated with increases in the magnitude of the sensory reinforcement effect, at least within the range of complexity studied in the present experiment.

Glanzer (1958) has suggested the relevance of information theory in interpreting phenomena rather analogous to the sensory reinforcement effect. With respect to the present findings, an extension of Glanzer's position may be developed by considering stimulus complexity as an inverse function of the information redundancy in a stimulus pattern (Attneave, 1954). Attneave's analysis leads to the conclusion that the stimuli employed in the present experiment are aligned circle, square, and X in order of increasing complexity, with the Multiple group presenting classification difficulty. It may be concluded that the magnitude of the sensory reinforcement effect is related to the amount of information presented to S by the sensory reinforcer, decreasing redundancy leading to increasing magnitudes of reinforcement.

The observed differences between the Circle, Square, and X groups of the present study support the suggestion of Welker (1956b, 1956c) and Berlyne (1955) that increases in novelty and/or complexity of stimulus objects result in enhancement of associated response tendencies. However, Berlyne and Slater (1957) have gone on to distinguish between two kinds of stimulus complexity: (*a*) simultaneous complexity, which results from increases in the degree of variety of stimuli presented simultaneously (as among the Circle, Square, and X groups of the present study); and (*b*) successive complexity, which results from increases in the degree of variety of stimuli presented successively (as in the Multiple group of the present study). Although Berlyne and Slater have not stated that successive complexity has greater reinforcing potential than simultaneous complexity, a reasonable extension of their viewpoint would be that changing patterns of stimulation should generate more "novelty," and presumably higher response rates, than unchanging patterns of stimulation. But application of this extension of the novelty hypothesis to the findings of the present study, while predicting the observed superiority of the Multiple group over the Circle and Square groups, cannot account for the absence of any real differences between the Multiple group and the X group.

The limitations of a stimulus novelty explanation of the present findings stem, at least in part, from lack of specificity in definitions of novelty. For example, the consequences to be expected from successive presentation of stimulus patterns varying in their simultaneous complexity are not clear. In all fairness, however, it must also be pointed out that alternative explanations are not readily available, and the development of such explanations awaits future research.

[11]
Facilitation of Exploration by Hunger in Rats [1]

PHILIP G. ZIMBARDO and NEAL E. MILLER

Recent experiments on the effects of hunger and thirst on the exploratory behavior of rats have yielded equivocal results. The purpose of the present study was to try to remove a particular source of difficulty in these experiments and, thus, to determine more de-

[1] This investigation was supported in part by a research grant, M 647, from the National Institute of Mental Health of the National Institutes of Health, Public Health Service, and by a research grant, G-930, from the National Science Foundation.

SOURCE: Philip G. Zimbardo and Neal E. Miller, "Facilitation of Exploration by Hunger in Rats," *Journal of Comparative and Physiological Psychology*, 1958, **51**, 43–46. Reprinted by permission of the American Psychological Association and P. G. Zimbardo and N. E. Miller.

finitively the relationship between hunger and exploratory behavior.

Montgomery (1953c) found that hunger decreased exploration in a Y maze, and Zimbardo and Montgomery (1957) reproduced this result in a square maze. However, Thompson (1953) failed to obtain significant differences, and Adlerstein and Fehrer (1955) found the opposite result, that hunger increased the exploration of an irregular maze, each unit of which was relatively small.

In all these experiments, exploratory drive was inferred from the number of maze sections entered per unit of time. Although "activity" may be a useful measurement of drive in some cases, it seems inappropriate for fatigue, fear, and perhaps for exploratory drive. In the studies cited, the Ss may have been in a conflict between tendencies to continue to explore the immediate environment more thoroughly and to move on to explore the next unit. These conflicting tendencies may account for the contradictory results because the total number of units traversed is confounded with the amount of exploration within each unit. By confining S in a given unit until it has thoroughly satiated its tendency to explore it, the conflicting tendency to remain in that unit is minimized. Consequently, the speed of entering the next unit will be a purer measure of exploratory performance.

The apparatus was reduced to its simplest form, a straight alley, separated by a door into two compartments. A 2×2 design was used to test the hypothesis. One hungry and one satiated group were tested without confinement—a procedure comparable to that used in the preceding studies (Adlerstein & Fehrer, 1955; Montgomery, 1953c; Thompson, 1953; Zimbardo & Montgomery, 1957). Another hungry and another satiated group were tested with the improved procedure of a delay in the first compartment. After all groups had reached asymptote, the novelty of the two compartments was increased, a change which should accentuate any differences dependent on exploratory drive.

METHOD

Subjects

The Ss were 20 female albino Wistar rats of the Charles River strain, about 120 days old at the start of the experiment. They were maintained on an ad lib. diet of water and Purina Lab Checkers before the experiment proper. All Ss were housed in individual cages and were tamed by handling for one week prior to the experiment.

Apparatus

The Ss were tested in a modified Miller acquired-drive apparatus which is diagrammed elsewhere (Miller, 1951, p. 437). It consisted of two compartments each 25 by 6 by 8 in., separated by a metal guillotine door. The compartments were made as similar as possible, each having a metal floor, wooden walls, a hinged top, and a glass front. Everything but the glass was painted a flat gray. The floors of both compartments were balanced on springs, so that S's weight in the starting compartment would close a circuit, automatically dropping open the door between the compartments either immediately or after a 2-min. delay period. A timer started when the door dropped, and stopped when S climbed over the 1-in. portion of the door (which remained as a distinctive hurdle) and placed all four feet on the floor of the second compartment.

A separate apparatus was used for habituating the animals to the sight and sound of a moving door and to going from one compartment to another. It consisted of two identical mesh cages the same as the cages in which the Ss had been housed, each cage measuring 20 by 8 by 10 in. The cages were separated by a door which was manually operated by E. Each S was allowed to explore the second cage for 1 min. after entering it.

Procedure

On the basis of exploration scores (number of Y maze units entered in a 10-min. trial) the Ss were divided into approximately equated groups which were randomly assigned to four experimental conditions:

1. *Satiated-Immediate* (SI), Ss on ad lib. diet throughout the experiment, and door in apparatus dropped immediately upon their placement in the start box.

2. *Hunger-Immediate* (HI), Ss on a deprivation schedule of a specified number of grams of food every 24 hr. (see below), and door dropped immediately.

3. *Satiated-Delay* (SD), Ss on an ad lib. diet throughout the experiment and allowed to explore the start box for 2 min. before the door dropped and the timer started.

4. *Hunger-Delay* (HD), Ss on food deprivation schedule (see below) and allowed to explore the start box for 2 min. before the door dropped and the timer started.

In order to insure a high constant level of drive throughout the experiment, thereby reducing the danger of distortion of our data resulting from a continuing elevation of drive (Reid & Finger, 1955), the Hunger rats were maintained on a food-deprivation cycle for 29 days before the start of testing. For two weeks the Hunger Ss were on a schedule of 7 gm. of Lab Checkers every 24 hrs. This, however, appeared to be too severe, for several Ss died. Following a day of ad lib. feeding, the Hunger groups had their diet increased to 10.5 gm. a day and were maintained on this schedule for an additional 15 days. Over the period of almost a month of testing, the deprived Ss lost an average of only 0.5 gm.

Four trials were run in the habituation apparatus to help reduce the fear-evoking aspects of the dropping door and the sudden presentation of a novel environment, i.e., the second compartment to be explored.

On the exploratory-acquisition trials proper, the Ss were placed in the far end of the start box. In order to minimize any systematic influences resulting from one experimental condition's always being followed by another, the running order of the rats was determined by means of a systematic latin square. The Delay animals were allowed to explore the second compartment freely for 1 min. after entering it, but were removed from the apparatus if they did not go into the second box 2 min. after the door dropped. Re-entry into the start box was prevented by raising the door after S had gone into the second compartment. In order to control for preferences and "position sets," half the animals were run from the left compartment into the right one, while half ran in the opposite direction. To control for the possibility that the Delayed groups might not be facing the door when it dropped, while the Immediate groups always would, Ss were placed in the start box facing the door every other day and facing the back on the alternate days. Analysis of the data revealed no consistent or significant differences in running speed within or between any of the four experimental groups between those trials when the Ss were placed facing toward the door and those when they were facing the back of the apparatus. The analysis of the data is in terms of pairs of trials in order to average out differences resulting from this procedure.

After completion of a trial, each S was placed in a detention cage for about 7 min. where, as in the apparatus, no food or water was ever present. The animals were fed 30 to 60 min. after testing in the apparatus; the deprived Ss received their specified diet, and the satiated Ss were given more food than they could consume in 24 hr.

All Ss were run one trial a day. Records were kept of: (a) the rat's weight, (b) the latency from door drop to entry in the second compartment (scores were converted by the formula, Speed = 100/seconds), (c) the rat's position in the apparatus at the time of door drop (only for Delay Ss), and (d) the number of feces and instances of urination during testing.

When the rats appeared to reach asymptote by the sixteenth trial in Part 1 of the experiment, the apparatus was modified, and all Ss were run an additional ten trials until their running speeds seemed to be leveling off. In this second part of the experiment, the Ss and procedure were maintained exactly as in Part 1, but the apparatus was modified to increase its novelty. The apparatus was designed so that painted metal inserts could be placed over the floors, walls, and top in order to change its appearance. Accordingly, one compartment was made white, and the other was made black. Several manipulatable objects were placed in each of the two compartments: springs, a bell, and a metal bar in one, and springs and a hollow can in the other.

Results and Discussion

Figure 1 shows mean running speed as a function of number of trials. This graph indicates that on the first trial the SI group ran faster to get into the second compartment than did the HI group.

This difference, which is reliable ($t = 2.45$, $p = .05$), is comparable to the result reported by Zimbardo and Montgomery (1957) that on the single test trial used, food deprivation leads to a decrement in exploratory maze behavior. The finding that the SI animals are faster, on the average, than the HI animals for the first four trials

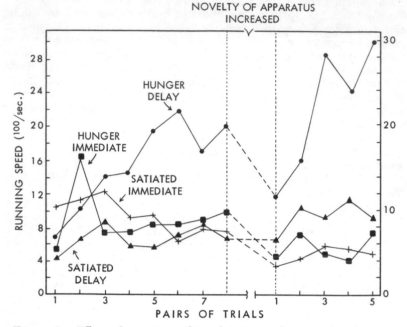

FIGURE 1.   Effect of experimental conditions on the response of running speed.

(although not statistically significant) is also in line with the result of prior research (Montgomery, 1953c). However, this difference is not maintained consistently over the entire course of testing (i.e., 16 test trials).

In contrast, it can be seen in Figure 1 that the HD group is performing at a higher level than the SD group on the first trial, and that this difference between the groups is consistent over trials. The observation that the curve for the HD group continues to rise and to diverge from the curves of the other groups is statistically substantiated by the significant interaction of Drive × Delay Period × Trials (see Table 1). The curve for the HD group looks like a learning curve.

Figure 1 also shows that increasing the novelty of the compart-

ments in Part 2 accentuated the difference between HD and SD
on one hand and between the Delayed and Immediate groups on the
other hand. After the scores for the asymptotic trials of the first and
second parts of the experiment were averaged separately, an analysis of covariance (see Table 2) was performed to determine whether
or not the differences obtained in Part 2 could be explained by the
results of Part 1. Furthermore, we wanted to determine whether or
not the increase in performance of the HD animals in Part 2 beyond
their level in Part 1 was significant. The analysis indicates that the

TABLE 1

Analysis of Variance of Running-Speed Data
(Last four pairs of trials in Part 1; repeated measurements on same Ss)

Source of Variance	df	MS	F
Uncorrelated:			
Drive	1	3,286.025	6.64*
Delay Period	1	1,203.583	2.43
Drive × Delay Period	1	2,563.372	5.18*
Between Ss in same group (ERROR)	13	494.572	
Correlated:			
Trials	3	2.126	—
Trials × Drive	3	65.027	—
Trials × Delay Period	3	42.129	—
Trials × Drive × Delay Period	3	431.613	6.54†
Pooled Ss × Trials (ERROR)	39	65.947	
Total	67		

* Indicates significance beyond the .05 level.
† Indicates significance beyond the .01 level.

TABLE 2

Summary of Analyses of Running-Speed Data
(Average of last four pairs of increased-novelty trials in Part 2)

Source of Variation	Analysis of Variance			Analysis of Covariance		
	df	MS	F	df	MS	F
Drive	1	224.799	8.42*	1	12.306	—
Delay Period	1	526.111	19.78†	1	222.647	15.25†
Drive × Delay Period	1	238.006	8.92*	1	208.635	14.29†
Error (within Groups)	13	26.694		12	14.600	

* Indicates significance beyond the .05 level.
† Indicates significance beyond the .01 level.

differences in Drive between the means of the groups in the second part of the experiment can be explained in terms of differences in Part 1. The consistency of this behavior is indicated by a rank-order correlation of .73 ($p < .001$, $df = 15$) between running speed in the two parts of the experiments. Nevertheless, differences between Delay Period and Drive $\times$ Delayed Period are still significant and cannot be accounted for by Part 1 differences. In other words, increasing the novelty produced a reliable increase in the differences.

A series of t tests to estimate the significance of the decline in response from the last trial in Part 1 to the first trial in Part 2 yielded no significant differences. Similarly, analysis of excretory behavior yielded negative results with regard to fear in the testing situation except for some Ss on the early trials of Part 1 and the first trial of Part 2.

The results of a χ^2 analysis of the data of the Delay Ss' orientation and location at the time the door was opened, points up a source of differences between the HD and SD animals. On a higher proportion of the trials for both Parts 1 and 2 the HD group was facing the door and was in the section of the compartment nearer to the door when it dropped than was the SD group. It might be interpreted that the HD Ss learned to be near the door and facing it when it opened, thus being in a more advantageous position to rapidly enter the second compartment.

Reinforcement

Since there is never any food or water in the apparatus and since the Ss apparently have no acquired fear of the start box, the question arises, What is reinforcing the response of going into the second compartment? There is no reinforcement associated with being returned to the home cage or being fed soon after making the running response because the Ss are put in a detention cage for 7 min. and not fed for at least 30 min. after being returned to the home cage. It is improbable that the rats go into the second compartment in order to escape confinement in the start box, because the two compartments are the same size. The hypothesis advanced is that opportunity to explore a "novel" environment or to effect a stimulus change in the environment is the reinforcing agent. Although the HD group is the only one that showed a learning-type curve, the other groups did maintain their performance with little evidence of extinction over 16 trials. Apparently, exploration of a "goal" box for only 1 min.

on distributed trials of one a day is not sufficient to satiate a rat's curiosity. If opportunity to explore the second compartment is reinforcing, it should follow that increasing the novelty of the compartment should serve to increase the magnitude of the reward or serve as an added incentive to making the running response. This appeared to be the case in Part 2 with the Delay groups. The running speeds for the Immediate groups did not increase with increases in novelty because once again the tendency to explore the first compartment (also made novel) is confounded with the tendency to enter the second novel compartment.

The Hunger-Delay Curve: Learning or Performance?

Without further experimental manipulation it cannot be determined whether the hunger affects (*a*) "curiosity" or (*b*) only the performance of curiosity-reinforced responses. The crucial test would be to run the Ss to asymptote and then reverse the drive conditions for half of each group. If hunger affects only performance (interpretation *b*), there should be an immediate reversal of the performance of the two subgroups changed to the opposite drive condition. If, however, hunger affects learning, then the HD animals will have acquired a stronger habit, which should cause part of the difference between the subgroups to persist.

[12]
Toward Some Integration of Learning Theories: The Concept of Optimal Stimulation [1]

CLARENCE LEUBA

After a careful review of learning theories in 1948, Hilgard concluded that they were in an "unsatisfactory state," and he added,

[1] In preparing this article, I am indebted to Dr. John Lacey for several suggestions.

SOURCE: Clarence Leuba, "Toward Some Integration of Learning Theories: The Concept of Optimal Stimulation," *Psychological Reports*, 1955, 1, 27–33. Reprinted by permission of Southern Universities Press and C. Leuba.

"there are no laws of learning which can be taught with confidence" (Hilgard, 1948, p. 326). This rather extreme view seems to have grown stronger among psychologists during the intervening years. One of the contributors to a recent symposium on learning indicated that he was opposed to "patching of what had better be thrown away" (Snygg, 1954, p. 130). This also is doubtless an extreme view; but there is no doubt that an increasing number of psychologists are questioning whether, for instance, the widely held drive- or tension-reduction view of learning is at all adequate to cover the non-maturational aspects of human development.

The observations of Harlow (1953b), Hebb (1954), Sheffield (1954), McClelland (1953), Montgomery (1954), Kish (1955), Kagan and Berkun (1954), and others are indicating ever more clearly that a variety of organisms learn many reactions which bring them increased, rather than decreased, stimulation. Thus, rats in darkness will press a bar more frequently if chance bar pressings are accompanied by dim illumination than if such pressings produce no increased stimulation (Kish, 1955). In another experiment, bar pressings became extremely frequent when each pressing was followed by electrical stimulation from electrodes placed in any one of numerous lower centers in the brain (Olds & Milner, 1954). Sheep learning a maze have been observed to pay little attention to the food at the end, and to be eager to return to the starting box, and to be absorbed in the maze itself (Liddell, 1954). Monkeys have learned to solve mechanical problems, involving hasps, hooks, etc. entirely under the influence of the increased stimulation produced by their manipulative activities (Harlow, 1953b). Hebb concludes that "mammals seek excitement . . . seek situations which even produce emotional stimulation to a mild degree" (Hebb & Thompson, 1954, p. 551). General observations of children indicate that they too tend to learn many things which are tension-producing and exciting. They often try to get as much stimulation as possible out of their environment.

There have been attempts to include such learning under the tension- or drive-reduction theory by assuming that there is an exploratory drive and that the actions which produce added stimulation reduce this drive. But why postulate the existence of an exploratory drive? Are we not playing the old game of assuming the existence in man of the very thing we are trying to explain? The assumption begs the question and violates the principle of parsimony. It would be better to admit, it seems to me, that the drive reduction theory explains some, but not all the facts of learning. Much animal learning and possibly most human learning seem to occur while the general drive state (the over-all stimulation) is increasing, rather than decreasing.

It seems surprising that, until very recently, we should have overlooked so completely the fact that much learning occurs under conditions of increasing drive. Perhaps it is partly because in most psychological laboratories, learning has been observed mainly in organisms driven by powerful biological or neurotic drives. The animals have been deprived of food or water for lengthy periods, or given electric shocks; some of the animals have been made neurotic by conflict situations, insolvable problems, noises, and blasts of air. These studies have been supplemented during recent decades by clinical ones of anxiety-ridden human beings. Under the circumstances in which the observations and experiments were made, organisms did learn to do the things which were tension-, drive-, or stimulation-reducing (Dollard & Miller, 1950; Keller, 1954; Maier, 1949; Mowrer, 1950; Skinner, 1953). The most obvious interpretation of this fact is that when organisms are overstimulated they will learn the reactions which lessen that stimulation and return it to more moderate levels.

Most human learning and development, however, does not occur when people are deprived of food or water for 12 or more hours, are given electric shocks, are under the influence of powerful neurotic drives, or are in any situations even remotely resembling these. Learning situations in the home, nursery, art room, trade school, on the playground, college campus, and so on, are frequently of a totally different sort.

Tension reduction would not seem to be a general or the only principle of learning. It may be only one aspect of a more general principle, a principle which might be called one of optimal stimulation: the organism tends to learn those reactions which will produce an optimal level of *total* stimulation. Hebb writes "animals will always act so as to produce an optimal level of excitation" (Hebb & Thompson, 1954, p. 552). That level is often higher than the one present at the moment.

Hilgard pointed out several years ago, that it might be "like a breath of fresh air in most learning laboratories" if some one were just to follow a child around and observe the situations in which he learns and what he learns (Hilgard, 1948, p. 352). Such observations would indicate, I believe, that at both home and school he is frequently living under circumstances which are lacking in adequate stimulation and are at least mildly boring. Actions which increase stimulation and produce excitement are strongly reinforced, sometimes to the dismay of parents and teachers, as compared with the reactions performed during more humdrum stimulation. Another way of saying this is that reactions which bring the environment to bear upon the sense organs and increase the stimulating capacities of the environment, are reinforced over other reactions; in everyday but somewhat misleading language, the child is animated by curiosity, by a desire to explore, and by a tendency to get reactions from things and people, as by teasing the latter. In the much rarer instances, when he is over-excited and over-stimulated, as during intense emotion, those actions, which are drive reducing, will gain the ascendancy.

Both the experimental evidence now available and general observations seem to indicate that the concept of optimal stimulation may have wide applicability in human development. *The organism tends to acquire those reactions which, when over-all stimulation is low, are accompanied by increasing stimulation; and when over-all stimulation is high, those which are accompanied by decreasing stimulation.*

It is the over-all stimulation which is significant rather than the intensity of any one particular stimulus. Even though, for instance, the stimulus to which the subject is responding may be a slight one, over-all stimulation may be intense, as when there is a high degree of proprioceptive stimulation from muscular tensions.

This principle of optimal stimulation may have a good deal to do with the gaining of ascendancy or priority by certain responses over others. Thus, during the infant's random movements, as in babbling, those gaining optimal stimulation are reinforced over others which are accompanied by either too little or too much total stimulation. Since exploratory behavior brings much of the environment to bear upon tactual and other sense organs, it will be most strongly reinforced, providing only that exploration does not produce excessive stimulation. This principle, as so far stated, explains only, however, why certain responses are reinforced as compared with others, but it does not explain why various situations or cues acquire the capacity to elicit those previously-reinforced reactions.

Classical conditioning may account for this connection of a response with a particular situation, so that the latter acquires the power to elicit it (Guthrie, 1935). Thus, there seem to be two steps clearly evident in the learning occurring during early child development: a first or reinforcing step, the strengthening of certain responses as compared with others, and a second or connective and associative step. But it is the very stimuli which strengthen a response that also become connected with it and acquire the power to elicit it; hence, both steps seem to be parts or aspects of the same process. The conditioning aspect of this process also occurs most effectively when the general level of stimulation is at least moderately high (Spence & Taylor, 1951; Spence, Farber, & Taylor, 1954).

In early child development, the typical sequence may be somewhat as follows: (a) general random behavior, (b) the reinforcement of activities accompanied by and producing increased stimulation (more rarely the reinforcement of stimulation-reducing activities), and (c) the connection of those activities to the reinforcement-producing stimuli (conditioning). This would make classical conditioning the end-result of a reinforcement process. At first, stimuli in the process of being conditioned merely reinforce an activity; eventually they can elicit it, first weakly and then more strongly.[2]

Experiments in which reactions have been conditioned to symbols and symbols to each other, or in which generalization of conditioned responses to symbols has occurred, indicate that classical conditioning may have much wider applications than is generally realized (Brogden, 1939; Lacey & Smith, 1954; Leuba & Dunlap, 1951; Menzies, 1937; Razran, 1949). It may account for sequences of symbols as in thinking, as well as for the connection of simple, reflex-like reactions to specific overt cues.

Contiguity and associationism are involved both in the reinforcement of activities by the general stimulation present at the time, and in the process of their conditioning to that stimulation as a whole and to various cues which form a part of it. Sometimes, however, reinforced activities seem to be followed by or to cause increased stimulation rather than to be accompanied by it; in Thorndikian terms, the reaction produces satisfying effects. But there is a well-

[2] Many observations point to the basic physiological importance of adequate stimulation. At least some neural structures fail to develop normally without adequate stimulation, as for instance, the cortical visual area in cases of early eye defects; and when once developed, neural structures tend to atrophy when unstimulated. It has repeatedly been shown that animals which have grown up in sensorily impoverished enviroments have failed to show normal abilities. A significant factor in producing the dire results allegedly due to the absence of human mother love, may be that neglected children sometimes lack the intensity and variety of stimulation required for normal development.

known tendency for reactions to be made to earlier and earlier stimuli in a sequence (anticipation). The excitement and increased stimulation which occur when the baby sees his bottle eventually take place in response to cues normally preceding the appearance of the bottle. The rat at first perks up and runs fast only when the food is in sight in the goal box; but eventually this occurs in response to cues preceding the sight of the goal (goal gradient). The reinforcing proprioceptive impulses from muscular tensions which occurred to begin with only as a consequence of an action, may eventually occur simultaneously with it and thereby reinforce it. The child becomes excited not only while playing with his father. He is already excited during the presence of the cues preceding a play period and, therefore, while performing the actions which will lead to or produce it. Anticipation or expectation of exciting circumstances may play an important role in the reinforcement of activities (Meehl & MacCorquodale, 1953; Tolman, Ritchie, & Kalish, 1946).

If we assume that changes from either minimal or excessive stimulation toward an optimal level tend to be experienced as more satisfying and pleasant than those involving changes in the opposite direction, then the concept of optimal stimulation can also be stated in familiar subjective terms. Agreeable reactions can be said to gain the ascendancy or priority over less pleasant ones. To demonstrate that changes in the direction of optimal stimulation may actually coincide with pleasantness would require a separate paper.[3]

The concept of optimal stimulation should be described in relative rather than absolute terms and in terms of the whole situation, internal as well as external, rather than in terms of specific stimuli. It is not assumed that any particular external situation is necessarily either optimally or excessively stimulating, pleasant or unpleasant. Whether it will be experienced as one or the other or as neutral, depends upon the *total* stimulation at the moment and what the stimulation has just been. It is the direction of the change that may be important: whether from too much or too little toward a middle range; as compared with from the latter toward the extremes. Even the stimulation of pain sense organs, as when a child wiggles a loose tooth or picks at a scab, may be pleasant and irresistible if there is a change in over-all stimulation from a minimum toward an optimal level. Identical stimulation of the same pain sense organs might be

[3] In the chapter on learning of a text, *Man—A General Psychology*, I try to demonstrate this connection (New York: Doubleday, in press).

unpleasantly painful if against a background of excessive stimulation as during a state of anxiety. In this case, stimulation of the pain sense organs is added to an already excessive general level of stimulation.

When external circumstances are only mildly stimulating, as in the case of the usual eyelid conditioning experiments, one would expect tense neurotic individuals to condition most rapidly. Under conditions of high external stimulation, however, the latter's already high level of internal stimulation might lead to an over-all state of excessive stimulation unfavorable to conditioning. In general, it might be predicted that the relaxed individual would condition best when a fairly high level of motivation and stimulation prevailed during learning; and conversely for the tense individual.

Over-all stimulation at any one moment may be anywhere along a continuum from minimal to excessive. Optimal stimulation could be represented by a band somewhere between those two extremes. This band would not maintain a fixed position, however, for it would shift at least slightly up and down depending upon such factors as sense organ sensitivity and the connections and conditions in the nervous system. A stimulus impinging upon fresh sense organs and initiating nerve impulses in fibers possibly sensitized by a hormone or a drug, may have far more stimulating effects than similar stimuli impinging upon fatigued sense organs or when a depressant drug is circulating in the blood stream. It is conceivable, as we have seen, that a stimulus which at one time was part of a reinforcing state of affairs might at another time be part of an overstimulating state. It is only as that stimulus is seen in its entire context that a generalization may be possible. The suggested principle of optimal stimulation emerges from the total situation; and its existence may be overlooked by those occupied in studying the reactions of organisms to specific stimuli.

For those attempting to modify behavior, as through education or counseling, the implications of a principle of optimal motivation may be great. Quite different procedures are indicated if learning in daily life occurs rarely, rather than ordinarily, through tension reduction. One function of the teacher may be, for most pupils, to increase tensions somewhat and to make the school situation a rather exciting one. Learning may occur best when stimulation is strong enough to provide maximum reinforcement, but not strong enough to be disruptive.

[13]
Drives and the C.N.S. (Conceptual Nervous System) [1]

D. O. HEBB

The problem of motivation of course lies close to the heart of the general problem of understanding behavior, yet it sometimes seems the least realistically treated topic in the literature. In great part, the difficulty concerns that c.n.s., or "conceptual nervous system," which Skinner disavowed and from whose influence he and others have tried to escape. But the conceptual nervous system of 1930 was evidently like the gin that was being drunk about the same time; it was homemade and none too good, as Skinner pointed out, but it was also habit-forming; and the effort to escape has not really been successful. Prohibition is long past. If we *must* drink we can now get better liquor; likewise, the conceptual nervous system of 1930 is out of date and—if we must neurologize—let us use the best brand of neurology we can find.

Though I personally favor both alcohol and neurologizing, in moderation, the point here does not assume that either is a good thing. The point is that psychology is intoxicating itself with a worse brand than it need use. Many psychologists do not think in terms of neural anatomy; but merely adhering to certain classical frameworks shows the limiting effect of earlier neurologizing. Bergmann (1953) has recently said again that it is logically possible to escape influence. This does not change the fact that, in practice, it has not been done.

Further, as I read Bergmann, I am not sure that he really thinks, deep down, that we should swear off neurologizing entirely, or at

---

[1] Presidential address, Division 3, at American Psychological Association, New York, September, 1954. The paper incorporates ideas worked out in discussion with fellow students at McGill, especially Dalbir Bindra and Peter Milner, as well as with Leo Postman at California, and it is a pleasure to record my great indebtedness to them.

SOURCE: D. O. Hebb, "Drives and the C.N.S. (Conceptual Nervous System)," *Psychological Review*, 1955, 62, 243–254. Reprinted by permission of the American Psychological Association and D. O. Hebb.

least that we should all do so. He has made a strong case for the functional similarity of intervening variable and hypothetical construct, implying that we are dealing more with differences of degree than of kind. The conclusion I draw is that both can properly appear in the same theory, using intervening variables to whatever extent is most profitable (as physics for example does), and conversely not being afraid to use some theoretical conception merely because it might become anatomically identifiable.

For many conceptions, at least, MacCorquodale and Meehl's (1948) distinction is relative, not absolute; and it must also be observed that physiological psychology makes free use of "dispositional concepts" as well as "existential" ones. Logically, this leaves room for some of us to make more use of explicitly physiological constructs than others, and still lets us stay in communication with one another. It also shows how one's views concerning motivation, for example, might be more influenced than one thinks by earlier physiological notions, since it means that an explicitly physiological conception might be restated in words that have—apparently—no physiological reference.

What I propose, therefore, is to look at motivation as it relates to the c.n.s.—or conceptual nervous system—of three different periods: as it was before 1930, as it was say 10 years ago, and as it is today. I hope to persuade you that some of our current troubles with motivation are due to the c.n.s. of an earlier day, and ask that you look with an open mind at the implications of the current one. Today's physiology suggests new psychological ideas, and I would like to persuade you that they make psychological sense, no matter how they originated. They might even provide common ground—not necessarily agreement, but communication, something nearer to agreement—for people whose views at present may seem completely opposed. While writing this paper I found myself having to make a change in my own theoretical position, as you will see, and though you may not adopt the same position you may be willing to take another look at the evidence, and consider its theoretical import anew.

Before going on it is just as well to be explicit about the use of the terms *motivation* and *drive*. *Motivation* refers here in a rather general sense to the energizing of behavior, and especially to the sources of energy in a particular set of responses that keep them temporarily dominant over others and account for continuity and direction in behavior. *Drive* is regarded as a more specific conception about the way in which this occurs: a hypothesis of motivation, which makes the energy a function of a special process distinct from those S-R or cognitive functions that are energized. In some contexts, therefore, *motivation* and *drive* are interchangeable.

MOTIVATION IN THE CLASSICAL (PRE-1930) C.N.S.

The main line of descent of psychological theory, as I have recently tried to show (Hebb, 1953), is through associationism and the stimulus-response formulations. Characteristically, stimulus-response theory has treated the animal as more or less inactive unless subjected to special conditions of arousal. These conditions are first, hunger, pain, and sexual excitement; and secondly, stimulation that has become associated with one of these more primitive motivations.

Such views did not originate entirely in the early ideas of nervous function, but certainly were strengthened by them. Early studies of the nerve fiber seemed to show that the cell is inert until something happens to it from outside; therefore, the same would be true of the collection of cells making up the nervous system. From this came the explicit theory of drives. The organism is thought of as like a machine, such as the automobile, in which the steering mechanism—that is, stimulus-response connections—is separate from the power source, or drive. There is, however, this difference: the organism may be endowed with three or more different power plants. Once you start listing separate ones, it is hard to avoid five: hunger, thirst, pain, maternal, and sex drives. By some theorists, these may each be given a low-level steering function also, and indirectly the steering function of drives is much increased by the law of effect. According to the law, habits—steering functions—are acquired only in conjunction with the operation of drives.

Now it is evident that an animal is often active and often learns when there is little or no drive activity of the kinds listed. This fact has been dealt with in two ways. One is to postulate additional drives—activity, exploratory, manipulatory, and so forth. The other is to postulate acquired or learned drives, which obtain their energy, so to speak, from association with primary drives.

It is important to see the difficulties to be met by this kind of formulation, though it should be said at once that I do not have any decisive refutation of it, and other approaches have their difficulties, too.

First, we may overlook the rather large number of forms of behavior in which motivation cannot be reduced to biological drive plus learning. Such behavior is most evident in higher species, and may be forgotten by those who work only with the rat or with restricted segments of the behavior of dog or cat. (I do not suggest that we put human motivation on a different plane from that of animals [Brown, 1953b]; what I am saying is that certain peculiarities of motivation increase with phylogenesis, and though most evident in man can be clearly seen with other higher animals.) What is the drive that produces panic in the chimpanzee at the sight of a model of a human head; or fear in some animals, and vicious aggression in others, at the sight of the anesthetized body of a fellow chimpanzee? What about fear of snakes, or the young chimpanzee's terror at the sight of strangers? One can accept the idea that this is "anxiety," but the anxiety, if so, is not based on a prior association of the stimulus object with pain. With the young chimpanzee reared in the nursery of the Yerkes Laboratories, after separation from the mother at birth, one can be certain that the infant has never seen a snake before, and certainly no one has told him about snakes; and one can be sure that a particular infant has never had the opportunity to associate a strange face with pain. Stimulus generalization does not explain fear of strangers, for other stimuli in the same class, namely, the regular attendants, are eagerly welcomed by the infant.

Again, what drive shall we postulate to account for the manifold forms of anger in the chimpanzee that do not derive from frustration objectively defined (Hebb & Thompson, 1954)? How account for the petting behavior of young adolescent chimpanzees, which Nissen (1953) has shown is independent of primary sex activity? How deal with the behavior of the female who, bearing her first infant, is terrified at the sight of the baby as it drops from the birth canal, runs away, never sees it again after it has been taken to the nursery for rearing; and who yet, on the birth of a *second* infant, promptly picks it up and violently resists any effort to take it from her?

There is a great deal of behavior, in the higher animal especially, that is at the very best difficult to reduce to hunger, pain, sex, and maternal drives, plus learning. Even for the lower animal it has been clear for some time that we must add an exploratory drive (if we are to think in these terms at all), and presumably the motivational phenomena recently studied by Harlow and his colleagues (Butler, 1953; Harlow, 1953a; Harlow, Harlow, & Meyer, 1950) could also be comprised under such a drive by giving it a little broader specification. The curiosity drive of Berlyne (1950) and Thompson and Solomon (1954), for example, might be considered to cover both investigatory and manipulatory activities on the one hand, and exploratory, on the other. It would also comprehend the "problem-seeking" behavior recently studied by Mahut and Havelka at McGill (unpublished studies). They have shown that the rat which is offered a short, direct path to food, and a longer, variable and indirect pathway involving a search for food, will very frequently prefer the more difficult, but more "interesting" route.

But even with the addition of a curiosity-investigatory-manipulatory drive, and even apart from the primates, there is still behavior that presents difficulties. There are the reinforcing effects of incomplete copulation (Sheffield, Wulff, & Backer, 1951) and of saccharin intake (Sheffield & Roby, 1950; Carper & Polliard, 1953), which do not reduce to secondary reward. We must not multiply drives beyond reason, and at this point one asks whether there is no alternative to the theory in this form. We come, then, to the conceptual nervous system of 1930 to 1950.

MOTIVATION IN THE C.N.S. OF 1930–1950

About 1930 it began to be evident that the nerve cell is not physiologically inert, does not have to be excited from outside in order to discharge (Hebb, 1949, p. 8). The nervous system is alive, and living things by their nature are active. With the demonstration of spontaneous activity in c.n.s. it seemed to me that the conception of a drive system or systems was supererogation.

For reasons I shall come to later, this now appears to me to have been an oversimplification; but in 1945 the only problem of motivation, I thought, was to account for the *direction* taken by behavior. From this point of view, hunger or pain might be peculiarly effective in guiding or channeling activity but not needed for its arousal. It was not surprising, from this point of view, to see human beings liking intellectual work, nor to find evidence that an animal might learn something without pressure of pain or hunger.

The energy of response is not in the stimulus. It comes from the food, water, and oxygen ingested by the animal; and the violence of an epileptic convulsion, when brain cells for whatever reason decide to fire in synchrony, bears witness to what the nervous system can do when it likes. This is like a whole powder magazine exploding at once. Ordinary behavior can be thought of as produced by an organized series of much smaller explosions, and so a "self-motivating" c.n.s. might still be a very powerfully motivated one. To me, then, it was astonishing that a critic could refer to mine as a "motivation-less" psychology. What I had said in short was that any organized process in the brain is a motivated process, inevitably, inescapably; that the human brain is built to be active, and that as long as it is supplied with adequate nutrition will continue to be active. Brain activity is what determines behavior, and so the only behavioral problem becomes that of accounting for *in*activity.

It was in this conceptual frame that the behavioral picture seemed to negate the notion of drive, as a separate energizer of behavior. A pedagogical experiment reported earlier (Hebb, 1930) had been very impressive in its indication that the human liking for work is not a rare phenomenon, but general. All of the 600-odd pupils in a city school, ranging from 6 to 15 years of age, were suddenly informed that they need do no work whatever unless they wanted to, that the punishment for being noisy and interrupting others' work was to be sent to the playground to play, and that the reward for being good was to be allowed to do more work. In these circumstances, *all* of the pupils discovered within a day or two that, within limits, they preferred work to no work (and incidentally learned more arithmetic and so forth than in previous years).

The phenomenon of work for its own sake is familiar enough to all of us, when the timing is controlled by the worker himself, when "work" is not defined as referring alone to activity imposed from without. Intellectual work may take the form of trying to understand what Robert Browning was trying to say (if anything), to discover what it is in Dali's paintings that can interest others, or to predict the outcome of a paperback mystery. We systematically underestimate the human need of intellectual activity, in one form or another, when we overlook the intellectual component in art and in games. Similarly with riddles, puzzles, and the puzzle-like games of strategy such as bridge, chess, and *go;* the frequency with which man has devised such problems for his own solution is a most significant fact concerning human motivation.

It is, however, not necessarily a fact that supports my earlier view, outlined above. It is hard to get these broader aspects of human behavior under laboratory study, and when we do we may expect to have our ideas about them significantly modified. For my views on the problem, this is what has happened with the experiment of Bexton, Heron, and Scott (1954). Their work is a long step toward dealing with the realities of motivation in the well-fed, physically comfortable, adult human being, and its results raise a serious difficulty for my own theory. Their subjects were paid handsomely to do nothing, see nothing, hear or touch very little, for 24 hours a day. Primary needs were met, on the whole, very well. The subjects suffered no pain, and were fed on request. It is true that they could not copulate, but at the risk of impugning the virility of Canadian college students I point out that most of them would not have been copulating anyway and were quite used to such long stretches of three or four days without primary sexual satisfaction. The secondary reward, on the other hand, was high: $20 a day plus room and board is more than $7000 a year, far more than a student could earn by other means. The subjects then should be highly motivated to continue the experiment, cheerful and happy to be allowed to contribute to scientific knowledge so painlessly and profitably.

In fact, the subject was well motivated for perhaps four to eight hours, and then became increasingly unhappy. He developed a need for stimulation of almost any kind. In the first preliminary exploration, for example, he was allowed to listen to recorded material on request. Some subjects were given a talk for 6-year-old children on the dangers of alcohol. This might be requested, by a grown-up male college student, 15 to 20 times in a 30-hour period. Others were offered, and asked for repeatedly, a recording of an old stock-market report. The subjects looked forward to being tested, but paradoxically tended to find the tests fatiguing when they did arrive. It is hardly necessary to say that the whole situation was rather hard to take, and one subject, in spite of not being in a special state of primary drive arousal in the experiment but in real need of money outside it, gave up the secondary reward of $20 a day to take up a job at hard labor paying $7 or $8 a day.

This experiment is not cited primarily as a difficulty for drive theory although three months ago that is how I saw it. It *will* make difficulty for such theory if exploratory drive is not recognized; but we have already seen the necessity, on other grounds, of including a sort of exploratory-curiosity-manipulatory drive, which essentially comes down to a tendency to seek varied stimulation. This would on the whole handle very well the motivational phenomena observed by Heron's group.

Instead, I cite their experiment as making esential trouble for my own treatment of motivation (Hebb, 1949) as based on the conceptual nervous system of 1930 to 1945. If the thought process is internally organized and motivated, why should it break down in conditions of perceptual isolation, unless emotional disturbance intervenes? But it did break down when no serious emotional change was observed, with problem-solving and intelligence-test performance significantly impaired. Why should the subjects themselves report (*a*) after four or five hours in isolation that they could not follow a connected train of thought, and (*b*) that their motivation for study or the like was seriously disturbed for 24 hours or more after coming out of isolation? The subjects were reasonably well adjusted, happy, and able to think coherently for the first four or five hours of the experiment; why, according to my theory, should this not continue, and why should the organization of behavior not be promptly restored with restoration of a normal environment?

You will forgive me perhaps if I do not dilate further on my own theoretical difficulties, paralleling those of others, but turn now to the conceptual nervous system of 1954 to ask what psychological values we may extract from it for the theory of motivation. I shall not attempt any clear answer for the difficulties we have considered —the data do not seem yet to justify clear answers—but certain conceptions can be formulated in sufficiently definite form to be a background for new research, and the physiological data contain suggestions that may allow me to retain what was of value in my earlier proposals while bringing them closer to ideas such as Harlow's (1953a) on one hand and to reinforcement theory on the other.

MOTIVATION AND C.N.S. IN 1954

For psychological purposes there are two major changes in recent ideas of nervous function. One concerns the single cell, the other an "arousal" system in the brain stem. The first I shall pass over briefly; it is very significant, but does not bear quite as directly upon our present problem. Its essence is that there are two kinds of activity in the nerve cell: the spike potential, or actual firing, and the dendritic potential, which has very different properties. There is now clear evidence (Clare & Bishop, 1955) that the dendrite has a "slow-burning" activity which is not all-or-none, tends not to be transmitted, and lasts 15 to 30 milliseconds instead of the spike's one millisecond. It facilitates spike activity (Li & Jasper, 1953), but often occurs independently and may make up the greater part of the EEG record. It is still true that the brain is always active, but the activity is not always the transmitted kind that conduces to behavior. Finally, there is decisive evidence of primary inhibition in nerve function (Lloyd, 1941; Eccles, 1953) and of a true fatigue that may last for a matter of minutes instead of milliseconds (Brink, 1951; Burns, 1955). These facts will have a great effect on the hypotheses of physiological psychology, and sooner or later on psychology in general.

Our more direct concern is with a development to which attention has already been drawn by Lindsley (1951): the nonspecific or diffuse projection system of the brain stem, which was shown by Moruzzi and Magoun (1949) to be an *arousal* system whose activity in effect makes organized cortical activity possible. Lindsley showed the relevance to the problem of emotion and motivation; what I shall attempt is to extend his treatment, giving more weight to cortical components in arousal. The point of view has also an evident relationship to Duffy's (1941).

The arousal system can be thought of as representing a second major pathway by which all sensory excitations reach the cortex, as shown in the upper part of Figure 1; but there is also feedback from

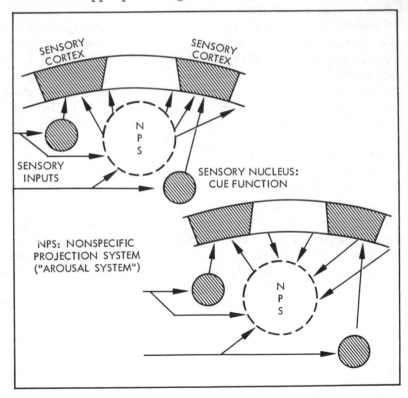

FIGURE 1.

the cortex and I shall urge that the *psychological* evidence further emphasizes the importance of this "downstream" effect.

In the classical conception of sensory function, input to the cortex was via the great projection systems only: from sensory nerve to sensory tract, thence to the corresponding sensory nucleus of the thalamus, and thence directly to one of the sensory projection areas of the cortex. These are still the direct sensory routes, the quick efficient transmitters of information. The second pathway is slow and inefficient; the excitation, as it were, trickles through a tangled thicket of fibers and synapses, there is a mixing up of messages, and the scrambled messages are delivered indiscriminately to wide cortical areas. In short, they are messages no longer. They serve, instead, to tone up the cortex, with a background supporting action that is completely necessary if the messages proper are to have their effect. Without the arousal system, the sensory impulses by the direct route reach the sensory cortex, but go no farther; the rest of the cortex is unaffected, and thus learned stimulus-response relations are lost. The waking center, which has long been known, is one part of this larger system; any extensive damage to it leaves a permanently inert, comatose animal.

Remember that in all this I am talking conceptual nervous system: making a working simplification, and abstracting for psychological purposes; and all these statements may need qualification, especially since research in this area is moving rapidly. There is reason to think, for example, that the arousal system may not be homogeneous, but may consist of a number of subsystems with distinctive functions (Olzewski, 1954). Olds and Milner's (1954) study, reporting "reward" by direct intracranial stimulation, is not easy to fit into the notion of a single homogeneous system. Sharpless' (1954b) results also raise doubt on this point, and it may reasonably be anticipated that arousal will eventually be found to vary qualitatively as well as quantitatively. But in general terms, psychologically, we can now distinguish two quite different effects of a sensory event. One is the *cue function*, guiding behavior; the other, less obvious but no less important, is the *arousal* or *vigilance function*. Without a foundation of arousal, the cue function cannot exist.

And now I propose to you that, whatever you wish to call it, arousal in this sense is synonymous with a general drive state, and the conception of drive therefore assumes anatomical and physiological identity. Let me remind you of what we discussed earlier: the drive is an energizer, but not a guide; an engine but not a steering gear. These are precisely the specifications of activity in the arousal system. Also, learning is dependent on drive, according to drive theory, and this too is applicable in general terms—no arousal, no learning; and efficient learning is possible only in the waking, alert, responsible animal, in which the level of arousal is high.

Thus I find myself obliged to reverse my earlier views and accept the drive conception, not merely on physiological grounds but also on the grounds of some of our current psychological studies. The conception is somewhat modified, but the modifications may not be entirely unacceptable to others.

Consider the relation of the effectiveness of cue function, actual or potential, to the level of arousal (Figure 2). Physiologically, we

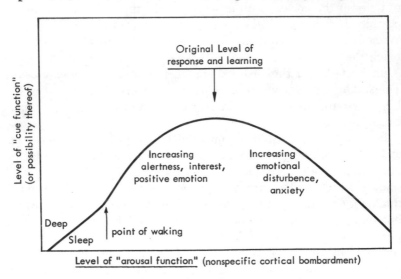

Level of "arousal function" (nonspecific cortical bombardment)

FIGURE 2.

may assume that cortical synaptic function is facilitated by the diffuse bombardment of the arousal system. When this bombardment is at a low level an increase will tend to strengthen or maintain the concurrent cortical activity; when arousal or drive is at a low level, that is, a response that produces increased stimulation and greater arousal will tend to be repeated. This is represented by the rising curve at the left. But when arousal is at a high level, as at the right, the greater bombardment may interfere with the delicate adjustments involved in cue function, perhaps by facilitating irrelevant responses (a high D arouses conflicting $_sH_R$'s?). Thus there will be an optimal level of arousal for effective behavior, as Schlosberg (1954) has suggested. Set aside such physiologizing completely, and we have a significant behavioral conception left, namely, that the same stimulation in mild degree may attract (by prolonging the pattern of response that leads to this stimulation) and in strong degree repel (by disrupting the pattern and facilitating conflicting or alternative responses).

The significance of this relation is in a phenomenon of the greatest importance for understanding motivation in higher animals. This is the *positive attraction of risk taking,* or mild fear, *and of problem solving,* or mild frustration, which was referred to earlier. Whiting and Mowrer (1943) and Berlyne (1950) have noted a relation between fear and curiosity—that is, a tendency to seek stimulation from fear-provoking objects, though at a safe distance. Woodworth (1921) and Valentine (1930) reported this in children, and Woodworth and Marquis (1947) have recently emphasized again its importance in adults. There is no doubt that it exists. There is no doubt, either, that problem-solving situations have some attraction for the rat, more for Harlow's (1953a) monkeys, and far more for man. When you stop to think of it, it is nothing short of extraordinary what trouble people will go to in order to get into more trouble at the bridge table, or on the golf course; and the fascination of the murder story, or thriller, and the newspaper accounts of real-life adventure or tragedy, is no less extraordinary. This taste for excitement *must* not be forgotten when we are dealing with human motivation. It appears that, up to a certain point, threat and puzzle have positive motivating value, beyond that point negative value.

I know this leaves problems. It is not *any* mild threat, *any* form of problem, that is rewarding; we still have to work out the rules for this formulation. Also, I do not mean that there are not secondary rewards of social prestige for risk taking and problem solving—or even primary reward when such behavior is part of lovemaking. But the animal data show that it is not always a matter of extrinsic reward; risk and puzzle can be attractive in themselves, especially for higher animals such as man. If we can accept this, it will no longer be necessary to work out tortuous and improbable ways to explain why human beings work for money, why school children should learn without pain, why a human being in isolation should dislike doing nothing.

One other point before leaving Figure 2: the low level of the curve to the right. You may be skeptical about such an extreme loss of adaptation, or disturbance of cue function and S-R relations, with high levels of arousal. Emotion is persistently regarded as energizing and organizing (which it certainly is at the lower end of the scale, up to the optimal level). But the "paralysis of terror" and related states do occur. As Brown and Jacobs (1949, p. 753) have noted, "the presence of fear may act as an energizer . . . and yet lead in certain instances to an increase in immobility." Twice in the past eight months, while this address was being prepared, the Montreal newspapers reported the behavior of a human being who, suddenly finding himself in extreme danger but with time to escape, simply made no move whatever. One of the two was killed; the other was not, but only because a truck driver chose to wreck his truck and another car instead. Again, it is reported by Marshall (1947), in a book that every student of human motivation should read carefully, that in the emotional pressure of battle no more than 15 to 25 per cent of men under attack even fire their rifles, let alone use them efficiently.

Tyhurst's (1951) very significant study of behavior in emergency and disaster situations further documents the point. The adult who is told that his apartment house is on fire, or who is threatened by a flash flood, may or may not respond intelligently. In various situations, 12 to 25 per cent did so; an equal number show "states of confusion, paralyzing anxiety, inability to move out of bed, 'hysterical' crying or screaming, and so on." Three-quarters or more show a clear impairment of intelligent behavior, often with aimless and irrelevant movements, rather than (as one might expect) panic reactions. There seems no doubt: the curve at the right must come down to a low level.

Now back to our main problem: If we tentatively identify a general state of drive with degree of arousal, where does this leave hunger, pain, and sex drives? These may still be anatomically separable, as Stellar (1954) has argued, but we might consider instead the possibility that there is just one general drive state that can be aroused in different ways. Stellar's argument does not seem fully convincing. There are certainly regions in the hypothalamus that control eating, for example; but is this a *motivating* mechanism? The very essence of such a conception is that the mechanism in question should energize *other* mechanisms, and Miller, Bailey, and Stevenson (1950) have shown that the opposite is true.

But this issue should not be pressed too far, with our present knowledge. I have tried to avoid dogmatism in this presentation in the hope that we might try, for once, to see what we have in common in our views on motivation. One virtue of identifying arousal with drive is that it relates differing views (as well as bringing into the focus of attention data that may otherwise be neglected). The important thing is a clear distinction between cue function and arousal function, and the fact that at low levels an increase of drive intensity may be rewarding, whereas at high levels it is a decrease that rewards. Given this point of view and our assumptions about arousal mechanisms, we see that what Harlow has emphasized is the exteroceptively aroused, but still low-level, drive, with cue function of course directly provided for. In the concept of anxiety, Spence and Brown emphasize the higher-level drive state, especially where there is no guiding cue function that would enable the animal to escape threat. The feedback from cortical functioning makes intelligible Mowrer's (1952) equating anxiety aroused by threat of pain, and anxiety aroused in some way by cognitive processes related to ideas of the self. Solomon and Wynne's (1950) results with sympathectomy are also relevant, since we must not neglect the arousal effects of interoceptor activity; and so is clinical anxiety due to metabolic and nutritional disorders, as well as that due to some conflict of cognitive processes.

Obviously these are not explanations that are being discussed, but possible lines of future research; and there is one problem in particular that I would urge should not be forgotten. This is the cortical feedback to the arousal system, in physiological terms: or in psychological terms, the *immediate drive value of cognitive processes*, without intermediary. This is psychologically demonstrable, and *has* been demonstrated repeatedly.

Anyone who is going to talk about acquired drives, or secondary motivation, should first read an old paper by Valentine (1930). He showed that with a young child you can easily condition fear of a caterpillar or a furry animal, but cannot condition fear of opera glasses, or a bottle; in other words, the fear of some objects, that seems to be learned, was there, latent, all the time. Miller (1951) has noted this possibility but he does not seem to have regarded it very seriously, though he cited a confirmatory experiment by Bregman; for in the same passage he suggests that my own results with chimpanzee fears of certain objects, including strange people, may be dealt with by generalization. But this simply will not do, as Riesen and I noted (Hebb & Riesen, 1943). If you try to work this out, for the infant who is terrified on *first* contact with a stranger, an infant who has never shown such terror before, and who has always responded with eager affection to the only human beings he has made contact with up to this moment, you will find that this is a purely verbal solution.

Furthermore, as Valentine observed, you cannot postulate that the cause of such fear is simply the strange event, the thing that has never occurred before. For the chimpanzee reared in darkness, the first sight of a human being is of course a strange event, by definition; but fear of strangers does not occur until later, until the chimpanzee has had an opportunity to learn to recognize a few persons. The fear is not "innate" but depends on some sort of cognitive or cortical conflict of learned responses. This is clearest when the baby chimpanzee, who knows and welcomes attendant A and attendant B, is terrified when he sees A wearing B's coat. The role of learning is inescapable in such a case.

The cognitive and learning element may be forgotten in other motivations, too. Even in the food drive, some sort of learning is fundamentally important: Ghent (1951) has shown this, Sheffield and Campbell (1954) seem in agreement, and so does the work of Miller and his associates (Berkun, Kessen, & Miller, 1952; Miller, 1953; Miller & Kessen, 1952) on the greater reinforcement value of food by mouth, compared to food by stomach tube. Beach (1939) has shown the cortical-and-learning element in sex behavior. Melzack (1954) has demonstrated recently that even pain responses involve learning. In Harlow's (1953a) results, of course, and Montgomery's (1953b), the cognitive element is obvious.

These cortical or cognitive components in motivation are clearest when we compare the behavior of higher and lower species. Application of a *genuine* comparative method is essential, in the field of motivation as well as of intellectual functions (Hebb & Thompson, 1954). Most disagreements between us have related to so-called "higher" motivations. But the evidence I have discussed today need not be handled in such a way as to maintain the illusion of a complete separation between our various approaches to the problem. It *is* an illusion, I am convinced; we still have many points of disagreement as to relative emphasis, and as to which of several alternative lines to explore first, but this does not imply fundamental and final opposition. As theorists, we have been steadily coming together in respect of ideational (or representative, or mediating, or cognitive) processes; I believe that the same thing can happen, and is happening, in the field of motivation.

[14]
Conflict and Information-Theory Variables as Determinants of Human Perceptual Curiosity [1]

D. E. BERLYNE [2]

The much-needed integration of the theory of perception with general behavior theory would seem to require some account of the motivational factors underlying perception. In laboratory experiments, Es usually induce artificial motives in human Ss by imposing specific tasks on them. Spontaneous human perceptual activities outside the laboratory, on the other hand, have been ascribed by some writers to such motives as "effort after meaning" (Bartlett, 1932) or "will to perceive" (Woodworth, 1947), reminiscent of the exploratory drives that are commonly invoked to explain exploratory behavior in animals (Berlyne, 1950; Harlow, Harlow, & Meyer, 1950; Montgomery, 1954).

The application of the concepts of "drive" and "drive-reduction" to this new area calls for some circumspection and some justification, as there may be more parsimonious ways of describing the facts. For example, the investigatory-reflex theory (Pavlov, 1927; Sokolov, 1955) may perhaps be adequate to account for orienting movements which afford a clearer or intenser perception of some stimulus object to which an organism is already exposed. The theory is, however, inapplicable when the response resulting in optimal perception is not innate but arbitrarily selected by E, and the stimulus object in question is absent at the time the response is made.

These conditions obtained in the experiments to be reported in

[1] The author is indebted to Mr. S. E. Burgess, who carried out a pilot study with children and is responsible for the preparation of most of the stimulus material.

[2] Now temporarily at the Center for Advanced Study in the Behavioral Sciences.

SOURCE: D. E. Berlyne, "Conflict and Information-Theory Variables as Determinants of Human Perceptual Curiosity," *Journal of Experimental Psychology*, 1957, **53**, 399–404. Reprinted by permission of the American Psychological Association and D. E. Berlyne.

this article. Tachistoscopic exposures of visual figures resulted from pressing a finger key, and Ss were free to expose themselves to each figure as many times as they wished. After each exposure, Ss found themselves in darkness. Fluctuations in the probability of making another response can therefore be attributed to some internal stimulus condition or drive. If this probability turns out to depend on the nature of the figure just exposed and the number of times it has already been seen, these variables can be regarded as drive-conditions, influencing the strength of the drive. If the probability of a further response decreases as a particular figure is repeatedly exposed, the exposures can be said to bring about the satiation or reduction of the drive.

By analogy with such drives as hunger or thirst, which are commonly measured by amount of consummatory activity (*cf.* Berkun, Kessen, & Miller, 1952), the number of exposures of a particular figure before S gave up responding was taken as an indication of the intensity of the drive aroused by that figure. The ultimate cessation of responding can be attributed, as with eating and drinking, both to a reduction in the energizing effect of the drive and to changes in internal stimuli. Of these, the latter would seem to be more important. It would not seem to be a matter of extinction in either case, as the response is immediately restored to its original strength when motivation is renewed.

A drive which is reduced by perception has been called *perceptual curiosity* and provisionally distinguished from *epistemic curiosity*, which is reduced by the acquisition of knowledge (Berlyne, 1954b). One class of variable that appears to increase perceptual curiosity in lower animals is the complexity of a stimulus situation (Berlyne, 1955; Berlyne & Slater, 1957; Butler, 1954; Welker, 1956b). This is related to relative entropy, the inverse of redundancy (Shannon & Weaver, 1949) which Attneave (1954) has shown to be an important attribute of visual figures. One of the principal determinants of epistemic curiosity, according to a theory proposed by the writer (Berlyne, 1954a, 1954b, 1954c) is the degree of learned conflict between the symbolic responses aroused by a stimulus situation, a variable which is related to the information theorist's entropy or uncertainty (Shannon & Weaver, 1949). An important case of such conflict is *incongruity-conflict*, aroused by a stimulus pattern with characteristics which S has been trained to regard as incompatible. Another is *surprise-conflict*, produced when a stimulus pattern fails to confirm an expectation evoked by what preceded it.

Secondly, the theory implied that epistemic curiosity will increase with the number of previous gratifications of the drive in similar situations. If all these factors can be shown to affect human perceptual curiosity, then the grounds for differentiating between perceptual and epistemic curiosity will become more tenuous.

METHOD

Apparatus

A tachistoscope (a simplified version of the one described in Humphrey, Dawe, & Mandell, 1955), operating with two short-decay phosphor fluorescent tubes and taking 6-in. square cards, was connected with a finger key. Whenever the key, which resembled the bar of a Skinner box, was depressed, the card in the tachistoscope became visible for .14 sec.

Subjects

Sixteen undergraduates from the first- and second-year psychology classes served as Ss.

Procedure

The S sat in a darkened room, 4 ft. from the tachistoscope, with his right hand holding the key. The use of the key was explained and demonstrated with two sample cards reserved for this purpose. He was told that the experiments were intended solely to show how interesting certain pictures were. The E would insert a card in the tachistoscope, and S was to begin pressing the key when E said "Now." The S was to continue to press the key for as long as he wanted to continue seeing the card. When he no longer wanted to see it, he was to say "Yes." and E would insert a new card. It was emphasized that no questions about the cards would be asked at any time.

Design

Each S underwent four experiments, which followed one another without interruption, used the same procedure, and differed only in stimulus material. Different Ss had the four experiments in four different sequences so that the design took the form of four replications of a counter-balanced 4 × 4 latin square (Bugelski, 1949).

Stimulus Material

Experiment 1 (Incongruity-Conflict). There was a series of seven pictures of Animals and a series of seven pictures of Birds (Figure 1). Cards 2 and 4 of the Animals series and 3 and 5 of the Birds series bore *incongruous* pictures. Half of the Ss received the Animals series first and the other half the Birds series first.

Experiment 2 (Meaningful Sequence). There was a series of six cards which began with a circle and developed by progressive addition of details into a picture of a Bear and a similar series of six cards changing

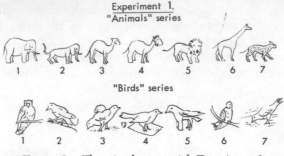

Experiment 1.
"Animals" series

"Birds" series

FIGURE 1.   The stimulus material, Experiment 1.

from a circle into a picture of a Clown (Figure 2). Each S received one series in this meaningful order and the other series in a random order. The four possible sequences—Bear meaningful Clown random, Clown meaningful Bear random, Bear random Clown meaningful, and Clown random Bear meaningful—were used with equal numbers of Ss.

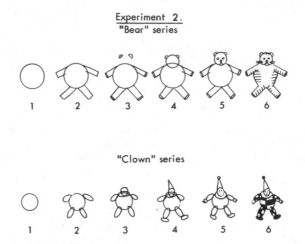

Experiment 2.
"Bear" series

"Clown" series

FIGURE 2.   The stimulus material, Experiment 2.

Experiment 3 (Surprise-Conflict). There were 12 cards bearing geometrical patterns made up of colored spots (Figure 3). The patterns of Cards 1–6 were composed of red triangles, those of Cards 7–11 of green circles, and that of Card 12 of violet squares.

Experiment 4 (Relative Entropy). There were three series of cards each bearing patterns differing in redundancy. As Attneave (1954) shows, redundancy varies directly with orderly arrangement, with symmetry and with similarity between parts of a figure, and inversely with changes in contour. Series A contained a card bearing nine crosses in a regular matrix pattern and a card bearing nine crosses in an irregular arrangement (Figure 4). Series B consisted of four cards bearing a circle, a square, an

Experiment 3.

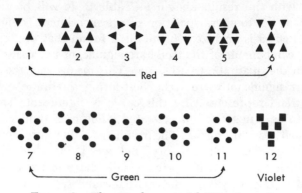

FIGURE 3. The stimulus material, Experiment 3.

Experiment 4.

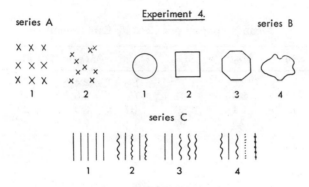

FIGURE 4. The stimulus material, Experiment 4.

octagon, and an irregular closed curve, all of approximately equal perimeter. These figures have, respectively, zero, four, eight, and an infinite set of points at which the curvature changes and hence represent progressively smaller degrees of redundancy. The four cards of Series C present patterns of five straight lines, of two straight and three wavy lines arranged symmetrically, of two straight and three wavy lines arranged asymmetrically and of five lines of different sorts. Redundancy therefore increases from the first card to the last.

Two sequences, based on random numbers, were worked out for all 10 cards, and each sequence was used with half the Ss.

RESULTS AND DISCUSSION

Determinants of Curiosity

PREVIOUS GRATIFICATIONS OF THE DRIVE. The mean numbers of responses per card were worked out for Ss by experiments and are displayed in Table 1. They were then subjected to an analysis of variance, with the results shown in Table 2. It will be seen that the effect of the temporal position of an experiment is significant. When this effect is analyzed further, it is found that the linear and quadratic components of the trend are significant but that the deviation from the quadratic trend is not. This means that the data do not depart significantly from the best-fitting quadratic curve and that the trend represented by this curve is significant. The curve happens to be a negatively accelerated rising one, similar in shape to the usual learning curve. The results are therefore compatible with the assumptions of the theory (Berlyne, 1954a, 1954b), according to which curiosity will increase with the number of previous opportunities to gratify it in similar circumstances.

TABLE 1
Mean Responses per Card by Experiments

Exp.	Mean	SD	Order	Mean	SD
1	3.8	1.32	I	2.4	.84
2	2.4	.91	II	2.6	1.20
3	2.1	.80	III	3.0	1.20
4	2.7	.92	IV	2.7	1.40
All	2.8	.84			

TABLE 2
Between-Experiments Analysis of Variance

Source	df	MS	F
Sequences	3	1.088	
Ss within sequences	12	2.806	
Total between Ss	15	2.462	10.42†
Experiments	3	9.106	38.58†
Temporal positions:			
a. linear component	1	1.435	6.08*
b. quadratic component	1	1.331	5.64*
c. deviation from quadratic trend	1	0.740	3.14
Temporal positions: total	3	1.169	4.95*
Residual (error)	42	0.236	
Total	63		

* Significant at .05 level.
† Significant at .001 level.

INCONGRUITY-CONFLICT. In Experiment 1, the mean numbers of responses per card were 5.8 for the four incongruous pictures and 3.0 for the 10 nonincongruous pictures. As the analysis of variance summarized in Table 3 shows, the difference is highly significant, and so the predicted importance of incongruity-conflict is vindicated.

MEANINGFULNESS OF SEQUENCE. Although meaningfulness of sequence was not one of the variables figuring in the theory, it was tested in Experiment 2 as a factor likely to be influential. The means were, however, 2.4 responses per card for both meaningful-sequence

TABLE 3

Analysis of Variance: Exp. 1

Source	df	MS	F	
Incongruous/Nonincongruous I/NI	1	382.00	(a)	32.73†
Ss	15	26.20	(b)	6.44†
Ss × I/NI (a)	15	11.67	(b)	2.87°
Residual (b)	192	4.07		
Total	223			

° Significant at .01 level.
† Significant at .001 level.

and random-sequence series, and so no effect can be attributed to this factor.

SURPRISE-CONFLICT. In Experiment 3, the two cards which introduced unexpected changes were Cards 7 and 12. These were compared with the remainder, with the exception of Card 1. Card 1 was disregarded because of its equivocal status at the beginning of the series. The two surprise cards produced a mean of 2.4 responses and the nine nonsurprise cards a mean of 2.0 responses. As the analysis of variance in Table 4 shows, the difference, which follows the predicted direction, is significant.

RELATIVE ENTROPY. The three series of cards in Experiment 4 each provided a separate test for the relative-entropy variable. In Series A, the mean numbers of responses were 2.6 for Card I and 4.2 for Card 2. A t test leads to a P-value of less than .05 ($t = 2.43$, $df = 15$). The means for cards 1–4, respectively, of Series B were 1.2, 1.6, 1.8, and 3.2. For Cards 1–4, respectively, of Series C, they were 1.7, 2.6, 2.8, and 3.3. In both of these series, therefore, the means followed exactly the predicted order (out of 24 possible permutations in each case). Ranking analyses of variance demonstrate that the differences, for both series, reach the .01 level of significance ($\chi^2_r = 18.47$ for Series B and 15.69 for Series C, $df = 3$).

ABSOLUTE ENTROPY. The variable tested in Experiment 4 was relative entropy or uncertainty. This is the ratio of the amount of information received from a figure to the maximum that could be received from a figure with the same quantity of material. In other words, it is a measure of the extent to which parts of the figure are unexpected in view of the nature of the other parts or, more briefly, a measure of the amount of variety in the figure.

TABLE 4

Analysis of Variance: Exp. 3

Source	df	MS	F
Surprise/Nonsurprise (S/NS)	1	4.00	6.35*
Ss	15	6.80	10.79†
Ss × S/NS	15	.47	
Residual (error)	144	.63	
Total	175		

* Significant at .01 level by one-tailed test.
† Significant at .001 level.

TABLE 5

Analysis of Variance: Exp. 2

Source	df	MS	F	
Amounts of detail (D)	2	19.50	(a)	9.90*
Ss	15	10.13	(b)	13.51*
Ss × D (a)	30	1.97	(b)	2.63*
Residual (b)	144	.75		
Total	191			

* Significant at .001 level.

All three series consisted of figures with approximately equal amounts of material. Experiment 4, therefore, showed that curiosity increases with relative entropy if maximum entropy is held constant. The figures in each series thus varied both in relative and in absolute entropy, and the question arises whether the *absolute* amount of information as such has an influence on curiosity.

Affirmative evidence on this question is provided by Experiment 2. It will be seen that the cards of both series numbered 1, 2–5 and 6 form three sets differing markedly in amount of nonrepetitive detail. The mean responses per card for these three sets are 1.6, 2.3, and 3.1, respectively, and, as Table 5 shows, the F value for this comparison is significant. The differences between figures varying in amount of detail can be described in terms of statistical information theory (Shannon & Weaver, 1949), if the parts of the figures are regarded as signals. But the concept of "structural information" (Mackay, 1950) is clearly also relevant.

Alternative Theories

The Pavlovian concept of an "investigatory reflex" (Pavlov, 1927; Sokolov, 1955) cannot account for our results, as the response was not a receptor adjustment but an arbitrary learned movement and, furthermore, the visual stimulus investigated was not present until the response had been performed. Estes (1956, p. 11), referring to experiments which purport to demonstrate learning under the influence of an exploratory drive, claims that Guthrie's contiguity theory could equally well handle the facts. It is not easy to see how this theory could handle our data, without assuming some internal stimulus condition which would amount to much the same as a curiosity drive.

Comparison with Children

Burgess (1956) performed Experiment 1 and slightly modified versions of Experiment 2 and 3 with 18 5-yr.-old children and with a .014-sec. exposure. The principal differences from our results were: (a) the children responded many more times per card (mean = 12.1, $SD = 7.75$); and (b) no effect of incongruity or surprise was manifested. In order to ascertain whether the first difference was due to the age of the children or to the shorter exposure, four Ss from the fourth-year psychology class were put through Experiments 1–4 with a latin-square design and a .014-sec. exposure. Their mean number of responses per card for Experiment 1–3 came to 2.3, with an SD of .70. A Cochran-Cox test (Lindquist, 1953, pp. 97–98) shows the difference between their mean and that of the children to be significant at the .01 level. One can therefore conclude that the children's greater resistance to satiation was not due to the shorter exposure alone. Without further experimentation, it is not possible to reach any conclusion with respect to the other difference. The fact that the children exhibited more curiosity than the adults is in harmony with Welker's finding (1956b) that young chimpanzees indulge in more exploratory manipulation of objects than their elders.

Bibliography

Adlerstein, A., & Fehrer, E.   The effect of food deprivation on exploratory behavior in a complex maze. *J. comp. physiol. Psychol.*, 1955, **48**, 250–253.

Antonitis, J. J., & Barnes, G. W.   Group operant behavior: an extension of individual research methodology. *J. genet. Psychol.*, 1961, **98**, 95–111.

Attneave, F.   Some informational aspects of visual perception. *Psychol. Rev.*, 1954, **61**, 183–193.

Barnes, G. W., & Baron, A.   Stimulus complexity and sensory reinforcement. *J. comp. physiol. Psychol.*, 1961, **54**, 466–469. (a)

Barnes, G. W., & Baron, A.   The effects of sensory reinforcement on extinction behavior. *J. comp. physiol. Psychol.*, 1961, **54**, 461–465. (b)

Barnes, G. W., & Kish, G. B.   On some properties of visual reinforcement. *Amer. Psychologist,* 1958, **13**, 417. (Abstract)

Barnes, G. W., & Kish, G. B.   Reinforcing properties of the onset of auditory stimulation. *J. exp. Psychol.*, 1961, **62**, 164–170.

Bartlett, F. C.   *Remembering.* Cambridge, Mass.: Cambridge Univer. Press, 1932.

Bartley, S. H.   Fatigue and efficiency.   In H. Helson (Ed.), *Theoretical foundations of psychology.* Princeton, N.J.: Van Nostrand, 1951. Pp. 318–348.

Beach, F. A.   The neural basis of innate behavior. III. Comparison of learning ability and instinctive behavior in the rat. *J. comp. Psychol.*, 1939, **28**, 225–262.

Beach, F. A.   The descent of instinct. *Psychol. Rev.*, 1955, **62**, 401–410.

Bergmann, G.   Theoretical psychology. *Annu. Rev. Psychol.*, 1953, **4**, 435–458.

Berkun, M. M., Kessen, Marion L., & Miller, N. E.   Hunger-reducing effects of food by stomach fistula versus food by mouth measured by a consummatory response. *J. comp. physiol. Psychol.*, 1952, **45**, 550–554.

Berlyne, D. E.   Novelty and curiosity as determinants of exploratory behavior. *Brit. J. Psychol.*, 1950, **41**, 68–80.

Berlyne, D. E.   Attention, perception and behavior theory. *Psychol. Rev.*, 1951, **58**, 137–146.

Berlyne, D. E.   An experimental study of human curiosity. *Brit. J. Psychol.*, 1954, **45**, 256–265. (a)

Berlyne, D. E.   A theory of human curiosity. *Brit. J. Psychol.*, 1954, **45**, 180–191. (b)

Berlyne, D. E.   Knowledge and stimulus-response psychology. *Psychol. Rev.*, 1954, **61**, 245–254. (c)

Berlyne, D. E.   The arousal and satiation of perceptual curiosity in the rat. *J. comp. physiol. Psychol.*, 1955, **48**, 238–246.

Berlyne, D. E.   Conflict and information-theory variables as determinants of human perceptual curiosity. *J. exp. Psychol.*, 1957, **53**, 399–404.

Berlyne, D. E.   *Conflict, arousal, and curiosity*. New York: McGraw-Hill, 1960.

Berlyne, D. E.   Motivational problems raised by exploratory and epistemic behavior. In S. Koch (Ed.), *Psychology: a study of a science*, Vol. 5. New York: McGraw-Hill, 1963. Pp. 284–364.

Berlyne, D. E., & Slater, J.   Perceptual curiosity, exploratory behavior and maze learning. *J. comp. physiol. Psychol.*, 1957, **50**, 228–232.

Bernard, L. L.   *Instinct*. New York: Holt, 1924.

Bexton, W. H., Heron, W., & Scott, T. H.   Effects of decreased variation in the sensory environment. *Canad. J. Psychol.*, 1954, **8**, 70–76.

Bindra, D.   *Motivation: a systematic reinterpretation*. New York: Ronald, 1959.

Birch, H. G.   The relation of previous experience to insightful problem-solving. *J. comp. Psychol.*, 1945, **38**, 367–383.

Bolles, R. C.   The usefulness of the drive concept. In M. R. Jones (Ed.), *Nebraska symposium on motivation*. Lincoln: Univer. Nebraska Press, 1958. Pp. 1–33.

Brink, F.   Excitation and conduction in the neuron. In S. S. Stevens (Ed.), *Handbook of experimental psychology*. New York: Wiley, 1951. Pp. 50–93.

Brogden, W. J.   Sensory preconditioning. *J. exp. Psychol.*, 1939, **24**, 323–332.

Brown, J. S.   Comments on Professor Harlow's paper. In *Current theory and research in motivation*. Lincoln: Univer. Nebraska Press, 1953. Pp. 49–54. (a)

Brown, J. S.   Problems presented by the concept of acquired drives. In *Current theory and research in motivation*. Lincoln: Univer. Nebraska Press, 1953. Pp. 1–21. (b)

Brown, J. S.   *The motivation of behavior*. New York: McGraw-Hill, 1961.

Brown, J. S., & Jacobs, A.   The role of fear in the motivation and acquisition of responses. *J. exp. Psychol.*, 1949, **39**, 747–759.

Bugelski, B. R.   A note on Grant's discussion of the Latin square principle in the design and analysis of psychological experiments. *Psychol. Bull.*, 1949, **46**, 49–50.

Burgess, S. E.   A study of curiosity as motivation for a key-pressing response in children. Unpubl. Ed. B. thesis, Univer. of Aberdeen, Scotland, 1956.

Burns, B. D.   The mechanism of afterbursts in cerebral cortex. *J. Physiol.*, 1955, **127**, 168–188.

Butler, R. A.   Discrimination learning by rhesus monkeys to visual-exploration motivation. *J. Comp. physiol. Psychol.*, 1953, **46**, 95–98.

Butler, R. A.   Incentive conditions which influence visual exploration. *J. exp. Psychol.*, 1954, **48**, 19–23.

Butler, R. A.   Discrimination learning by rhesus monkeys to auditory incentives. *J. comp. physiol. Psychol.*, 1957, **50**, 239–241. (a)

Butler, R. A.   The effect of deprivation of visual incentives on visual exploration motivation in monkeys. *J. comp. physiol. Psychol.*, 1957, **50**, 177–179. (b)

Butler, R. A., & Alexander, H. M.   Daily patterns of visual exploratory behavior in monkeys. *J. comp. physiol. Psychol.*, 1955, **48**, 247–249.

Butler, R. A., & Harlow, H. F.   Persistence of visual exploration in monkeys. *J. comp. physiol. Psychol.*, 1954, **47**, 258–263.

Buxton, C. E.   Latent learning and the goal gradient hypothesis. *Contr. Psychol. Theor.*, 1940, **2**, No. 2.

Cannon, W. B.   *The wisdom of the body.* New York: Norton, 1932.

Carmichael, L.   An experimental study in the prenatal guinea-pig of the origin and development of reflexes and patterns of behavior in relation to the stimulation of specific receptor areas during the period of active fetal life. *Genet. Psychol. Monogr.*, 1934, **16**, 337–491.

Carper, J. W., & Polliard, F. A.   Comparison of the intake of glucose and saccharin solutions under conditions of caloric need. *Amer. J. Psychol.*, 1953, **66**, 479–482.

Carr, H. A.   The alternation problem: a preliminary study. *J. Anim. Behav.*, 1917, **7**, 365–384.

Carr, H. A.   Length of time interval in successive association. *Psychol. Rev.*, 1919, **26**, 335–353.

Carr, H. A.   *Psychology, a study of mental activity.* New York: Longmans, Green, 1925.

Chance, M. R. A., & Mead, A. P.   Competition between feeding and investigation in the rat. *Behaviour*, 1955, **8**, 174–182.

Chapman, R. M., & Levy, N.   Hunger drive and reinforcing effect of novel stimuli. *J. comp. physiol. Psychol.*, 1957, **50**, 233–238.

Clare, M. H., & Bishop, G. H.   Properties of dendrites; apical dendrites of the cat cortex. *EEG clin. Neurophysiol.*, 1955, **7**, 85–98.

Clayton, F. L.   Light reinforcement as a function of water deprivation. *Psychol. Rep.*, 1958, **4**, 63–66.

Crespi, L. P.   Quantitative variation of incentive and performance in the white rat. *Amer. J. Psychol.*, 1942, **55**, 467–517.

Crowder, W. F., & Crowder, T. H.   Duration of weak-light reinforcement. *Psychol. Rep.*, 1961, **8**, 130.

Crozier, W. J.   The study of living organisms. In C. Murchinson (Ed.), *The foundations of experimental psychology.* Worcester, Mass.: Clark Univer. Press, 1929.

Darchen, R.   Sur le comportement d'exploration de *Blatella germancia.* Exploration d'un plan. *J. Psychol. norm. path.,* 1957, **54,** 190–205.

Darwin, C.   *On the origin of species.* London: Murray, 1859.

Darwin, C.   *The expression of emotions in man and animals.* London: Murray, 1872.

Dashiell, J. F.   A quantitative demonstration of animal drive. *J. comp. Psychol.,* 1925, **5,** 205–208.

Dashiell, J. F.   *Fundamentals of objective psychology.* Boston: Houghton Mifflin, 1928.

Davis, J. D.   The reinforceing effect of weak-light onset as a function of amount of food deprivation. *J. comp. physiol. Psychol.,* 1958, **51,** 496–498.

Davis, R. T., Settlage, P. H., & Harlow, H. F.   Performance of normal and brain operated monkeys on mechanical puzzles with and without food incentive. *J. genet. Psychol.,* 1950, **77,** 305–311.

deLorge, J., & Bolles, R. C.   Effects of food deprivation on exploratory behavior in a novel situation. *Psychol. Rep.,* 1961, **9,** 599–606.

Dember, W. N.   Response by the rat to environmental change. *J. comp. physiol. Psychol.,* 1956, **49,** 93–95.

Dember, W. N., Earl, R. W., & Paradise, N.   Response by rats to differential stimulus complexity. *J. comp. physiol. Psychol.,* 1957, **50,** 514–518.

Dember, W. N., & Fowler, H.   Spontaneous alternation behavior. *Psychol. Bull.,* 1958, **55,** 412–428.

Dember, W. N., & Millbrook, Barbara A.   Free-choice by the rat of the greater of two brightness changes. *Psychol. Rep.,* 1956, **2,** 465–467.

Dennis, W.   A comparison of the rat's first and second explorations of a maze unit. *Amer. J. Psychol.,* 1935, **47,** 488–490.

Dennis, W.   Spontaneous alternation in rats as an indicator of persistence of stimulus effects. *J. comp. Psychol.,* 1939, **28,** 305–312.

Dennis, W., & Sollenberger, R. T.   Negative adaptation in the maze exploration of albino rats. *J. comp. Psychol.,* 1934, **18,** 197–206.

Dollard, J., & Miller, N. E.   *Personality and psychotherapy.* New York: McGraw-Hill, 1950.

Duffy, Elizabeth.   An explanation of "emotional" phenomena without the use of the concept "emotion." *J. gen. Psychol.,* 1941, **25,** 283–293.

Dunlap, K.   Are there any instincts? *J. abnorm. Psychol.,* 1919–20, **14,** 307–311.

Eccles, J. C.   *The neurophysiological basis of mind.* London: Oxford Univer. Press, 1953.

Estes, W. K.   Learning. *Ann. Rev. Psychol.,* 1956, **7,** 1–38.

Estes, W. K.   Comments on Dr. Bolles' paper. In M. R. Jones (Ed.), *Nebraska symposium on motivation.* Lincoln: Univer. Nebraska Press, 1958. Pp. 33–34.

Fehrer, E.   The effects of hunger and familiarity of locale on exploration. *J. comp. physiol. Psychol.*, 1956, **49**, 549–552.

Fisher, A. E.   Effects of stimulus variation on sexual satiation in the male rat. *J. comp. physiol. Psychol.*, 1962, **55**, 614–620.

Fiske, D. W., & Maddi, S. R.   A conceptual framework. In D. W. Fiske and S. R. Maddi (Eds.), *Functions of varied experience.* Homewood, Ill.: Dorsey, 1961. Pp. 11–56.

Flynn, J. P., & Jerome, E. A.   Learning in an automatic multiple-choice box with light as incentive. *J. comp. physiol. Psychol.*, 1952, **45**, 336–340.

Forgays, D. G., & Levin, H.   Learning as a function of sensory stimulation in food-deprived and food-satiated animals. *J. comp. physiol. Psychol.*, 1958, **51**, 50–54.

Forgays, D. G., & Levin, H.   Discrimination and reversal learning as function of change of sensory stimulation. *J. comp. physiol. Psychol.*, 1959, **52**, 191–194.

Forgays, D. G., & Levin, H.   Learning as a function of change of sensory stimulation: distributed vs. massed trials. *J. comp. physiol. Psychol.*, 1961, **54**, 59–62.

Fowler, H.   Response to environmental change: A positive replication. *Psychol. Rep.*, 1958, **4**, 506.

Fowler, H.   The concept of motivation in exploratory behavior. Paper read at the East. Psychol. Ass., Atlantic City, 1959.

Fowler, H.   Exploratory motivation and animal handling: the effect on runway performance of start-box exposure time. *J. comp. physiol. Psychol.*, 1963, **56**, 866–871.

Fowler, H., Blond, Joyce, & Dember, W. N.   Alternation behavior and learning: the influence of reinforcement magnitude, number, and contingency. *J. comp. physiol. Psychol.*, 1959, **52**, 609–614.

Fowler, H., Fowler, D. E., & Dember, W. N.   The influence of reward on alternation behavior. *J. comp. physiol. Psychol.*, 1959, **52**, 220–224.

Fowler, H., & Whalen, R. E.   Variation in incentive stimulus and sexual behavior in the male rat. *J. comp. physiol. Psychol.*, 1961, **54**, 68–71.

Ghent, Lila.   The relation of experience to the development of hunger. *Canad. J. Psychol.*, 1951, **5**, 77–81.

Girdner, J. B.   An experimental analysis of the behavioral effects of a perceptual consequence unrelated to organic drive states. *Amer. Psychologist*, 1953, **8**, 354–355. (Abstract)

Glanzer, M.   Stimulus satiation as an explanation of spontaneous alternation in rats. Unpublished doctoral dissertation, Univer. of Michigan, 1952.

Glanzer, M.   Stimulus satiation: an explanation of spontaneous alternation and related phenomena. *Psychol. Rev.*, 1953, **60**, 257–268. (a)

Glanzer, M.   The role of stimulus satiation in spontaneous alternation. *J. exp. Psychol.*, 1953, **45**, 387–393. (b)

Glanzer, M. Curiosity, exploratory drive, and stimulus satiation. *Psychol. Bull.*, 1958, **55**, 302–315.

Glanzer, M. Changes and interrelations in exploratory behavior. *J. comp. physiol. Psychol.*, 1961, **54**, 433–438.

Glickman, S. E., & Jensen, G. D. The effects of hunger and thirst on Y-maze exploration. *J. comp. physiol. Psychol.*, 1961, **54**, 83–85.

Guthrie, E. R. *The psychology of learning.* New York: Harper, 1935.

Guthrie, E. R. *The psychology of learning.* (Rev. ed.) New York: Harper, 1952.

Haney, G. W. The effect of familiarity on maze performance of albino rats. *Univer. Calif. Publ. Psychol.*, 1931, **4**, 319–333.

Harlow, H. F. Learning and satiation of response in intrinsically motivated complex puzzle performance by monkeys. *J. comp. physiol. Psychol.*, 1950, **43**, 289–294.

Harlow, H. F. Primate learning. In C. P. Stone (Ed.), *Comparative Psychology.* (3rd ed.) Englewood Cliffs, N.J.: Prentice-Hall, 1951.

Harlow, H. F. Mice, monkeys, men, and motives. *Psychol. Rev.*, 1953, **60**, 23–32. (a)

Harlow, H. F. Motivation as a factor in the acquisition of new responses. In *Current theory and research in motivation.* Lincoln: Univer. Nebraska Press, 1953. Pp. 24–49. (b)

Harlow, H. F., Blazek, Nancy C., & McClearn, G. E. Manipulatory motivation in the infant rhesus monkey. *J. comp. physiol. Psychol.*, 1956, **49**, 444–448.

Harlow, H. F., Harlow, Margaret K., & Meyer, D. R. Learning motivated by a manipulatory drive. *J. exp. Psychol.*, 1950, **40**, 228–234.

Harlow, H. F., & McClearn, G. E. Object discrimination learned by monkeys on the basis on manipulation motives. *J. comp. physiol. Psychol.*, 1954, **47**, 73–76.

Heathers, G. L. The avoidance of repetition of a maze reaction in the rat as a function of the time between trials. *J. Psychol.*, 1940, **10**, 359–380.

Hebb, D. O. Elementary school methods. *Teach. Mag.* (Montreal), 1930, **12**, 23–26.

Hebb, D. O. *The organization of behavior.* New York: Wiley, 1949.

Hebb, D. O. On human thought. *Canad. J. Psychol.*, 1953, **7**, 99–110.

Hebb, D. O. Drives and the C.N.S. (conceptual nervous system) *Psychol. Rev.*, 1955, **62**, 243–254.

Hebb, D. O., & Riesen, A. H. The genesis of irrational fears. *Bull. Canad. Psychol. Ass.*, 1943, **3**, 49–50.

Hebb, D. O., & Thompson, W. R. The social significance of animal studies. In G. Lindzey (Ed.), *Handbook of social psychology.* Cambridge, Mass.: Addison-Wesley, 1954. Pp. 532–561.

Hefferline, R. F. An experimental study of avoidance. *Genet. Psychol. Monogr.*, 1950, **42**, 231–334.

Heron, W. T., & Skinner, B. F.   Changes in hunger during starvation. *Psychol. Rec.*, 1937, **1**, 51–60.

Hilgard, E. R.   *Theories of learning.* New York: Appleton-Century-Crofts, 1948.

Horenstein, Betty.   Performance of conditioned responses as a function of strength of hunger drive. *J. comp. physiol. Psychol.*, 1951, **44**, 210–224.

Hull, C. L.   *Principles of behavior.* New York: Appleton-Century-Crofts, 1943.

Hull, C. L.   *A behavior system.* New Haven: Yale Univer. Press, 1952.

Humphrey, G., Dawe, P. G. M., & Mandell, B.   New high-speed electronic tachistoscope. *Nature*, 1955, **176**, 1–9.

Hunter, W. S.   Delayed reaction in animals and children. *Behav. Monogr.*, 1913, **2**, No. 6.

Hunter, W. S.   The temporal maze and kinaesthetic sensory processes in the white rat. *Psychobiol.*, 1920, **2**, 1–17.

Hunter, W. S.   A further consideration of the sensory control of the maze habit in the white rat. *J. Genet. Psychol.*, 1930, **38**, 3–19.

Hunter, W. S., & Nagge, J.   The white rat and the double alternation temporal maze. *J. Genet. Psychol.*, 1931, **39**, 303–319.

Hurwitz, H. M. B.   Conditioned responses in rats reinforced by light. *Brit. J. anim. Behav.*, 1956, **4**, 31–33.

Hurwitz, H. M. B., & De, S. C.   Studies in light reinforced behavior. II. The effect of food deprivation and stress. *Psychol. Rep.*, 1958, **4**, 71–77.

Jackson, M. M.   Reactive tendencies in the white rat in running and jumping situations. *J. comp. physiol. Psychol.*, 1941, **31**, 255–262.

James, W.   *The principles of psychology.* New York: Holt, 1890.

Jennings, H. S.   *Behavior of the lower organisms.* New York: Columbia Univer. Press, 1906.

Jensen, K.   Differential reactions to taste and temperature stimuli in newborn infants. *Genet. Psychol. Monogr.*, 1932, **12**, 361–476.

Jones, A.   Supplementary report: information deprivation and irrelevant drive as determiners of an instrumental response. *J. exp. Psychol.*, 1961, **62**, 310–311.

Jones, A., Wilkinson, H. J., & Braden, I.   Information deprivation as a motivational variable. *J. exp. Psychol.*, 1961, **62**, 126–137.

Kagan, J., & Berkun, M.   The reward value of running activity. *J. comp. physiol. Psychol.*, 1954, **47**, 108.

Karsten, Anitra.   Untersuchungen zur Handlungs—und Affektpsychologie: V. Psychische Sättigung. *Psychol. Forsch.*, 1928, **10**, 142–154.

Keller, F. S.   Light aversion in the white rat. *Psychol. Rec.*, 1941, **4**, 235–250.

Keller, F. S.   *Learning: reinforcement theory.* Garden City, N.Y.: Doubleday, 1954.

Kinsey, A. C., Pomeroy, W. B., & Martin, C. E. *Sexual behavior in the human male.* Philadelphia: W. B. Saunders, 1948.

Kish, G. B. Learning when the onset of illumination is used as reinforcing stimulus. *J. comp. physiol. Psychol.,* 1955, 48, 261–264.

Kish, G. B., & Antonitis, J. J. Unconditioned operant behavior in two homozygous strains of mice. *J. genet. Psychol.,* 1956, 88, 121–124.

Kivy, P. N., Earl, R. W., & Walker, E. L. Stimulus context and satiation. *J. comp. physiol. Psychol.,* 1956, 49, 90–92.

Kling, J. W., Horowitz, L., & Delhagen, J. E. Light as a positive reinforcer for rat responding. *Psychol. Rep.,* 1956, 2, 337–340.

Klüver, H. *Behavior mechanisms in monkeys.* Chicago: Univer. Chicago Press, 1933.

Koch, S. Psychological science versus the science-humanism antinomy. *Amer. Psychol.,* 1961, 16, 629–639.

Koch, S., & Daniel, W. J. The effect of satiation on the behavior mediated by a habit of maximum strength. *J. exp. Psychol.,* 1945, 35, 162–185.

Krechevsky, I. Brain mechanisms and variability. II. Variability where no learning is involved. *J. comp. Psychol.,* 1937, 23, 139–163. (a)

Krechevsky, I. Brain mechanisms and variability. III. Limitations of the effect of cortical injury upon variability. *J. comp. Psychol.,* 1937, 23, 351–364. (b)

Kuo, Z. Y. The fundamental error of the concept of purpose and the trial and error fallacy. *Psychol. Rev.,* 1928, 35, 414–433.

Lacey, J., & Smith, R. Conditioning and generalization of unconscious anxiety, *Science,* 1954, 120, 1045–1052.

Langworthy, O. R. The behavior of pouch-young opossums correlated with the myelinization of tracts in the nervous system. *J. comp. Neurol.,* 1928, 46, 201–248.

Lashley, K. S. The mechanism of vision. II. The influence of cerebral lesions upon the threshold of discrimination for brightness in the rat. *J. genet. Psychol.,* 1930, 37, 461–480.

Leuba, C. Toward some integration of learning theories: the concept of optimal stimulation. *Psychol. Rep.,* 1955, 1, 27–33.

Leuba, C., & Dunlap, R. Conditioning imagery. *J. exp. Psychol.,* 1951, 41, 352–355.

Levin, H., & Forgays, D. G. Learning as a function of sensory stimulation of various intensities. *J. comp. physiol. Psychol.,* 1959, 52, 195–201.

Li, Choh-Luh, & Jasper, H. Microelectrode studies of the cerebral cortex in the cat. *J. Physiol.,* 1953, 121, 117–140.

Liddell, H. S. Conditioning and emotions. *Sci. Amer.,* 1954, 190, 48–57.

Lindquist, E. F. *Design and analysis of experiments in psychology and education.* Boston: Houghton Mifflin, 1953.

Lindsley, D. B. Emotion. In S. S. Stevens (Ed.), *Handbook of experimental psychology.* New York: Wiley, 1951. Pp. 473–516.

Lloyd, D. P. C.   A direct central inhibitory action of dromically conducted impulses. *J. Neurophysiol.*, 1941, **4**, 184–190.

Loeb, J.   *Forced movements, tropisms and animal conduct.* Philadelphia: Lippincott, 1918.

Loucks, R. B.   The efficacy of the rat's motor cortex in delayed alternation. *J. comp. Neurol.*, 1931, **53**, 511–567.

MacCorquodale, K., & Meehl, P. E.   A distinction between hypothetical constructs and intervening variables. *Psychol. Rev.*, 1948, **55**, 95–107.

Mackay, D. M.   Quantal aspects of scientific information. *Phil. Mag.*, 1950, **41**, 289–311.

Maier, N. R. F.   *Frustration.* New York: McGraw-Hill, 1949.

Marshall, S. L. A.   *Men against fire.* New York: Morrow, 1947.

Marx, M. H., Henderson, R. L., & Roberts, C. L.   Positive reinforcement of the bar-pressing response by a light stimulus following dark operant pretests with no after effect. *J. comp. physiol. Psychol.*, 1955, **48**, 73–76.

Maslow, A. H.   A theory of human motivation. *Psychol. Rev.*, 1943, **50**, 370–396.

McClelland, D. C., Atkinson, J. W., Clark, R. A., & Lowell, E. L.   *The achievement motive.* New York: Appleton-Century-Crofts, 1953.

McDougall, W.   *An introduction to social psychology.* (5th ed.) London: Methuen, 1912.

McDougall, W.   *Outline of psychology.* New York: Scribner, 1923.

Meehl, P., & MacCorquodale, K.   Drive conditioning as a factor in latent learning. *J. exp. Psychol.*, 1953, **45**, 20–24.

Melzack, R.   The effects of early experience on the emotional responses to pain. Unpublished doctoral dissertation, McGill Univer., 1954.

Menzies, R.   Conditioned vasomotor responses in human subjects. *J. Psychol.*, 1937, **4**, 75–120.

Meyer, D. R.   Food deprivation and discrimination reversal learning by monkeys. *J. exp. Psychol.*, 1951, **41**, 10–16.

Miles, R. C.   Effect of food deprivation on manipulatory reactions in cat. *J. comp. physiol. Psychol.*, 1962, **55**, 358–362.

Miller, G. A., & Frick, F. C.   Statistical behavioristics and sequences of responses. *Psychol. Rev.*, 1949, **56**, 311–324.

Miller, N. E.   Experiments on the strength of acquired drives based on hunger. *Amer. Psychologist*, 1947, **2**, 303. (Abstract)

Miller, N. E.   Studies of fear as an acquirable drive: I. Fear as motivation and fear-reduction as reinforcement in the learning of new responses. *J. exp. Psychol.*, 1948, **38**, 89–101.

Miller, N. E.   Learnable drives and rewards. In S. S. Stevens (Ed.) *Handbook of experimental psychology.* New York: Wiley, 1951. Pp. 435–472.

Miller, N. E.   Some studies of drive and drive reduction. Paper read at Amer. Psychol. Ass., Cleveland, September, 1953.

Miller, N. E., Bailey, C. J., & Stevenson, J. A. F.   Decreased "hunger" but increased food intake from hypothalamic lesions. *Science*, 1950, **112**, 256–259.

Miller, N. E., & Dollard, J. *Social learning and imitation*. New Haven: Yale Univer. Press, 1941.

Miller, N. E., & Kessen, Marion L. Reward effects of food via stomach fistula compared with those via mouth. *J. comp. physiol. Psychol.*, 1952, **45**, 555–564.

Montgomery, K. C. "Spontaneous alternation" as a function of time between trials and amount of work. *J. exp. Psychol.*, 1951, **42**, 82–93. (a)

Montgomery, K. C. The relationship between exploratory behavior and spontaneous alternation in the white rat. *J. comp. physiol. Psychol.*, 1951, **44**, 582–589. (b)

Montgomery, K. C. A test of two explanations of spontaneous alternation. *J. comp. physiol. Psychol.*, 1952, **45**, 287–293. (a)

Montgomery, K. C. Exploratory behavior and its relation to spontaneous alternation in a series of maze exposures. *J. comp. physiol. Psychol.*, 1952, **45**, 50–57. (b)

Montgomery, K. C. Exploratory behavior as a function of "similarity" of stimulus situations. *J. comp. physiol. Psychol.*, 1953, **46**, 129–133. (a)

Montgomery, K. C. The effect of activity deprivation upon exploratory behavior. *J. comp. physiol. Psychol.*, 1953, **46**, 438–441. (b)

Montgomery, K. C. The effect of hunger and thirst drives upon exploratory behavior. *J. comp. physiol. Psychol.*, 1953, **46**, 315–319. (c)

Montgomery, K. C. The role of the exploratory drive in learning. *J. comp. physiol. Psychol.*, 1954, **47**, 60–64.

Montgomery, K. C., & Segall, M. Discrimination learning based upon the exploratory drive. *J. comp. physiol. Psychol.*, 1955, **48**, 225–228.

Moon, L. E., & Lodahl, T. M. The reinforcing effect of changes in illumination on lever-pressing in the monkey. *Amer. J. Psychol.*, 1956, **69**, 288–290.

Moruzzi, G., & Magoun, H. W. Brain stem reticular formation and activation of the EEG. *EEG clin. Neurophysiol.*, 1949, **1**, 455–473.

Moss, F. A. Study of animal drives. *J. exp. Psychol.*, 1924, **7**, 165–185.

Mowrer, O. H. A stimulus-response analysis of anxiety and its role as a reinforcing agent. *Psychol. Rev.*, 1939, **46**, 553–565.

Mowrer, O. H. *Learning theory and personality dynamics*. New York: Ronald, 1950.

Mowrer, O. H. Motivation. *Annu. Rev. Psychol.*, 1952, **3**, 419–438.

Myers, A. K., & Miller, N. E. Failure to find a learned drive based on hunger; evidence for learning motivated by "exploration." *J. comp. physiol. Psychol.*, 1954, **47**, 428–436.

Nicholls, Edith E. A study of the spontaneous activity of the guinea pig. *J. comp. Psychol.*, 1922, **2**, 303–330.

Nissen, H. W. A study of exploratory behavior in the white rat by means of the obstruction method. *J. genet. Psychol.*, 1930, **37**, 361–376.

Nissen, H. W.   Instinct as seen by a psychologist. *Psychol. Rev.*, 1953, **60**, 291–294.

Nissen, H. W.   The nature of the drive as innate determinant of behavioral organization. In M. R. Jones (Ed.), *Nebraska Symposium on Motivation.* Lincoln: Univer. Nebraska Press, 1954. Pp. 281–321.

Olds, J., & Milner, P.   Positive reinforcement produced by electrical stimulation of septal area and other regions of the rat brain. *J. comp. physiol. Psychol.*, 1954, **47**, 419–427.

Olszewski, J.   The cytoarchitecture of the human reticular formation. In E. D. Adrian, F. Bremer, & H. H. Jasper (Eds.), *Brain mechanisms and consciousness.* Oxford: Blackwell, 1954.

Pavlov, I. P.   *Conditioned reflexes.* London: Oxford Univer. Press, 1927.

Platt, J. R.   Beauty: pattern and change. In D. W. Fiske & S. R. Maddi (Eds.), *Functions of varied experience.* Homewood, Ill.: Dorsey, 1961. Pp. 402–430.

Premack, D., Collier, G., & Roberts, C. L.   Frequency of light-contingent bar pressing as a function of the amount of deprivation of light. *Amer. Psychologist*, 1957, **12**, 411. (Abstract)

Razran, G.   Semantic and phonetographic generalization of salivary conditioning to verbal stimuli. *J. exp. Psychol.*, 1949, **39**, 642–652.

Reid, L. S., & Finger, F. W.   The rat's adjustment to 23-hour food deprivation cycles. *J. comp. physiol. Psychol.*, 1955, **48**, 110–113.

Richards, W. J., & Leslie, G. R.   Food and water deprivation as influences on exploration. *J. comp. physiol. Psychol.*, 1962, **55**, 834–837.

Richter, C. P.   A behavioristic study of the activity of the rat. *Comp. Psychol. Monogr.*, 1922, **1**, No. 2.

Richter, C. P.   Animal behavior and internal drives. *Quart. Rev. Biol.*, 1927, **2**, 307–343.

Roberts, C. L., Marx, M. H., & Collier, G.   Light onset and light offset as reinforcers for the albino rat. *J. comp. physiol. Psychol.*, 1958, **51**, 575–579.

Robinson, J.   Light as a reinforcer for bar pressing in rats as a function of adaptation, illumination level and direction of light change. *Amer. Psychologist*, 1957, **12**, 411. (Abstract)

Robinson, J. S.   Light onset and termination as reinforcers for rats under normal light conditions. *Psychol. Rep.*, 1959, **5**, 793–796.

Robinson, J. S.   The reinforcing effects of response-contingent light increment and decrement in hooded rats. *J. comp. physiol. Psychol.*, 1961, **54**, 470–473.

Rothkopf, E. Z., & Zeaman, D.   Some stimulus controls of alternation behavior. *J. Psychol.*, 1952, **34**, 235–255.

Schlosberg, H.   Three dimensions of emotion. *Psychol. Rev.*, 1954, **61**, 81–88.

Seward, J. P., Levy, N., & Handlon, J. H., Jr. Incidental learning in the rat. *J. comp. physiol. Psychol.*, 1950, **43**, 240–251.

Shannon, C. E., & Weaver, W. *The mathematical theory of communication.* Urbana: Univer. of Ill. Press, 1949.

Sharpless, S. Habituation of the arousal mechanism. Paper read at East. Psychol. Ass., New York, April, 1954. (a)

Sharpless, S. K. Role of the reticular formation in habituation. Unpublished doctoral dissertation, McGill Univer., 1954. (b)

Sheffield, F. D., & Campbell, B. A. The role of experience in the "spontaneous" activity of hungry rats. *J. comp. physiol. Psychol.*, 1954, **47**, 97–100.

Sheffield, F. D., & Roby, T. B. Reward value of a non-nutritive sweet taste. *J. comp. physiol. Psychol.*, 1950, **43**, 471–481.

Sheffield, F. D., Roby, T. B., & Campbell, B. A. Drive reduction vs. consummatory behavior as determinants of reinforcement. *J. comp. physiol. Psychol.*, 1954, **47**, 349–354.

Sheffield, F. D., Wulff, J. J., & Backer, R. Reward value of copulation without sex drive reduction. *J. comp. physiol. Psychol.*, 1951, **44**, 3–8.

Skinner, B. F. *Behavior of organisms.* New York: Appleton-Century-Crofts, 1938.

Skinner, B. F. *Science and human behavior.* New York: Macmillan, 1953.

Snygg, D. Learning; an aspect of personality development. In *Learning theory, personality theory, and clinical research: the Kentucky Symposium.* New York: Wiley, 1954.

Sokolov, E. N. The higher nervous activity and the problems of perception. *Proc. XIV Int. Cong. Psychol.*, 1955, 134–135.

Solomon, R. L. The role of effort in the production of several related behavior phenomena. Unpublished doctoral dissertation, Brown Univer., 1947.

Solomon, R. L., & Wynne, L. C. Avoidance conditioning in normal dogs and in dogs deprived of normal autonomic functioning. *Amer. Psychologist*, 1950, **5**, 264. (Abstract)

Spence, K. W. The nature of theory construction in contemporary psychology. *Psychol. Rev.*, 1944, **51**, 47–68.

Spence, K. W. *Behavior theory and conditioning.* New Haven: Yale Univer. Press, 1956.

Spence, K., Farber, I. E., & Taylor, E. The relation of electric shock and anxiety to level of performance in eyelid conditioning. *J. exp. Psychol.*, 1954, **48**, 404–408.

Spence, K., & Taylor, J. Anxiety and strength of the UCS as determiners of the amount of eyelid conditioning. *J. exp. Psychol.*, 1951, **42**, 183–188.

Stellar, E. The physiology of motivation. *Psychol. Rev.*, 1954, **61**, 5–22.

Stetson, R. H., & Dashiell, J. F. A multiple unit system of maze construction. *Psychol. Bull.*, 1919, **16**, 223–230.

Stewart, J.   Reinforcing effect of light as a function of intensity and reinforcement schedule. *J. comp. physiol. Psychol.*, 1960, **53**, 187–193.

Strassburger, R. C.   Resistance to extinction of a conditioned operant as related to drive level at reinforcement. *J. exp. Psychol.*, 1950, **40**, 473–487.

Thomson, R. H.   The reward-value for the rat of changes in illumination. Unpublished Master's thesis, Univer. of Aberdeen, Scotland, 1955.

Thompson, W. R.   Exploratory behavior as a function of hunger in "bright" and "dull" rats. *J. comp. physiol. Psychol.*, 1953, **46**, 323–326.

Thompson, W. R., & Solomon, L. M.   Spontaneous pattern discrimination in the rat. *J. comp. physiol. Psychol.*, 1954, **47**, 104–107.

Thorndike, E. L.   *Animal intelligence*. New York: Macmillan, 1911.

Tolman, E. C.   Purpose and cognition: the determiners of animal learning. *Psychol. Rev.*, 1925, **32**, 285–297. (a)

Tolman, E. C.   The nature of fundamental drives. *J. abnorm. soc. Psychol.*, 1925–26, **20**, 349–358. (b)

Tolman, E. C.   *Purposive behavior in animals and men*. New York: Appleton-Century-Crofts, 1932.

Tolman, E. C., Ritchie, B. F., & Kalish, D.   Studies in spatial learning. I. Orientation and the short-cut. *J. exp. Psychol.*, 1946, **36**, 13–24.

Tyhurst, J. S.   Individual reactions to community disaster; the natural history of psychiatric phenomena. *Amer. J. Psychiat.*, 1951, **107**, 764–769.

Valentine, C. W.   The innate bases of fear. *J. genet. Psychol.*, 1930, **37**, 394–419.

Walker, E. L., Dember, W. N., Earl, R. W., Fawl, C. L., & Karoly, A. J.   Choice alternation: III. Response intensity vs. response discriminability. *J. comp. physiol. Psychol.*, 1955, **48**, 80–85.

Walker, E. L., Dember, W. N., Earl, R. W., Fliege, S. E., & Karoly, A. J.   Choice alternation: II. Exposure to stimulus or stimulus and place without choice. *J. comp. physiol. Psychol.*, 1955, **48**, 24–28.

Walker, E. L., Dember, W. N., Earl, R. W., & Karoly, A. J.   Choice alternation: I. Stimulus vs. place vs. response. *J. comp. physiol. Psychol.*, 1955, **48**, 19–23.

Warner, L. H.   A study of sex behavior in the white rat by means of the obstruction method. *Comp. Psychol. Monogr.*, 1927, **4**, No. 22.

Warner, L. H.   A study of thirst behavior in the white rat by means of the obstruction method. *J. genet. Psychol.*, 1928, **35**, 178–192.

Watson, J. B.   *Behavior: An introduction to comparative psychology*. New York: Holt, 1914.

Watson, J. B.   *Behaviorism*. New York: Norton, 1925.

Welker, W. I.   Effects of age and experience on play and exploration of young chimpanzees. *J. comp. physiol. Psychol.*, 1956, **49**, 223–226. (a)

Welker, W. I.   Some determinants of play and exploration in chimpanzees. *J. comp. physiol. Psychol.*, 1956, **49**, 84–89. (b)

Welker, W. I.   Variability of play and exploratory behavior in chimpanzees. *J. comp. physiol. Psychol.*, 1956, **49**, 181–185. (c)

White, R. W.   Motivation reconsidered: the concept of competence. *Psychol. Rev.*, 1959, **66**, 297–333.

Whiting, J. W. M., & Mowrer, O. H.   Habit progression and regression —a laboratory study of some factors relevant to human socialization. *J. comp. Psychol.*, 1943, **36**, 229–253.

Williams, C. D., & Kuchta, J. C.   Exploratory behavior in two mazes with dissimilar alternatives. *J. comp. physiol. Psychol.*, 1957, **50**, 509–513.

Wiln, E. C.   *The theories of instinct, a study in the history of psychology.* New Haven: Yale Univer. Press, 1925.

Wingfield, R. C.   Some factors influencing spontaneous alternation in human subjects. *J. comp. physiol. Psychol.*, 1943, **35**, 237–243.

Wingfield, R. C., & Dennis, W.   The dependence of the rat's choice of pathways upon the length of the daily trial series. *J. comp. Psychol.*, 1934, **18**, 135–147.

Woods, P. J., & Jennings, S.   Response to environmental change: a further confirmation. *Psychol. Rep.*, 1959, **5**, 560.

Woodworth, R. S.   *Dynamic Psychology.* New York: Columbia Univer. Press, 1918.

Woodworth, R. S.   *Psychology.* New York: Holt, 1921.

Woodworth, R. S.   Reinforcement of perception. *Amer. J. Psychol.*, 1947, **60**, 119–125.

Woodworth, R. S., & Marquis, D. G.   *Psychology.* (5th ed.) New York: Holt, 1947.

Yamaguchi, H. G.   Drive (D) as a function of hours of hunger (h). *J. exp. Psychol.*, 1951, **42**, 108–117.

Yerkes, R. M., & Dodson, J. D.   The relation of strength of stimulus to rapidity of habit-formation. *J. comp. neurol. Psychol.*, 1908, **18**, 459–482.

Young, P. T.   Food-seeking drive, affective process, and learning. *Psychol. Rev.*, 1949, **56**, 98–121.

Zeaman, D.   Response latency as a function of amount of reinforcement. *J. exp. Psychol.*, 1949, **39**, 466–483.

Zeaman, D., & House, Betty J.   Response latency at zero drive after varying numbers of reinforcements. *J. exp. Psychol.*, 1950, **40**, 570–583.

Zeaman, D., & House, Betty J.   The growth and decay of reactive inhibition as measured by alternation behavior. *J. exp. Psychol.*, 1951, **41**, 177–186.

Zimbardo, P. G., & Miller, N. E.   Facilitation of exploration by hunger in rats. *J. comp. physiol. Psychol.*, 1958, **51**, 43–46.

Zimbardo, P. G., & Montgomery, K. C.   The relative strengths of consummatory responses in hunger, thirst, and exploratory drive. *J. comp. physiol. Psychol.*, 1957, **50**, 504–508.

Index